6th Workshop on Indian Language Data: Resources and Evaluation (WILDRE-6)

Held at LREC 2022

Marseille, France
20 – 25 June 2022

Editors:

Girish Nath Jha
Sobha L
Kalika Bali
Atul Kr. Ojha

ISBN: 978-1-7138-6143-0

Printed from e-media with permission by:

Curran Associates, Inc.
57 Morehouse Lane
Red Hook, NY 12571

Some format issues inherent in the e-media version may also appear in this print version.

Association for Computational Linguistics
209 N. Eighth Street
Stroudsburg, Pennsylvania 18360

Phone: 1-570-476-8006
Fax: 1-570-476-0860

acl@aclweb.org

Additional copies of this publication are available from:

Curran Associates, Inc.
57 Morehouse Lane
Red Hook, NY 12571 USA
Phone: 845-758-0400
Fax: 845-758-2633
Email: curran@proceedings.com
Web: www.proceedings.com

LREC 2022 Workshop
Language Resources and Evaluation Conference
20-25 June 2022

6th Workshop on Indian Language Data: Resources and Evaluation (WILDRE-6)

PROCEEDINGS

Editors:
Girish Nath Jha, Sobha L, Kalika Bali, Atul Kr. Ojha

Proceedings of the 6th Workshop on Indian Language Data: Resources and Evaluation (WILDRE-6 2022)

Edited by:
Girish Nath Jha, Sobha L., Kalika Bali, Atul Kr. Ojha

For more information:
European Language Resources Association (ELRA)
9 rue des Cordelières
75013, Paris
France
http://www.elra.info
Email: lrec@elda.org

Preface

WILDRE – the 6th Workshop on Indian Language Data: Resources and Evaluation is being organized in Marseille, France on June 20th, 2022 under the LREC platform. India has a huge linguistic diversity and has seen concerted efforts from the Indian government and industry towards developing language resources. European Language Resource Association (ELRA) and its associate organizations have been very active and successful in addressing the challenges and opportunities related to language resource creation and evaluation. It is, therefore, a great opportunity for resource creators of Indian languages to showcase their work on this platform and also to interact and learn from those involved in similar initiatives all over the world.

The broader objectives of the 6th WILDRE will be

- to map the status of Indian Language Resources
- to investigate challenges related to creating and sharing various levels of language resources
- to promote a dialogue between language resource developers and users
- to provide an opportunity for researchers from India to collaborate with researchers from other parts of the world

The call for papers received a good response from the Indian language technology community. This year, we selected only three papers for oral, and thirteen for a poster presentations.

Workshop Chairs

Girish Nath Jha, Jawaharlal Nehru University, India
Kalika Bali, Microsoft Research India Lab, Bangalore
Sobha L, AU-KBC, Anna University

Workshop Organizers

Atul Kr. Ojha, National University of Ireland Galway, Ireland & Panlingua Language Processing LLP, India
Girish Nath Jha, Jawaharlal Nehru University, India
Kalika Bali, Microsoft Research India Lab, Bangalore
Sobha L, AU-KBC, Anna University

Program Committee

Adil Amin Kak, Kashmir University
Alessandro Panunzi, University of Florence, Italy
Arul Mozhi, University of Hyderabad
Atul Kr. Ojha, National University of Ireland Galway, Ireland & Panlingua Language Processing LLP, India
Bharathi Raja Asoka Chakravarthi, National University of Ireland Galway, Irelnad
Bogdan Babych, Heidelberg University, Germany
Chao-Hong Liu, Potamu Research Ltd, Ireland
Claudia Soria, CNR-ILC, Italy
Dafydd Gibbon, Universität Bielefeld, Germany
Daan van Esch, Google, USA
Dan Zeman, Charles University, Prague, Czech Republic
Delyth Prys, Bangor University, UK
Dorothee Beermann, Norwegian University of Science and Technology (NTNU)
Elizabeth Sherley, IITM-Kerala, Trivandrum
Esha Banerjee, Google
Georg Rehm, DFKI, Germany
Girish Nath Jha, Jawaharlal Nehru University, New Delhi
Jan Odijk, Utrecht University, The Netherlands
Jolanta Bachan, Adam Mickiewicz University, Poland
Joseph Mariani, LIMSI-CNRS, France
Jyoti D. Pawar, Goa University
Kalika Bali, Microsoft Research India Lab, Bangalore
Khalid Choukri, ELRA, France
Lars Hellan, NTNU, Norway
Malhar Kulkarni, IIT Bombay
Massimo Monaglia, University of Florence, Italy
Monojit Choudhary, MSRI Bangalore
Nicoletta Calzolari, ILC-CNR, Pisa, Italy
Niladri Shekhar Dash, ISI Kolkata
Partha Talukdar, Google Research, India

Pinky Nainwani, Cognizant Technology Solutions, Bangalore
Pushpak Bhattacharya, IIT Bombay
Rajeev R R, ICFOSS, Trivandrum
Ritesh Kumar, Agra University
Shantipriya Parida, Silo AI, Helsinki, Finland
S.S. Agrawal, KIIT, Gurgaon, India
Sobha L, AU-KBC Research Centre, Anna University
Stelios Piperidis, ILSP, Greece
Subhash Chandra, Delhi University
Vishal Goyal, Punjabi University, Patiala
Zygmunt Vetulani, Adam Mickiewicz University, Poland

Table of Contents

Conference Program

Monday, June 20, 2022

14:00–14:45 Inaugural session

14:00–14:05 ***Welcome by Workshop Chairs***

14:25–15:00 ***Keynote Lecture***

15:00–16:00 Oral Session-I

15:00–15:30 *Introducing EM-FT for Manipuri-English Neural Machine Translation*
Rudali Huidrom and Yves Lepage

15:30–16:00 *L3Cube-HingCorpus and HingBERT: A Code Mixed Hindi-English Dataset and BERT Language Models*
Ravindra Nayak and Raviraj Joshi

16:00–16:30 Coffee break/Poster Session

16:00–16:30 *Leveraging Sub Label Dependencies in Code Mixed Indian Languages for Part-Of-Speech Tagging using Conditional Random Fields.*
Akash Kumar Gautam

16:00–16:30 *HindiWSD: A package for word sense disambiguation in Hinglish & Hindi*
Mirza Yusuf, Praatibh Surana and Chethan sharma

16:00–16:30 *Pāṇinian Phonological Changes: Computation and Development of Online Access System*
Sanju . and Subhash Chandra

16:00–16:30 *L3Cube-MahaNER: A Marathi Named Entity Recognition Dataset and BERT models*
Onkar Litake, Maithili Ravindra Sabane, Parth Sachin Patil, Aparna Abhijeet Ranade and Raviraj Joshi

16:00–16:30 *Identifying Emotions in Code Mixed Hindi-English Tweets*
Sanket Sonu, Rejwanul Haque, Mohammed Hasanuzzaman, Paul Stynes and Pramod Pathak

Monday, June 20, 2022 (continued)

16:00–16:30 *Digital Accessibility and Information Mining of Dharmaśāstric Knowledge Traditions*
Arooshi Nigam and Subhash Chandra

16:00–16:30 *Language Resource Building and English-to-Mizo Neural Machine Translation Encountering Tonal Words*
Vanlalmuansangi Khenglawt, Sahinur Rahman Laskar, Santanu Pal, Partha Pakray and Ajoy Kumar Khan

16:00–16:30 *Classification of Multiword Expressions in Malayalam*
Treesa Cyriac and Sobha Lalitha Devi

16:00–16:30 *Bengali and Magahi PUD Treebank and Parser*
Pritha Majumdar, Deepak Alok, Akanksha Bansal, Atul Kr. Ojha and John P. McCrae

16:00–16:30 *Makadi: A Large-Scale Human-Labeled Dataset for Hindi Semantic Parsing*
Shashwat Vaibhav and Nisheeth Srivastava

16:00–16:30 *Automatic Identification of Explicit Connectives in Malayalam*
Kumari Sheeja S and Sobha Lalitha Devi

16:00–16:30 *Web based System for Derivational Process of Kṛdanta based on Pāṇinian Grammatical Tradition*
Sumit Sharma and Subhash Chandra

16:00–16:30 *Universal Dependency Treebank for Odia Language*
Shantipriya Parida, Kalyanamalini Shabadi, Atul Kr. Ojha, Saraswati Sahoo, Satya Ranjan Dash and Bijayalaxmi Dash

16:00–16:30 *Computational Referencing System for Sanskrit Grammar*
Baldev Khandoliyan and Ram Kishor

Monday, June 20, 2022 (continued)

16:30–17:00 Oral Session-II

16:30–17:00 *L3Cube-MahaCorpus and MahaBERT: Marathi Monolingual Corpus, Marathi BERT Language Models, and Resources*
Raviraj Joshi

17:00–17:45 Panel discussion

17:45–17:55 ***Valedictory Session***

17:55–18:00 ***Vote of Thanks***

Proceedings of the WILDRE-6 Workshop @LREC2020, pages 1–6
Marseille, 20 June 2022

Introducing EM-FT for Manipuri-English Neural Machine Translation

Rudali Huidrom and Yves Lepage
Waseda University
Kitakyushu, Japan
{rudali.huidrom@ruri, yves,lepage@}waseda.jp

Abstract

This paper introduces pretrained word embeddings for Manipuri, a low-resourced Indian language. The pretrained word embeddings based on fastText is capable of handling the highly agglutinative language Manipuri (mni). We then perform machine translation (MT) experiments using neural network (NN) models. In this paper, we confirm the following observations. Firstly, the reported BLEU score of the Transformer architecture with fastText word embedding model EM-FT performs better than without in all the NMT experiments. Secondly, we observe that adding more training data from a different domain of the test data negatively impacts translation accuracy. The resources reported in this paper are made available in the ELRA catalogue to help the low-resourced languages community with MT/NLP tasks.

Keywords: neural machine translation, low resource language, language technology

1. Introduction

Manipuri, a highly agglutinative low-resourced Indian language from the Sino-Tibetan language family, is reported as an extremely low-resourced language for MT/NLP tasks and developing an MT system for the already available size of data is a true challenge (Huidrom and Lepage, 2020). Manipuri is a morphologically-rich in nature. We introduce the creation of a pretrained word embedding model for Manipuri based on fastText that we call **EM-FT** (meaning, a **F**ast**T**ext word embedding model exclusively trained on Manipuri from the EM Corpus (Huidrom et al., 2021)) especially, for use in MT of Manipuri-English language pair.

The objective of this paper is to introduce word embeddings (Mikolov et al., 2013b; Peters et al., 2018) during MT. We trained the word embeddings using the monolingual Manipuri (locally known as Meiteilon) data of 1.88 million sentences from the EM Corpus. In particular, introducing this embeddings help in initialization and/or transfer learning for NLP/MT tasks and in cross-lingual transfer (Kakwani et al., 2020) for learning multilingual embeddings. The quality of the embeddings depends on the size of the monolingual data (Mikolov et al., 2013a; Bojanowski et al., 2017) which is a resource that is not widely available for many languages. In our case, the monolingual data of 1.88 million sentences is one of the largest among the available monolingual corpora of Manipuri.

In this paper, we report experiments for MT using the PMIndia data set and the *EM Corpus*. Furthermore, we report experiments on MT where we introduce our pretrained embeddings (*EM-FT*) during training.

The main contributions of our work are as follows:

- This is the first work to create a pretrained word embedding model trained from comparatively large Manipuri monolingual data and introduce it during MT of Manipuri–English language pair.
- We have shown the impact in the differences of the domains used for test data and training data in our experiments on MT.

The structure of the paper is as follows. Section 2 describes previous work. Section 3 gives details about the data set used. Section 4 presents the methodology. Section 5 describes the experiments, their results and provides an analysis. Section 7 concludes and proposes future directions.

2. Related Work

Word embeddings (Mikolov et al., 2013b; Peters et al., 2018) are a way of representing words in real-valued vector representations (Ortiz Suárez et al., 2019) and it can encode morphology, semantics, syntax etc. to some extent and it provides transfer learning in NLP tasks. Some examples of word embeddings are word2vec (Mikolov et al., 2013b), GloVe (Pennington et al., 2014) and fastText (Bojanowski et al., 2017). These models are context-free in nature: a given word has a single vector representation independent of context. Some of the existing word embeddings trained for Indian languages are The Polyglot (Al-Rfou' et al., 2013), IndicFT (Kakwani et al., 2020) and, fastText (Bojanowski et al., 2017; Mikolov et al., 2018; Grave et al., 2018) trained on Wikipedia and Common Crawl data. None of these includes Manipuri trained on large corpora or even a limited corpus.

Although NMT models are trained end-to-end with continuous representations that mitigate the sparsity problem in comparison to the rigid SMT architectures (Koehn et al., 2003), NMT (Sutskever et al., 2014; Bahdanau et al., 2015; Cho et al., 2014) possess a risk for low translation accuracy for low-resourced languages of small amounts (Koehn and Knowles, 2017). However, it is to note that SMT is still superior in training for corpus which are not big enough.

Data set	Language pair	sentence pairs	words / sent.	word types
PMIndia	Manipuri	7,419	15	22,289
	English		19	18,502
EM Corpus	Manipuri	124,975	21	74,516
	English		26	64,501

Table 1: Statistics on the data set used.

Our work consists of creating a pretrained word embeddings for Manipuri, which is one of a kind available for this low-resourced Indian language. We analyse how introducing our word embeddings to the NMT model during its training and further adding sentences from EM Corpus to the training set from base data set impact the translation quality and its results. In this paper, we propose to introduce word embeddings for Manipuri, EM-FT and study the impact of it.

3. Dataset

In this section, we discuss the nature of the low-resourced language, Manipuri, and the data set in use for our experiments, namely the PMIndia data set and the EM Corpus.

3.1. Manipuri (Meiteilon)

Manipuri, also known as Meiteilon, is an Indian language from the Sino-Tibetan language family. It follows the SOV (Subject-Object-Verb) syntax structure. Manipuri is predominately spoken in the Indian state Manipur with about two million native speakers. Manipuri is classified as 'vulnerable language' by UNESCO (Moseley and Nicolas, 2010), it is one of the two Indian languages listed in the 8th Schedule of the Indian Constitution as endangered.
Manipuri has two writing systems: Eastern Nagari Script (also known as the Bengali Script) and Meitei Mayek. We use Manipuri written in Eastern Nagari Script for all of our works. Again, Manipuri is a low-resourced language that has not been explored much in computational linguistics. One of the reasons being the limited amount of available resources. In this paper, we aim to bridge this gap by sharing our resources publicly.

3.2. PMIndia dataset

The PMIndia data set[1] (Haddow and Kirefu, 2020) is used as our base data set and with EM Corpus for MT. This data set (monolingual and parallel corpora) contains the official documents from the Prime Minister Office of the Government of India. There are 13 Indian languages and English in it. We use the parallel corpora of the Manipuri–English language pair for our experiments. Statistics about the data are described in Table 1. There are 7,419 sentences in parallel for the Manipuri–English language pair with the average number of words per sentence in Manipuri and English as 15 and 19. The available number of sentences in the monolingual corpora for Manipuri reported as 41,699 sentences.

3.3. EM Corpus

The Ema-lon Manipuri Corpus (translation: our mother tongue Manipuri Corpus), abbreviated as the EM Corpus[2] (Huidrom et al., 2021) is a comparable corpus created by collecting news articles daily from a newspaper website known as "The Sangai Express," which is available in both languages. An average of 14,000 sentences is crawled for this language pair daily. The reported data is being collected from August 2020 to March 2021. The domain of the EM Corpus (Rudali Huidrom and Yves Lepage, 2021) includes general articles, news on state, national and international affairs, sports and entertainment news, and the editorial.
The monolingual and parallel corpora contain 3.33 million and 124,975 sentences in total for both languages, along with the number of words per sentence in Manipuri and English to be 21 and 26. It is to note that the number of word types in each language reflects the number of sentences and the structure of the language: it is natural that the more the sentence pairs, the higher the number of word types as reported in Table 1.

4. Methodology

Our first series of experiments introduces the creation of a pretrained word embedding model exclusively for Manipuri. In particular, we chose fastText as it is capable of integrating subword information using character n-gram embeddings during training (Kakwani et al., 2020). Some of the previously published results on pretrained word embeddings suggests that fastText performs better than word-level algorithms like GloVe, word2vec for morphologically rich languages (Mikolov et al., 2013b; Pennington et al., 2014). We trained skipgram models on the monolingual data of EM corpus of 1.88 million sentences of Manipuri. We introduced the pretrained word embeddings during the training of the NMT models.
Our second series of experiments introduces the performance of MT task by iteratively increasing the amount of training data. We use 5,000 sentences from our base data set, PMIndia data set in the NMT models in the first iteration. It is the baseline of our experiment. The training data other than the base data set is created by adding 10,000 sentences each sampled from the EM corpus to its previous iteration. All our models are validated and tested on 1,000 sentences each from the PMIndia dataset. The training data from the base data set share the same domain with the test and validation data set.

[1] https://data.statmt.org/PMIndia/

[2] http://catalog.elra.info/en-us/repository/browse/ELRA-W0316/

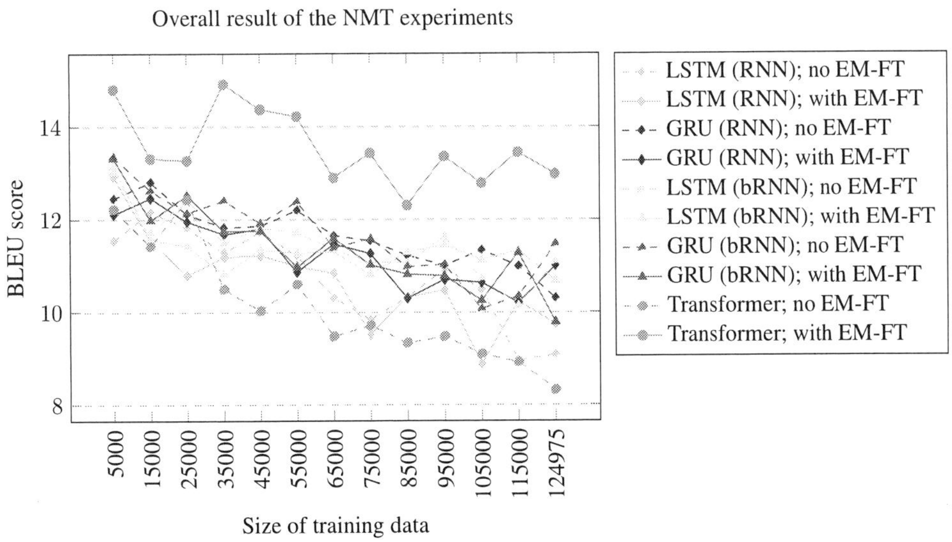

Figure 1: shows the result from the NMT experiments. All the experiments with s EM-FT are represented by a solid line otherwise, a dashed line. The results are color-coded and marked by different shapes for NMT architecture with different RNN type and/or different encoder & decoder respectively.

5. Experiments and results

5.1. EM-FT: fastText word embeddings

We train fastText (Bojanowski et al., 2017) word embeddings for Manipuri. In context to similar works, one of the most notable examples is when (Mikolov et al., 2018) first trained fastText in English using Common Crawl and for other 157 languages (Grave et al., 2018). However, there are no word embeddings reported for Manipur so far until our work. We train 300-dimensional word embeddings on our monolingual corpus obtained from the EM corpus. In particular, we chose fastText as it is capable of integrating subword information using character n-gram embeddings during training, and fastText is said to perform well among other word embeddings for morphologically rich languages (Kakwani et al., 2020). We trained skipgram models on our monolingual data of 1.88 million sentences of Manipuri for five epochs with a maximum and minimum character length as 2 and 5, size of the context window as 5 and 5 negative examples for each instance.

5.2. Machine Translation

To provide validation in the corpus, we perform NMT on the PMIndia data set as a base data set and later on, PMIndia data set + EM Corpus. As mentioned in 4, as the first series of experiments, MT is performed by further adding 10,000 sentences each sampled from the EM corpus to the base data set for every iteration and are validated and tested on 1,000 sentences of validation and test data set from the PMIndia data set. It is to note that the training data other than the base data set belong to a different domain. In the second series of experiments, we introduce our Manipuri word embeddings EM-FT during the training in the NMT models. We use Joint Byte-Pair Encoding (BPE) (Sennrich et al., 2016) to address the problem of rare words by using sub-word segmentation. We apply BPE on all of our selected data set with 30,000 merge operations to obtain a vocabulary representation of the Manipuri–English language pair. For all of our NMT experiments, we use the OpenNMT-py toolkit (Klein et al., 2017). We preprocess the training and validation data set for the Manipuri–English language pair after applying BPE. We train our model on a 2-layered RNN model with a bidirectional RNN as encoder and a simple RNN as a decoder, and on simple RNN as encoder and decoder. In addition, we train our model on a 2-layered Transformer architecture (Vaswani et al., 2017). We later introduce fastText word embeddings for Manipuri during the training of NMT models. We also train MT models on SMT architecture (Koehn et al., 2003) to validate our data set. We measure the translation accuracy of all our experiments using BLEU with confidence at 95 % (Koehn, 2004).

- **Model Configuration.** Firstly, we choose the default seq2seq architecture with attention mechanism (Luong et al., 2015) provided by OpenNMT-py toolkit (Klein et al., 2017) where both the encoders and decoders are LSTM cells (Hochreiter and Schmidhuber, 1997). Most of the hyper-parameters are the default ones provided by the toolkit. Secondly, we choose the Transformer architecture (Vaswani et al., 2017). (Lakew et al., 2018) reports that the transformer architecture usually outperforms the recurrent ones in all their

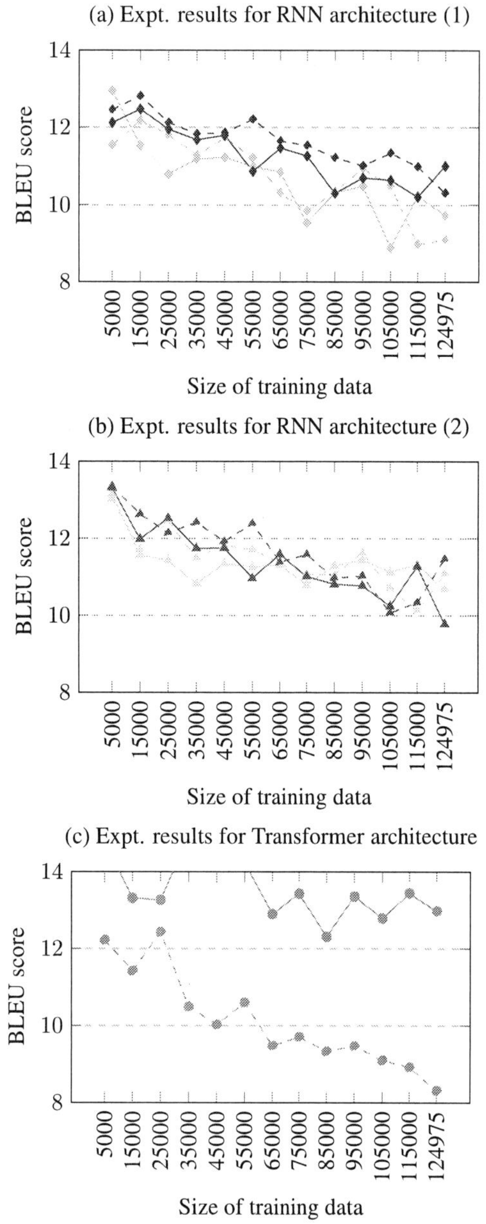

Figure 2: This figure is extracted from Figure 1. The results in (a) are from the NMT experiments for RNN architecture (diamond) with RNN Type as LSTM (pink) and GRU (violet) of encoder type and decoder type as RNN The results in (b) are from the NMT experiments for RNN architecture (triangle) with RNN Type as LSTM (lime) and GRU (teal) of encoder type and decoder type as bRNN & RNN. The results in (c) are from the Transformer architecture. Experiments with s EM-FT are represented by a solid line otherwise, a dashed line.

systems.

- **Training Settings.** The hyper-parameters are uniform throughout all the models in our experiments. Firstly, we train the NMT model on a two-layered RNN model having a layer size of 64 for embeddings and 500 for inner layers. The LSTM is trained on encoder type as bidirectional RNN and decoder as a simple RNN, and on simple RNN as encoder and decoder. We also use the general typed global attention mechanism onto the RNN models. The models are trained with 10,000 training steps with checkpoints at every 5,000 steps and a drop-out (Srivastava et al., 2014) rate of 0.3 (Gal and Ghahramani, 2016) across all the NMT experiments. For optimization of the model during training, we use the Adam (Kingma and Ba, 2015) optimizer with a learning rate of 0.001. The number of steps set before dropping the learning rate is 50,000. The decay frequency is the number of steps at which the learning rate starts to drop at each training step taken is 10,000. Secondly, for the Transformer, we used the recommended setting by the OpenNMT-py toolkit, except for the learning rate of 0.001.

6. Results and Analysis

In this particular experimental setting for validating and testing against training data from different domain, it is observed that Transformer with our word embeddings EM-FT outperforms the rest. See results in Figure 1.

As we progress with the adding more training data, we observe a decrease in the BLEU score which is expected. It is to be noted that the decrease is not linear in nature. The data that we add other than the base data set are obtained from the news crawls which are not standardised translated data. Although, the sentences are aligned, the parallel sentences are not exact translations of one another, instead comparable. Our validation and test data are from the PMIndia (Haddow and Kirefu, 2020) dataset whose domain is the official documents from the Prime Minister Office of India. In most of the experiments, the sudden increase of the BLEU score could be the result of seeing similar sentences crawled from the news articles related to the Prime Minister Office while training.

The NMT system reported in this paper did not perform well for Transformer architecture without EM-FT. It is followed by RNN architecture of RNN type as LSTM with encoder & decoder as RNN and with encoder & decoder as bRNN & RNN. Another interesting observation is that RNN architecture of RNN type as GRU with encoder & decoder as RNN as well as with encoder & decoder as bRNN & RNN are similar in nature irrespective of the presence of EM-FT. It is expected of RNN architecture with encoder & decoder as bRNN and RNN to perform better than the encoder & decoder as RNN as observed in the case of RNN architecture of LSTM with or without EM-FT.

In most of the experiments on RNN architecture, there

is a sudden change in BLEU score between 45,000 sentences and 65,000 sentences of training data.

7. Conclusion

This work provided an insight into creation of pretrained word embeddings for Manipuri–English language pair and to use it in NMT task. Firstly, we studied the creation of the pretrained word embeddings using fastText, EM-FT for Manipuri. Secondly, we performed MT on these data, given the condition that it is tested and validated on a data set of a completely different domain. All in all, we confirm the following observations.

First, it is observed in Figure 1 that the Transformer architecture with the EM-FT fastText word embeddings model performs better than without in all the NMT experiments.

Second, the impact of differences in domains used for test data and training data is clearly demonstrated in our experiments. Adding more data from a different domain negatively impacts the translation accuracy.

In the future, we would like to inspect the possibility of increasing the size of data from the same domain by using data-augmentation techniques, so as to increase the translation accuracy of NMT with a BERT (Devlin et al., 2018) model for Manipuri.

8. Bibliographical References

Al-Rfou', R., Perozzi, B., and Skiena, S. (2013). Polyglot: Distributed word representations for multilingual NLP. In *Proceedings of the Seventeenth Conference on Computational Natural Language Learning*, pages 183–192, Sofia, Bulgaria, August. Association for Computational Linguistics.

Bahdanau, D., Cho, K., and Bengio, Y. (2015). Neural machine translation by jointly learning to align and translate. In Yoshua Bengio et al., editors, *3rd International Conference on Learning Representations, ICLR 2015, San Diego, CA, USA, May 7-9, 2015, Conference Track Proceedings*.

Bojanowski, P., Grave, E., Joulin, A., and Mikolov, T. (2017). Enriching word vectors with subword information. *Transactions of the Association for Computational Linguistics*, 5:135–146.

Cho, K., van Merrienboer, B., Gulcehre, C., Bougares, F., Schwenk, H., and Bengio, Y. (2014). Learning phrase representations using rnn encoder-decoder for statistical machine translation. In *Conference on Empirical Methods in Natural Language Processing (EMNLP 2014)*.

Devlin, J., Chang, M.-W., Lee, K., and Toutanova, K. (2018). Bert: Pre-training of deep bidirectional transformers for language understanding. *arXiv preprint arXiv:1810.04805*.

Gal, Y. and Ghahramani, Z. (2016). Dropout as a bayesian approximation: Representing model uncertainty in deep learning. In Maria Florina Balcan et al., editors, *Proceedings of Machine Learning Research*, volume 48, pages 1050–1059, New York, New York, USA, 20–22 Jun. PMLR.

Grave, E., Bojanowski, P., Gupta, P., Joulin, A., and Mikolov, T. (2018). Learning word vectors for 157 languages. In *Proceedings of the Eleventh International Conference on Language Resources and Evaluation (LREC 2018)*, Miyazaki, Japan, May. European Language Resources Association (ELRA).

Haddow, B. and Kirefu, F. (2020). Pmindia - a collection of parallel corpora of languages of india. *ArXiv*, abs/2001.09907.

Hochreiter, S. and Schmidhuber, J. (1997). Long short-term memory. *Neural Computation*, 9(8):1735–1780, November.

Huidrom, R. and Lepage, Y. (2020). Zero-shot translation among Indian languages. In *Proceedings of the 3rd Workshop on Technologies for MT of Low Resource Languages*, pages 47–54, Suzhou, China, December. Association for Computational Linguistics.

Huidrom, R., Lepage, Y., and Khomdram, K. (2021). EM corpus: a comparable corpus for a less-resourced language pair Manipuri-English. In *Proceedings of the 14th Workshop on Building and Using Comparable Corpora (BUCC 2021)*, pages 60–67, Online (Virtual Mode), September. INCOMA Ltd.

Kakwani, D., Kunchukuttan, A., Golla, S., N.C., G., Bhattacharyya, A., Khapra, M. M., and Kumar, P. (2020). IndicNLPSuite: Monolingual corpora, evaluation benchmarks and pre-trained multilingual language models for Indian languages. In *Findings of the Association for Computational Linguistics: EMNLP 2020*, pages 4948–4961, Online, November. Association for Computational Linguistics.

Kingma, D. P. and Ba, J. (2015). Adam: A method for stochastic optimization. In Yoshua Bengio et al., editors, *3rd International Conference on Learning Representations, ICLR 2015, San Diego, CA, USA, May 7-9, 2015, Conference Track Proceedings*.

Klein, G., Kim, Y., Deng, Y., Senellart, J., and Rush, A. (2017). OpenNMT: Open-source toolkit for neural machine translation. In *Proceedings of ACL 2017, System Demonstrations*, pages 67–72, Vancouver, Canada, July. Association for Computational Linguistics.

Koehn, P. and Knowles, R. (2017). Six challenges for neural machine translation. In *Proceedings of the First Workshop on Neural Machine Translation*, pages 28–39, Vancouver, August. Association for Computational Linguistics.

Koehn, P., Och, F. J., and Marcu, D. (2003). Statistical phrase-based translation. In *Proceedings of the 2003 Human Language Technology Conference of the North American Chapter of the Association for Computational Linguistics*, pages 127–133.

Koehn, P. (2004). Statistical significance tests for machine translation evaluation. In *Proceedings of the 2004 Conference on Empirical Methods in Natural Language Processing*, pages 388–395, Barcelona, Spain, July. Association for Computational Linguistics.

Lakew, S. M., Cettolo, M., and Federico, M. (2018). A comparison of transformer and recurrent neural networks on multilingual neural machine translation. In *Proceedings of the 27th International Conference on Computational Linguistics*, pages 641–652, Santa Fe, New Mexico, USA, August. Association for Computational Linguistics.

Luong, T., Pham, H., and Manning, C. D. (2015). Effective approaches to attention-based neural machine translation. In *Proceedings of the 2015 Conference on Empirical Methods in Natural Language Processing*, pages 1412–1421, Lisbon, Portugal, September. Association for Computational Linguistics.

Mikolov, T., Chen, K., Corrado, G. S., and Dean, J. (2013a). Efficient estimation of word representations in vector space.

Mikolov, T., Sutskever, I., Chen, K., Corrado, G., and Dean, J. (2013b). Distributed representations of words and phrases and their compositionality. In *Proceedings of the 26th International Conference on Neural Information Processing Systems - Volume 2*, NIPS'13, page 3111–3119, Red Hook, NY, USA. Curran Associates Inc.

Mikolov, T., Grave, E., Bojanowski, P., Puhrsch, C., and Joulin, A. (2018). Advances in pre-training distributed word representations. In *Proceedings of the Eleventh International Conference on Language Resources and Evaluation (LREC 2018)*, Miyazaki, Japan, May. European Language Resources Association (ELRA).

Moseley, C. and Nicolas, A. (2010). *Atlas of the world's languages in danger*. UNESCO, France, 3 edition.

Ortiz Suárez, P. J., Sagot, B., and Romary, L. (2019). Asynchronous pipelines for processing huge corpora on medium to low resource infrastructures. In Piotr Bański, et al., editors, *Proceedings of the Workshop on Challenges in the Management of Large Corpora (CMLC-7) 2019. Cardiff, 22nd July 2019*, pages 9 – 16, Mannheim. Leibniz-Institut für Deutsche Sprache.

Pennington, J., Socher, R., and Manning, C. (2014). GloVe: Global vectors for word representation. In *Proceedings of the 2014 Conference on Empirical Methods in Natural Language Processing (EMNLP)*, pages 1532–1543, Doha, Qatar, October. Association for Computational Linguistics.

Peters, M., Neumann, M., Iyyer, M., Gardner, M., Clark, C., Lee, K., and Zettlemoyer, L. (2018). Deep contextualized word representations. In *Proceedings of the 2018 Conference of the North American Chapter of the Association for Computational Linguistics: Human Language Technologies, Volume 1 (Long Papers)*, pages 2227–2237, New Orleans, Louisiana, June. Association for Computational Linguistics.

Sennrich, R., Haddow, B., and Birch, A. (2016). Neural machine translation of rare words with subword units. In *Proceedings of the 54th Annual Meeting of the Association for Computational Linguistics (Volume 1: Long Papers)*, pages 1715–1725, Berlin, Germany, August. Association for Computational Linguistics.

Srivastava, N., Hinton, G., Krizhevsky, A., Sutskever, I., and Salakhutdinov, R. (2014). Dropout: A simple way to prevent neural networks from overfitting. *Journal of Machine Learning Research*, 15(56):1929–1958.

Sutskever, I., Vinyals, O., and Le, Q. V. (2014). Sequence to sequence learning with neural networks. In *Advances in neural information processing systems*, pages 3104–3112.

Vaswani, A., Shazeer, N., Parmar, N., Uszkoreit, J., Jones, L., Gomez, A. N., Kaiser, L. u., and Polosukhin, I. (2017). Attention is all you need. In I. Guyon, et al., editors, *Advances in Neural Information Processing Systems 30*, pages 5998–6008. Curran Associates, Inc.

9. Language Resource References

Rudali Huidrom and Yves Lepage. (2021). *Ema-lon Manipuri Corpus (including word embedding and language model)*. distributed via ELRA: ELRA-Id ELRA-W0316, ISLRN 588-170-827-016-7.

Proceedings of the WILDRE-6 Workshop @LREC2020, pages 7–12
Marseille, 20 June 2022

L3Cube-HingCorpus and HingBERT: A Code Mixed Hindi-English Dataset and BERT Language Models

Ravindra Nayak[1,3], **Raviraj Joshi** [2,3]
[1] Sri Jayachamarajendra College of Engineering, [2] Indian Institute of Technology Madras, [3] L3Cube Pune
[1] Mysore, Karnataka India, [2] Chennai, Tamilnadu India, [3] Pune, Maharashtra India
ravindranyk707@gmail.com, ravirajoshi@gmail.com

Abstract

Code-switching occurs when more than one language is mixed in a given sentence or a conversation. This phenomenon is more prominent on social media platforms and its adoption is increasing over time. Therefore code-mixed NLP has been extensively studied in the literature. As pre-trained transformer-based architectures are gaining popularity, we observe that real code-mixing data are scarce to pre-train large language models. We present L3Cube-HingCorpus, the first large-scale real Hindi-English code mixed data in a Roman script. It consists of 52.93M sentences and 1.04B tokens, scraped from Twitter. We further present HingBERT, HingMBERT, HingRoBERTa, and HingGPT. The BERT models have been pre-trained on codemixed HingCorpus using masked language modelling objectives. We show the effectiveness of these BERT models on the subsequent downstream tasks like code-mixed sentiment analysis, POS tagging, NER, and LID from the GLUECoS benchmark. The HingGPT is a GPT2 based generative transformer model capable of generating full tweets. Our models show significant improvements over currently available models pre-trained on multiple languages and synthetic code-mixed datasets. We also release L3Cube-HingLID Corpus, the largest code-mixed Hindi-English language identification(LID) dataset and HingBERT-LID, a production-quality LID model to facilitate capturing of more code-mixed data using the process outlined in this work. The dataset and models are available at `https://github.com/l3cube-pune/code-mixed-nlp`.

Keywords: Code mixed, BERT, code switch, Hinglish, English, Hindi, MBERT, XLM-RoBERTa, HingCorpus, HingBERT, GPT

1. Introduction

Popular languages like English have been penetrating non-English societies. The usage of English along with other local languages has drastically increased. As people are getting accustomed to it, there is also a need of understanding such code-mixed data. In this internet era, we see the usage of code-mixed data prevalently in social media and chat platforms (Kim, 2006). We observe that there is a mismatch between the scale at which this code-mixed language is used and the data that is available for further research.

As Hindi is the third most spoken language in the world after English and Mandarin[1]. The usage of Hinglish, a portmanteau of Hindi and English (Srivastava and Singh, 2021a; Gupta et al., 2020a) has become popular in the recent past in the Indian sub-continent. Since it is difficult to build a large scale code-mixed dataset, the literature has been more inclined toward building synthetic code-mixed datasets (Srivastava and Singh, 2021b). However, at the same time real code-mixed data has been shown to produce better results than synthetically generated datasets (Santy et al., 2021). We, therefore, aim to build a real Hinglish data corpora which can be used to enhance other code-mixed NLP tasks. In this work, we build L3Cube-HingCorpus a Hindi-English code-mixed corpus, containing 52.93M sentences and 1.04B tokens.

The unsupervised HingCorpus is further used to train BERT based language models. The BERT based architectures have gained traction recently, due to their various pre-training and fine-tuning techniques that have taken over initial deep learning techniques. The unsupervised pretraining has shown promising results on deep neural network architectures as they act like a regulariser to the model (Erhan et al., 2010). So we pretrain the model on the masked language modelling task and then further try to evaluate various downstream tasks.

We introduce transformer-based BERT models (Devlin et al., 2019), namely HingBERT, [2], HingMBERT, [34], and HingRoBERTa [56] all pre-trained on our Hinglish corpus. We release both roman and mixed script versions of these models trained on roman script text and roman + Devanagari text respectively. The models have been evaluated on various downstream tasks such as Language Identification(LID), Named Entity Recognition(NER), Part of Speech(POS) tagging and Sentiment analysis, which were part of the GLUECos benchmark dataset (Khanuja et al., 2020). We also release other resources like HingGPT [78] , a GPT2 (Radford et al., 2019) model trained on HingCorpus and

[1] `https://en.wikipedia.org/wiki/Hindi`

[2] `https://huggingface.co/l3cube-pune/hing-bert`
[3] `https://huggingface.co/l3cube-pune/hing-mbert`
[4] `https://huggingface.co/l3cube-pune/hing-mbert-mixed`
[5] `https://huggingface.co/l3cube-pune/hing-roberta`
[6] `https://huggingface.co/l3cube-pune/hing-roberta-mixed`
[7] `https://huggingface.co/l3cube-pune/hing-gpt`
[8] `https://huggingface.co/l3cube-pune/hing-gpt-devanagari`

HingFT, the fast text (Mikolov et al., 2018) based code-mixed Hindi-English word embeddings.

To facilitate further creation of code-mixed Hi-En corpus we release HingBERT-LID [9] , a token level Hindi-English language identification model trained on a large in-house LID dataset. The model can be utilized to select code-mixed Hi-En sentences and expand the HingCorpus using the process outlined in the paper. A subset of the LID dataset is released as a benchmark code mixed Hindi-English language identification dataset L3Cube-HingLID. This is the largest LID dataset for the Hi-En pair.

The data and models will be publicly [10] released to enable further research in Hinglish NLP.

2. Related Work

In this section, we will try to mainly discuss previous attempts in the creation of code-mixed datasets. User-generated content is the main source of code-mixed data, and preprocessing is necessary for tasks like profanity hate speech (Qin et al., 2020; Bohra et al., 2018; Kamble and Joshi, 2018; Santosh and Aravind, 2019; Nayak and Joshi, 2021), sentiment analysis, etc. Various attempts of scraping have been done before for the initial set of code-mixed data and later augmented synthetically using equivalence constraint theory (Pratapa et al., 2018), semi-supervised learning (Gupta et al., 2020b) and rule-based language-pair approaches (Srivastava and Singh, 2021b).

As BERT based architectures are gaining popularity, there have been studies around pre-training and fine-tuning them on various tasks. There have been variations around the BERT architecture like RoBERTa (Liu et al., 2019) and ALBERT (Lan et al., 2020), which have helped in various use cases like accuracy and latency related improvements. Models like multilingual-BERT, XLM-RoBERTa (Conneau et al., 2020), have focused mainly on multilingual and cross-lingual data representations.

While evaluating code-mixed tasks, it is also shown that training on code-mixed sentences has given better results compared to training them on multiple monolingual corpora (Ansari et al., 2021). Bertlogicomix (Santy et al., 2021) have shown that real code-mixed data works much better when compared to synthetically generated after fine-tuning on various BERT based architectures. All the above models have been pre-trained on not more than 100k real code-mixed sentences. GLUECoS, the benchmark dataset was also evaluated on models pre-trained using 5M sentences which was a mix of both real and synthetic code-mixed sentences. (Khanuja et al., 2020)

[9] https://huggingface.co/l3cube-pune/hing-bert-lid

[10] https://github.com/l3cube-pune/code-mixed-nlp

3. Curation of Dataset

Our data consists of tweets that were scraped using the framework Twint [11]. An initial vocabulary of commonly spoken Hindi words was iteratively built to scrape the tweets containing these words. The initial vocabulary was constantly updated to include the newly found words from the scraped data. As we focus only on the code-switched Roman script, the scraped data was then preprocessed to remove non-English characters. User mentions in the tweet were also removed to avoid privacy concerns.

The pre-processed data is passed through a word-level language classifier model to detect the language of each word. If both Hindi and English words are present in the sentence it is treated as a code-mixed sentence. The language classifier is initially a shallow subword-based LSTM as described in (Joshi and Joshi, 2022). The shallow model is shown to work well for Hindi-English language identification on limited data. The model is trained iteratively using a semi-supervised learning approach. A small labelled dataset with 5k sentences was created initially and further multiple versions of the models are trained using the pseudo-labels generated from the previous version. We manually verified less confident pseudo labels and corrected labels were fed for the next iteration of training. In the end, we create a dataset of around 44455 sentences using this process. Finally, the expanded dataset is used to fine-tune the base BERT model as it worked better than the LSTM counterpart. This ensured that we have a strong word language classifier in place while creating the target dataset. It was ensured that the LID model was highly accurate as the quality of the Hinglish corpus depended heavily on the LID accuracy. The details of the LID accuracy are discussed in the results section. We set a threshold to check whether a sufficient number of Hindi and English words are present in the sentence to consider it as code-mixed. A sentence is considered code-mixed if it has at least 2 Hindi and 2 English words. We have retained the case, punctuation and smileys in the sentences and the data were shuffled in the end for training.

The final dataset consists of nearly 52.93M sentences (1.04B tokens), out of which 47.79M (944M tokens) sentences were used for training and 5.13M sentences (99M tokens) for validation. The Devanagari version of HingCorpus is created using an in-house transliteration model. The Devanagari dataset contains an equal number of sentences and an approximately similar number of tokens. A code-mixing metric viz Mixed CMI index (Gambäck and Das, 2016) of 31.21 was obtained from final data, where 0 corresponds to monolingual data with no code-mixing and 100 is the highest degree of code-switching.

[11] https://github.com/twintproject/twint

Table 1: This table represents the F1 scores of test sets after fine-tuning on various downstream tasks of the GLUECoS dataset in Roman script

Model	LID	POS-UD	POS-FG	NER	Sentiment	HingLID
BERT	78.69	83.70	70.75	79.27	59.16	96.04
m-BERT	82.56	83.68	69.58	76.64	58.42	95.59
XLMRoBERTa	85.93	87.24	70.95	77.01	61.57	95.42
HingBERT	84.44	88.42	71.04	**81.80**	63.72	96.21
HingMBERT	84.90	89.47	71.55	80.09	63.51	96.27
HingRoBERTa	**86.69**	**90.17**	**71.69**	81.13	66.43	96.15
HingMBERT-mixed	83.26	90.06	70.34	81.12	63.51	96.29
HingRoBERTa-mixed	86.13	89.87	70.73	80.68	**66.73**	95.96
HingBERT-LID	-	-	-	-	-	**98.77**

4. Model Architecture

Our architecture includes various BERT model variations, that are trained on unsupervised learning tasks like masked language model (MLM) and next sentence prediction (NSP). Deep bi-directional transformers are the basic building block of these models. Their use has been prevalent due to their understanding of the long term dependencies of text. Moreover, they are capable of making use of contemporary hardware to train the models parallelly. We explore three variations of BERT-based models viz. BERT-base, m-BERT and XLM-RoBERTa.

- **BERT :** Also known as BERT-base (Devlin et al., 2019), it is a model that contains 12 transformer blocks, 12 self-attention heads, hidden size of 768. The input for BERT contains a maximum embedding of 512 words and it outputs a sequential representation. Special tokens like [CLS] and [SEP] are used to specify the start of a sentence and separation of sentences respectively. For a classification task, final encoder representations are considered and a softmax is applied to classify the representation.
- **Multilingual-BERT (m-BERT) :** This model's architecture is based on BERT-base. It has been trained in 102 languages with a word-piece vocabulary of size 110k (Devlin et al., 2019). It has shown promising results for zero-shot transfer learning on various downstream tasks and also helped in code-switched data tasks (Pires et al., 2019).
- **XLM-RoBERTa :** It is a transformer-based multi-lingual language model which has been trained on 100 languages (Conneau et al., 2020). It has shown great results in cross-lingual tasks and has outperformed m-BERT in various multilingual downstream tasks.

5. HingBERT Evaluation

5.1. Training

In this work, we consider three variations of BERT architectures i.e. BERT, m-BERT and XLM-RoBERTa for training. These models are further pre-trained on L3Cube-HingCorpus using MLM objective with a masking probability of 15%. The models were trained for 2 epochs with a learning rate of 1e-5 and a batch size of 64. We observed that 2 epochs were sufficient for the models to converge as we loaded the pre-trained weights of the respective models. Moreover, there was no significant decrease in the loss after 2 epochs. The respective models after Hinglish training are referred to as HingBERT, HingMBERT and HingRoBERTa and their validation perplexity on this task is shown in Table 4. These were further fine-tuned on the respective downstream tasks by considering the [CLS] or token embeddings and feeding it to feed-forward layers. We train two versions of models in Roman script and mixed script. The mixed script model is trained on both roman and Devanagari text. The mixed script model can be used for both roman or Devanagari code-mixed text. The mixed script HingBERT models are evaluated on the Devanagari version of the GLUECoS dataset.

Table 2: This table shows the evaluation of pre-training the model on the MLM task. Perplexity is a measure to validate how well the language model can predict the next word, in the case of BERT it would be the prediction of masked words.

Model	Validation Perplexity
HingBERT	5.72
HingMBERT	5.20
HingRoBERTa	7.82
HingMBERT-mixed	5.22
HingRoBERTa-mixed	9.39

5.2. Downstream Tasks

For the evaluation of our models, we use the EN-HI pair from GLUECoS, a code-switching benchmark dataset, for the below mentioned NLP tasks. The models were fine-tuned by adding a dense layer on top of the BERT encoder. These were fine-tuned for 5 epochs using early stopping w.r.t validation F1 score. A batch size of 64 and a learning rate of 3e-5 were used.

1. **Language Identification (LID)**: This task is to

Table 3: This table represents the F1 scores of test sets after fine-tuning on various downstream tasks of the GLUECoS dataset in mixed script including Roman and Devanagari script.

Model	LID	POS-UD	POS-FG	NER	Sentiment
SOTA	96.6	90.53	80.68	78.21	59.35
BERT	95.30	81.49	68.55	73.92	60.14
m-BERT	95.03	86.87	69.81	74.79	60.45
XLMRoBERTa	95.37	89.62	70.53	75.53	63.93
GLUECoS-mBERT	96.6	88.06	63.31	78.21	59.35
BERToLogicoMix	95.8	88.09	60.46	76.86	58.25
HingBERT	95.54	82.26	67.69	77.60	59.59
HingMBERT	95.68	86.71	70.15	78.78	60.72
HingRoBERTa	**96.30**	89.97	69.90	80.28	64.43
HingMBERT-mixed	95.65	89.31	70.52	79.66	62.93
HingRoBERTa-mixed	94.96	**90.81**	**70.61**	**81.72**	**66.07**

mainly identify the language for each word in the given sentence, with labels EN (English), HI (Hindi) and OTHER. This task contains 2631 training data points along with 500 dev and 406 test data, and the SOTA was achieved by the GLUECoS-mBERT model (Khanuja et al., 2020).

2. **Part of Speech (POS) tagging**: There are 2 datasets under this subtask which are named POS-UD and POS-FG. POS-UD has 16 labels to predict with 1384 data points for training and 215 & 215 for dev & test respectively. Similarly, POS-FG has 2104, 263 & 264 data points for training, dev and testing with nearly 35 unique labels. The highest score is mentioned state-of-the-art (SOTA) models for these tasks given by papers (Bhat et al., 2018) for POS-UD and (Sharma, 2015) for POS-FG.

3. **NER (Named Entity Recognition)**: This is a token level classification task for words consisting of 7 labels. There are 2467 training data sentences and 308 & 309 sentences for validation & testing. The SOTA was achieved by GLUECoS-mBERT model (Khanuja et al., 2020).

4. **Sentiment analysis**: This is a multi-class classification task of predicting the sentiment of the sentence as positive, negative or neutral. This dataset contains 10080, 1260 and 1261 sentences for train, dev and test sets respectively. GLUECoS-mBERT model was able to achieve SOTA on this task.

6. L3Cube-HingLID Corpus

The LID dataset used to train the LID model is termed L3Cube-HingLID and is released publicly as the benchmark dataset. The L3Cube-HingLID consists of 31756, 6420, and 6279 train, test, and validation samples respectively with an average of nearly 30 tokens per sentence across all the datasets. All the models considered in this work are also evaluated on this LID dataset. Note that the HingBERT-LID model released as a part of this work was trained on a bigger corpus and provides the best numbers on the L3Cube-HingLID test set as compared to the models trained only on its train set. It was ensured that the test and validation set were separate and not leaked during the training of HingBERT-LID. The original LID train set was further expanded using the first generation of the BERT model trained on this train set to label an equal amount of unlabelled datasets. Both the supervised data and unsupervised data were used to train the final model. This strong LID model with 98% of accuracy on the unseen test set was used for selecting sentences for HingCorpus.

Table 4: This table shows the token level details of HingLID dataset

Data	EN	HI
Train	274255	693977
Test	56723	136824
Validation	56143	137575

7. Other Resources

7.1. HingGPT

HingGPT is a standard GPT2 causal transformer model trained on HingCorpus using the language modelling task. The model has 12 standard transformer layers and is trained using the Causal Language Model (CLM) objective. With a learning rate of 5e-5, the model is trained for 2 epochs. We train both roman and Devanagari versions of the model and are capable of generating full tweets. The mixed script version is not relevant for GPT and hence is not considered. The model can be further used to either generate or evaluate the quality of synthetic code-mixed corpus. Some sample tweets generated using roman HingGPT are shown in Table 5.

7.2. HingFT

We train fast text style distributed word representations using the HingCorpus and term it as HingFT. A skip-

Table 5: This table shows some of the sentences generated by our HingGPT model. The words that are in bold are the initial text provided to the model to generate the sentences

Sentences generated by HingGPT
My name is Julien and I like to make food for you every hour and see the whole world without you , I can ' t even keep you happy , I know you will be missed You are the best but how do you forget to add , the world is the best , it has the ultimate universe .
mujhe iss duniya se jana , na ki zindagi se . mujhe bas apna rehna ... teri ek muskan se bhi mangi hui har kami ko hai . dil mein hai it ' s so weird to even see people who ask for their rights are just asking to follow .
The goal of life is not to lose trust of your own self . And it ' s more important than your own self .
The goal of life is not merely a mere lawyers document , it is a vehicle of life , and its spirit is always the spirit of age . - Dr . Khan
Corona has become worse . So , for now , for the benefit of the family , we have to pay enough to get our daughters vaccinated . If we had a booster , it ' s better our kids should ' ve.

gram model is used to train 300 dimension word embeddings using the standard training parameters. The model is trained for 10 epochs using a learning rate of 0.05. The fast text uses subwords to create word embeddings and is more suitable for code-mixed text.

7.3. Results and Discussions

All the HingBERT models are pre-trained with similar hyper-parameters and fine-tuned on different tasks. The models are evaluated on 3 token classification tasks POS, NER, LID and one sentence classification task of sentiment identification. These tasks are part of the GLUECoS benchmark. We use the F1 score as the metric for the evaluation of these models. The dataset for these tasks is present in roman and mixed script form. The mixed script is mostly in the Devnagari script along with some roman tokens. The results for all the tasks in Roman script are described in Table 1. Table 3 describes the results for tasks in mixed Devanagari + Roman script. Along with models introduced in this work we also evaluate baseline models like base BERT, m-BERT, and XLMRoBERTa. Table 3 also shows various SOTA F1 scores on all these tasks. The mixed script form of the dataset has been mainly evaluated in the literature so SOTA numbers are only added for the mixed script form. We observe that our models outperform SOTA numbers on NER and Sentiment tasks. They perform competitively on the LID and POS-UD tasks. They perform poorly only on the POS-FG mixed-script task where all the BERT models fail to compete with SOTA. However, our models consistently outperform the baseline BERT models on all the tasks. Both roman and mixed-script models perform better than their respective baselines on either of the script. We see that the roman models perform slightly better than the mixed script ones on the roman script tasks. Similarly, mixed-script models perform better than roman models on mixed-script tasks. The observations are consistent with the general assumption that the addition of Devanagari data will help the mixed-script tasks containing Devanagari words. Among the models introduced in this work, the RoBERTa based models mostly perform the best. It outperforms all the BERT based models and also achieves SOTA on three tasks except for the POS-FG and LID tasks. Overall we show that pre-training on real code-mixed corpus provides significant performance improvements.

8. Conclusion

In this paper, we expand the code mixed Hindi-English corpora, using various data mining and curation techniques. We present L3Cube-HingCorpus, the first major unsupervised Hindi-English code-mixed dataset. We have used these corpora in pre-training our BERT based models namely HingBERT, HingMBERT, HingRoBERTa. These models were later evaluated on various downstream NLP tasks. We observe that pretraining the models on real code mixed data have helped them outperform BERT models pre-trained on non-code-mixed corpus and synthetic code-mixed corpus and achieve SOTA on the majority of these tasks. We also release other resources like HingGPT, a GPT2 model and HingFT, a Hinglish fast-text model both trained on HingCorpus. We leave the evaluation of these models on downstream tasks to future work. Finally, we curate a new Hindi-English LID Corpus HingLID containing around 44k sentences and also release HingBERT-LID to further help augmentation of HingCorpus.

9. Bibliographical References

Ansari, M. Z., Beg, M. M. S., Ahmad, T., Khan, M. J., and Wasim, G. (2021). Language identification of hindi-english tweets using code-mixed bert.

Bhat, I., Bhat, R. A., Shrivastava, M., and Sharma, D. (2018). Universal Dependency parsing for Hindi-English code-switching. In *Proceedings of the 2018 Conference of the North American Chapter of the Association for Computational Linguistics: Human Language Technologies, Volume 1 (Long Papers)*, pages 987–998, New Orleans, Louisiana, June. Association for Computational Linguistics.

Bohra, A., Vijay, D., Singh, V., Akhtar, S. S., and Shrivastava, M. (2018). A dataset of hindi-english code-mixed social media text for hate speech detection. In *Proceedings of the second workshop on computational modeling of people's opinions, personality, and emotions in social media*, pages 36–41.

Conneau, A., Khandelwal, K., Goyal, N., Chaudhary, V., Wenzek, G., Guzmán, F., Grave, E., Ott, M., Zettlemoyer, L., and Stoyanov, V. (2020). Unsupervised cross-lingual representation learning at scale.

Devlin, J., Chang, M.-W., Lee, K., and Toutanova, K. (2019). Bert: Pre-training of deep bidirectional transformers for language understanding.

Erhan, D., Bengio, Y., Courville, A., Manzagol, P.-A., Vincent, P., and Bengio, S. (2010). Why does unsupervised pre-training help deep learning? *Journal of Machine Learning Research*, 11(19):625–660.

Gambäck, B. and Das, A. (2016). Comparing the level of code-switching in corpora. In Nicoletta Calzolari (Conference Chair), et al., editors, *Proceedings of the Tenth International Conference on Language Resources and Evaluation (LREC 2016)*, Paris, France, may. European Language Resources Association (ELRA).

Gupta, D., Ekbal, A., and Bhattacharyya, P. (2020a). A semi-supervised approach to generate the code-mixed text using pre-trained encoder and transfer learning. In *Findings of the Association for Computational Linguistics: EMNLP 2020*, pages 2267–2280.

Gupta, D., Ekbal, A., and Bhattacharyya, P. (2020b). A semi-supervised approach to generate the code-mixed text using pre-trained encoder and transfer learning. In *Findings of the Association for Computational Linguistics: EMNLP 2020*, pages 2267–2280, Online, November. Association for Computational Linguistics.

Joshi, R. and Joshi, R. (2022). Evaluating input representation for language identification in hindi-english code mixed text. In *ICDSMLA 2020*, pages 795–802. Springer.

Kamble, S. and Joshi, A. (2018). Hate speech detection from code-mixed hindi-english tweets using deep learning models. *arXiv preprint arXiv:1811.05145*.

Khanuja, S., Dandapat, S., Srinivasan, A., Sitaram, S., and Choudhury, M. (2020). Gluecos : An evaluation benchmark for code-switched nlp.

Kim, E. (2006). Reasons and motivations for code-mixing and code-switching. *Issues in EFL*, 4(1):43–61.

Lan, Z., Chen, M., Goodman, S., Gimpel, K., Sharma, P., and Soricut, R. (2020). Albert: A lite bert for self-supervised learning of language representations.

Liu, Y., Ott, M., Goyal, N., Du, J., Joshi, M., Chen, D., Levy, O., Lewis, M., Zettlemoyer, L., and Stoyanov, V. (2019). Roberta: A robustly optimized bert pretraining approach.

Mikolov, T., Grave, É., Bojanowski, P., Puhrsch, C., and Joulin, A. (2018). Advances in pre-training distributed word representations. In *Proceedings of the Eleventh International Conference on Language Resources and Evaluation (LREC 2018)*.

Nayak, R. and Joshi, R. (2021). Contextual hate speech detection in code mixed text using transformer based approaches. *arXiv preprint arXiv:2110.09338*.

Pires, T., Schlinger, E., and Garrette, D. (2019). How multilingual is multilingual bert?

Pratapa, A., Bhat, G., Choudhury, M., Sitaram, S., Dandapat, S., and Bali, K. (2018). Language modeling for code-mixing: The role of linguistic theory based synthetic data. In *Proceedings of the 56th Annual Meeting of the Association for Computational Linguistics (Volume 1: Long Papers)*, pages 1543–1553, Melbourne, Australia, July. Association for Computational Linguistics.

Qin, L., Ni, M., Zhang, Y., and Che, W. (2020). Cosda-ml: Multi-lingual code-switching data augmentation for zero-shot cross-lingual nlp.

Radford, A., Wu, J., Child, R., Luan, D., Amodei, D., Sutskever, I., et al. (2019). Language models are unsupervised multitask learners. *OpenAI blog*, 1(8):9.

Santosh, T. and Aravind, K. (2019). Hate speech detection in hindi-english code-mixed social media text. In *Proceedings of the ACM India joint international conference on data science and management of data*, pages 310–313.

Santy, S., Srinivasan, A., and Choudhury, M. (2021). Bertologicomix: How does code-mixing interact with multilingual bert? In *AdaptNLP EACL 2021*, April.

Sharma, A. (2015). Pos tagging for code-mixed indian social media text : Systems from iiit-h for icon nlp tools contest.

Srivastava, V. and Singh, M. (2021a). Challenges and considerations with code-mixed nlp for multilingual societies.

Srivastava, V. and Singh, M. (2021b). Hinge: A dataset for generation and evaluation of code-mixed hinglish text.

Proceedings of the WILDRE-6 Workshop @LREC2020, pages 13–17
Marseille, 20 June 2022

Leveraging Sub Label Dependencies in Code Mixed Indian Languages for Part-Of-Speech Tagging using Conditional Random Fields.

Akash Kumar Gautam
Department of Language Science and Technology (LST)
Saarland Informatics Campus, Saarland University, Saarbrücken, Germany
akga00001@stud.uni-saarland.de

Abstract

Code-mixed text sequences often lead to challenges in the task of correct identification of Part-Of-Speech tags. However, lexical dependencies created while alternating between multiple languages can be leveraged to improve the performance of such tasks. Indian languages with rich morphological structure and highly inflected nature provide such an opportunity. In this work, we exploit these sub-label dependencies using conditional random fields (CRFs) by defining feature extraction functions on three distinct language pairs (Hindi-English, Bengali-English, and Telugu-English). Our results demonstrate a significant increase in the tagging performance if the feature extraction functions employ the rich inner structure of such languages.

Keywords: Code-Mixed Text, Indian Languages, Part-Of-Speech Tagging

1. Introduction

In informal settings such as social media, people fluent in multiple languages often converse with each other by changing dialects and languages. This is a highly observable phenomenon among people in India, which is home to several languages. People having text conversations, frequently alternate between a common professional language such as English and other regional languages such as Hindi or Bengali in a single conversation. The primary reason for observing this phenomenon is that in short geo-spatial distances with language diversities, people know neighboring languages as well (Jamatia et al., 2015).

Code-switching has been explored as a research topic in fields such as sociolinguistics, and psycho-linguistics before as well (Joshi, 1982; Paolillo, 1996).

Since code-switching involves alternating between languages below clause level, it leads to creating lexical dependencies which can be leveraged to improve several downstream NLP tasks. In this work, we explore utilizing these sub-label dependencies for improving the part-of-speech (POS) tagging in such a setting.

Current research on POS tagging has concentrated on monolingual text. Hence traditional approaches to this task might not give the best results on specific settings involving code mixed text. To this end, we discuss POS tagging using conditional random fields (CRF) introduced by (Lafferty et al., 2001) in scenarios where there are rich fine-grained sub-labels for POS tags.

An example text which demonstrates this scenario is for transliterated Hindi word *achchhaaii*: translation (goodness), which can have multiple levels of tags such as: `ADJ` (adjective) which is the main category followed by subcategories, `QT_QTC`(cardinal quantifier), and `SG` (singular).

In this work, we show that utilizing the labels at multiple levels leads to an improvement in the task of correctly identifying POS tags for the complete text sequence. We achieve this by making use of CRFs, which have the ability to process feature functions given an observation space.

To the best of our knowledge, such an approach of utilizing sub-label dependencies for POS tag identification in code-mixed settings for Indian languages has not been presented before. We present our results on 3 language pairs: Hindi-English, Bengali-English, and Telugu-English. The results of this work indicate that exploiting sub-labels in the text sequences leads to an improvement in the tagging accuracy provided by fine-grained labels.

Contributions: We explain a methodology for defining feature extraction functions leveraging sub-label dependencies based on CRFs along with providing linguistic intuition for using such features in Indian languages (Section 3.). We report the statistical results of our experiments (Section 5.) along with describing various parameter settings (Section 4.) used for the work.

2. Related Work

One of the first approaches for POS tagging of Hindi text was made by (Sangal et al., 1995). Their approach would provide the root form of the word along with a generalized POS category. (Shrivastav et al., 2006) added decision tree-based classification along with this approach to improve the tagging accuracy. (Shrivastava and Bhattacharyya, 2008) made use of a stemmer to create suffixes, which then generated POS tags. Some prior works have also used conditional random fields along with morphological analyzer (Agarwal and Mani, 2006; PVS and Karthik, 2007). Similar attempts were made for Tamil and Bengali (Selvam and Natarajan, 2009; Dhanalakshmi et al., 2008; Ekbal et al., 2007) However, all of these were restricted to monolingual text.

POS tagging for code-mixed text as a research problem is still in its early stage. The earliest attempts made by (Solorio and Liu, 2008a) aimed to make use of machine learning approaches to predict code alternation points for code-mixed English-Spanish data. (Solorio and Liu, 2008b; Bali et al., 2014) used output of language-specific taggers for tagging code-mixed data. (Das and Gambäck, 2015) produced one of the first Indian code-mixed corpora for Hindi-Bengali-English. The traditional approach for automatic identification of such Indian languages utilized n-grams, part-of-speech, lemmas, dictionary-based word classification (Barman et al., 2014a; Barman et al., 2014b; Bali et al., 2014)

3. Methods

Given a sequence of tokens in a sentence consisting of $x = (x_1, \dots x_{|x|})$ and the relevant POS tags as, $y = (y_1, \dots y_{|x|})$, the CRF model (Lafferty et al., 2001) is considered as:

$$p(y \mid x; w) \propto \prod_{i=n}^{|x|} exp(w.\phi(y_{i-n}, \dots y_i, x, i)) \quad (1)$$

Here, n defines the model order, w is the model parameter, and ϕ is the feature extraction function. Each $y_i \in Y$ for $i \in 1 \dots |x|$, denotes the tag set. In the next sections, we describe the feature functions which can model sequence-based dependencies for code-mixed text. The baseline features define a naive set of functions that associate the relationship between the POS tag label and the token. Expanded features utilize the sub-label dependencies by exploiting the inner structure of fine-grained labels.

3.1. Baseline Feature Set

Based on work of (Ratnaparkhi and others, 1996; Silfverberg et al., 2014), the baseline features associates a set of functions for a word form x_i with y_i (label), where i is it's position in the sequence. These functions are:

- Bias, true irrespective of the input word-form.
- Word forms x_{i-2}, .., x_{i+2} for given x_i, including the length.
- Language of the current word form x_i.
- Prefix and suffix of the current word form of various lengths upto $\delta = 4$.
- Presence of url, user-mentions, hashtags in x_i, assigned by a boolean value.
- Boolean function indicating, if the word form x_i is an upper capital string or is a number.

These serve a practical purpose in Indian languages where case (nominative, accusative, genitive), number (singular, plural), and gender (masculine, feminine) are inflected through suffix and prefix in word-forms (Schmid and Laws, 2008). Most Indian languages follow case-based dependent marking. For the current task, these are defined for a word-form only if its length is more than 4. Capitalization of a word-form helps in identification whenever a token is used as a proper noun (Silfverberg et al., 2014). Hence, we can say that the mentioned feature functions are representative of the data highly prevalent on social media platforms and have the ability to capture sequence-based dependencies in code-mixed settings.

3.2. Expanded Feature Set

In this section, we describe the expanded feature set which has the ability to model the sub-label dependencies in a given sequence. Fine-grained labels include multiple levels of labeling for POS tags (sub-labels) which are used to indicate the main category of the token, followed by its sub-category. Such labels are known as compound labels.

Instead of associating feature functions for a word-form x_i with just label y_i, we partition any compound label into its sub-components (s). As an example, consider the Hindi word-form *tha*: translation (was), consisting of the compound label, { `V + VAUX` }, hence listing that this word-form has the main category as a verb, and within the given utterance, it occurs as an auxiliary verb.

Let S be the set of all sub-label components for a compound label. Then, we individually associate feature functions with all the sub-labels such that $s \in S$. We describe the process of partitioning a compound label in detail in section 4.2.. This approach aims to utilize the morphological rich structure of highly inflected Indian languages for improving the tagging accuracy.

3.3. Linguistic Motivation For Expanded Feature Set

This section aims to provide linguistic intuition behind selecting the mentioned expanded features and why leveraging sub-label dependencies for a token provides a better representation of a sequence for Indian languages.

Consider a noun based transliterated word-form in Hindi: *nadiya (NOUN)*: translation (river – plural). For such a word-form, the baseline feature set would just associate 2-suffix *-ya* to the compound label { `NOUN + PLURAL` }. In Hindi, morpheme `-ya` is used as a suffix based marker for plural.

The expanded feature set on the other hand would associate the 2-suffix *-ya* to both the main label `NOUN`, and the sub-label `PLURAL` individually. Such an approach of distribution of labels would be useful for correct identification of a different verb-based word-form in Hindi, *shaktiya (VERB)*: translation (power – plural) which is also formed by inflecting the 2-suffix morpheme *-ya* to the root word, *shakti*.

4. Experiments

In this section we describe constituents for the experiments, including data, tag-set and partitioning of labels for the expanded feature set.

4.1. Data

We use the dataset provided by (Jamatia et al., 2015) for the mentioned research problem. It contains text conversations recorded from social media platforms such as Twitter, WhatsApp, and Facebook, code-mixed in these language pairs: Hindi-English, Bengali-English, and Telugu-English. The mentioned conversations are labeled into appropriate fine-grained POS tags along with the language of each token in the utterance. Please refer to table 2 for an overview of the number of utterances for each language pair in the dataset.

[user]	why	not	hike	the	petrol	price	to	120	rs/Ltr	... ,	baar	baar	shock
@	QT_QTC	RP_NEG	V_VM	DT	JJ	N_NN	RP_RPD	$	N_NN	RD_PUNC	N_NNP	RP_RPD	V_VM
dene	se	accha	hai	ki	ek	baar	mein	hi	de	diya	jaye	!	
N_NNV	PSP	RB_AMN	V_AUX	PSP	QT_QTO	RP_RPD	PSP	RP_RPD	V_VM	V_VM	V_VAUX	RD_PUNC	

Table 1: Sample sentence from the dataset (Jamatia et al., 2015) with code-mixed Hindi-English text and fine-grained POS tag labels. Original utterances in the dataset includes Hindi words as transliterated text.

Language Pairs	**Hindi-English**	**Bengali-English**	**Telugu-English**
#Utterances	2630	624	1279

Table 2: Total number of text utterances for each language pair in the dataset (Jamatia et al., 2015).

POS-tags were assigned to each token by manual annotation with substantial agreement over the labels after deciding the utterance boundary. Labels over text conversations use tagset introduced by (Gimpel et al., 2010) for Twitter-specific data and a set of POS tags for Indian languages (Jha et al., 2009) for a fine-grained annotation scheme. Each instance of the datapoint includes the token, identified language for a token, and labeled POS tag. There are dedicated tags for identifying universal acronyms or punctuations as tokens in the dataset. Table 1 shows a sample sentence from the dataset with code mixed Hindi-English text and POS tag labels. Personally identifiable information for a social media user has been removed from the example presented.
The authors of the dataset mention that even though corpus is bi-lingual, there might be occasional instances of tri-quad-lingual mix in a single utterance as well. For each language pair, the total number of utterances were split into the ratio of 80:10:10 as train, test, and validation splits respectively.

4.2. Partitioning of Labels

In this section, we describe the process of splitting the compound labels mentioned in section 3.2. for an expanded feature set. A fine-grained annotation scheme for POS tags mentioned in (Jamatia et al., 2015) focuses on identifying the main category of the token, followed by a descriptive sub-category. Our distribution process aims to leverage that.
For example, given a compound label (V_VM) for a word-form, it is split in a way such that it identifies the main category of the token as (verb) and the sub-category of the token as a (main verb), hence such a label would be distributed into the set {V, VM}. Compound labels in the dataset for a token are identified by the presence of underscore (_) within a POS tag for a token. Not every label for a token in the dataset is a compound label. The described splitting scheme was followed before performing the experiments, hence they were not optimized through the development set.

4.3. Model Specifications

For the code-mixed settings for Indian languages, we explore the baseline feature set and the expanded feature set for first-order ($n = 1$) and second-order ($n = 2$) CRF models. The CRF model parameters in all the cases were estimated using Averaged Perceptron algorithm (Collins, 2002). We use sklearn crf-suite [1] open-source implementation for this work. The maximum number of iterations for the training algorithm was set to 100. The parameters were evaluated on the validation set, with the best-performing ones finally applied to the test set. Instances of the test set were decoded using the Viterbi algorithm.

5. Results and Discussions

Sub-Label Dependencies: Table 3 summarizes the weighted F1 scores of the baseline feature set and expanded feature set for the first-order and second-order CRF models for the 3 language pairs in the dataset. Compared to the standard baseline features, the expanded features show an improvement for all the language pairs, for both first and second-order models. These results are in line with the linguistic intuition for using sub-label dependencies for Indian languages.

Model Order: Another interesting observation is the increased weighted F1-score for first-order models with the expanded feature set, compared to baseline features for the second-order models. However, within the experiments performed, this is observed only for 2 language pair: Hindi-English, and Bengali-English. This suggests that as opposed to increasing the model order, utilizing sub-label dependencies for Indian languages might lead to a better improvement of results. The best set of results for all the language pairs was obtained using an expanded feature set within the second-order model. Tagging accuracy percentage of the models follows the same trend, as described previously for weighted F1 scores, however, for brevity, these have been omitted.

Feature Ablation: In table 4 we report the effects of individual features on the second-order CRF model for Hindi-English language pair on the expanded feature set. The performance is reported in terms of tagging accuracy percentage. From the table, it can be concluded that adding prefixes and suffixes of varying lengths (δ) to the feature extraction function leads to a considerable increment in the performance of the model. Finally identifying URLs, mentions and capitalization help improve the performance most for the text data, as these are efficiently able to capture sequence-based dependencies for social media text.

6. Conclusion

In this work, we evaluate the ability to utilize sub-label dependencies in Indian languages for improving the tagging accuracy of the code-mixed text. We analyze results

[1] https://sklearn-crfsuite.readthedocs.io/en/latest/api.html

	First Order ($n = 1$)		Second Order ($n = 2$)	
Language-Pairs	Baseline Features	Expanded Features	Baseline Features	Expanded Features
Hindi - English	0.70	0.77	0.71	**0.81**
Bengali - English	0.65	0.73	0.69	**0.83**
Telugu - English	0.70	0.71	0.71	**0.72**

Table 3: Table showing comparison between baseline feature set and expanded feature set for first order and second order CRF models explored for all language pairs through **weighted F1-score**. Best results are highlighted in **bold**.

Features	Accuracy %
Current word-form (x_i)	74.16
+ Language and Length	75.10
+ Prefix-Suffix (δ = 1)	76.81
+ Prefix-Suffix (δ = 2)	77.91
+ Prefix-Suffix (δ = 4)	78.87
+ Urls, mentions, capitalization	80.09

Table 4: Feature ablation for second order model (expanded feature set) on Hindi-English language pair. Performance measured through **tagging accuracy percentage.**

in three different language pairs: Hindi-English, Bengali-English, and Telugu-English over first and second-order CRF models. Preliminary conclusions from the results show a step in the right direction. We observe that expanded feature set making use of sub-label dependencies shows a vast improvement against the baseline.
In the future, we aim to utilize neural network architectures like LSTM's having the ability to process lexical sequences over feature functions defined by sub-label dependencies. Another direction to take this research could be to evaluate the performance by having a different splitting criterion for a compound label as opposed to the one described in this paper.

7. Acknowledgments

We would like to thank Dr. Alexander Koller for his initial suggestions regarding research in this paper. We also extend our gratitude to anonymous reviewers for their insightful comments on this work.

8. Bibliographical References

Agarwal, H. and Mani, A. (2006). Part of speech tagging and chunking with conditional random fields. In *the Proceedings of NWAI workshop*.

Bali, K., Sharma, J., Choudhury, M., and Vyas, Y. (2014). "i am borrowing ya mixing?" an analysis of english-hindi code mixing in facebook. In *Proceedings of the First Workshop on Computational Approaches to Code Switching*, pages 116–126.

Barman, U., Das, A., Wagner, J., and Foster, J. (2014a). Code mixing: A challenge for language identification in the language of social media. In *Proceedings of the first workshop on computational approaches to code switching*, pages 13–23.

Barman, U., Wagner, J., Chrupała, G., and Foster, J. (2014b). Dcu-uvt: Word-level language classification with code-mixed data. In *Proceedings of the first workshop on computational approaches to code switching*, pages 127–132.

Collins, M. (2002). Discriminative training methods for hidden markov models: Theory and experiments with perceptron algorithms. In *Proceedings of the 2002 conference on empirical methods in natural language processing (EMNLP 2002)*, pages 1–8.

Das, A. and Gambäck, B. (2015). Code-mixing in social media text: the last language identification frontier?

Dhanalakshmi, V., Anandkumar, M., Vijaya, M., Loganathan, R., Soman, K., and Rajendran, S. (2008). Tamil part-of-speech tagger based on svmtool. In *Proceedings of the COLIPS International Conference on Asian Language Processing*, pages 59–64.

Ekbal, A., Mondal, S., and Bandyopadhyay, S. (2007). Pos tagging using hmm and rule-based chunking. *The Proceedings of SPSAL*, 8(1):25–28.

Gimpel, K., Schneider, N., O'Connor, B., Das, D., Mills, D., Eisenstein, J., Heilman, M., Yogatama, D., Flanigan, J., and Smith, N. A. (2010). Part-of-speech tagging for twitter: Annotation, features, and experiments. Technical report, Carnegie-Mellon Univ Pittsburgh Pa School of Computer Science.

Jamatia, A., Gambäck, B., and Das, A. (2015). Part-of-speech tagging for code-mixed english-hindi twitter and facebook chat messages. Association for Computational Linguistics.

Jha, G. N., Gopal, M., and Mishra, D. (2009). Annotating sanskrit corpus: adapting il-posts. In *Language and Technology Conference*, pages 371–379. Springer.

Joshi, A. (1982). Processing of sentences with intra-sentential code-switching. In *Coling 1982: Proceedings of the Ninth International Conference on Computational Linguistics*.

Lafferty, J., McCallum, A., and Pereira, F. C. (2001). Conditional random fields: Probabilistic models for segmenting and labeling sequence data.

Paolillo, J. C. (1996). Language choice on soc. culture. punjab. *Electronic Journal of Communication/La revue électronique de communication*, 6(3).

PVS, A. and Karthik, G. (2007). Part-of-speech tagging and chunking using conditional random fields and transformation based learning. *Shallow Parsing for South Asian Languages*, 21:21–24.

Ratnaparkhi, A. et al. (1996). A maximum entropy model for part-of-speech tagging. In *EMNLP*, volume 1, pages 133–142. Citeseer.

Sangal, R., Chaitanya, V., and Bharati, A. (1995). *Natu-*

ral language processing: a Paninian perspective. PHI Learning Pvt. Ltd.

Schmid, H. and Laws, F. (2008). Estimation of conditional probabilities with decision trees and an application to fine-grained pos tagging. In *Proceedings of the 22nd International Conference on Computational Linguistics (Coling 2008)*, pages 777–784.

Selvam, M. and Natarajan, A. (2009). Improvement of rule based morphological analysis and pos tagging in tamil language via projection and induction techniques. *International journal of computers*, 3(4):357–367.

Shrivastav, M., Melz, R., Singh, S., Gupta, K., and Bhattacharyya, P. (2006). Conditional random field based pos tagger for hindi. *Proceedings of the MSPIL*, pages 63–68.

Shrivastava, M. and Bhattacharyya, P. (2008). Hindi pos tagger using naive stemming: harnessing morphological information without extensive linguistic knowledge. In *International Conference on NLP (ICON08), Pune, India*.

Silfverberg, M., Ruokolainen, T., Lindén, K., and Kurimo, M. (2014). Part-of-speech tagging using conditional random fields: Exploiting sub-label dependencies for improved accuracy. In *Proceedings of the 52nd Annual Meeting of the Association for Computational Linguistics (Volume 2: Short Papers)*, pages 259–264.

Solorio, T. and Liu, Y. (2008a). Learning to predict code-switching points. In *Proceedings of the 2008 Conference on Empirical Methods in Natural Language Processing*, pages 973–981.

Solorio, T. and Liu, Y. (2008b). Part-of-speech tagging for english-spanish code-switched text. In *Proceedings of the 2008 Conference on Empirical Methods in Natural Language Processing*, pages 1051–1060.

Proceedings of the WILDRE-6 Workshop @LREC2020, pages 18–23
Marseille, 20 June 2022

HindiWSD: A Package for Word Sense Disambiguation in Hinglish & Hindi

Mirza Yusuf, Praatibh Surana, Chethan Sharma*
Department of Information and Communication Technology, Manipal Institute of Technology, Manipal Academy of Higher Education, India
mirzayusuf1000@gmail.com, praatibhsurana@gmail.com, chethan.sharma@manipal.edu

Abstract

A lot of commendable work has been done, especially in high resource languages such as English, Spanish, French, etc. However, work done for Indic languages such as Hindi, Tamil, Telugu, etc is relatively less due to difficulty in finding relevant datasets, and the complexity of these languages. With the advent of IndoWordnet, we can explore important tasks such as word sense disambiguation, word similarity, and cross-lingual information retrieval, and carry out effective research regarding the same. In this paper, we worked on improving word sense disambiguation for 20 of the most common ambiguous Hindi words by making use of knowledge-based methods. We also came up with "hindiwsd", an easy- to-use framework developed in Python that acts as a pipeline for transliteration of Hinglish code-mixed text followed by spell correction, POS tagging, and word sense disambiguation of Hindi text. We also curated a dataset of these 20 most used ambiguous Hindi words. This dataset was then used to enhance a modified Lesk algorithm and more accurately carry out word sense disambiguation. We achieved an accuracy of about 71% using our customized Lesk algorithm which was an improvement to the accuracy of about 34% using the original Lesk algorithm on the test set.

Keywords: Word Sense Disambiguation, Code-Mixing, Indic Transliteration

1. Introduction

The use of a Hindi-English mix language usually referred to as Hinglish has been used prominently since the inception of social media. According to a recent survey, around 57% of the Indian population generally while conversing on any social media prefer to use Hinglish over Devanagari Hindi or English[1]. The popularity of Hinglish arises from the fact that it is easier than typing in Hindi due to the unavailability of Hindi characters on a common keyboard. Wordnets (George A. Miller. 1995) are used extensively for many NLP-related tasks. They are generally used for a number of processes in information systems, including word sense disambiguation (which from here on we will refer to as WSD), information retrieval, automatic text classification, automatic text summarization, machine translation, and even automatic crossword puzzle generation[2]. The Indian languages wordnet originated from the advent of the Hindi Wordnet (Bhattacharyya et al., 2008). Using this model as default, the wordnets for other Indic languages were developed. Eighteen of these languages have wordnets under a common platform known as the IndoWordNet (Pushpak Bhattacharyya, 2010). In Natural Language Processing, WSD is the problem of determining which sense of a word is being used in a particular sentence. Given a word, it can have multiple possible meanings which makes it difficult for a reader/system to understand the meaning of the word by itself. However, when the word is provided along with the context/sentence it is a part of, it becomes easier to gauge its meaning. The process of identifying this contextual meaning of the word is called Word Sense Disambiguation". For

example, the Hinglish sentence Mein sonaa chaahta hoon translates as I want to sleep, whereas in the sentence Mein sonaa khareednaa chaahta hoon translates as I want to buy gold, here the word sonaa is being used in two different contexts and hence has two different meanings; the first one being sleep and the other being gold. The presence of just 1 extra word was able to change the meaning of the word sonaa. Hence, one can see why it would be tough for a model to carry out WSD.

2. Related Work

WordNet is a large lexical database of English. Nouns, verbs, adjectives, and adverbs are grouped into sets of cognitive synonyms (synsets), each expressing a distinct concept. Synsets are interlinked by means of conceptual-semantic and lexical relations. WordNet is also freely and publicly available for download. Its structure makes it a useful tool for computational linguistics and natural language processing. In recent times, it has been developed in other languages as well such as French, German, and in our case Hindi as can be seen with the Hindi WordNet. Word Sense Disambiguation has been done for English by utilizing

[1] `https://www.milestoneloc.com/guide-to-hinglish-language/`

[2] `https://en.wikipedia.org/w/index.php?title=WordNet&oldid=1069690711`

the data from the original Wordnet, which contains a vast amount of relations between words. Various methods, both supervised, and unsupervised have been used. Apart from this, Banerjee and Pedersen (2002) also made use of knowledge-based methods such as the Lesk algorithm (Michael Lesk, 1986). Seo et al. (2004) made use of unsupervised methods on English data and then evaluated their model on Korean datasets. Mihalcea and Faruque (2004) made use of a supervised approach with a minimum amount of annotated data and achieved commendable results on SENSEVAL-3 (Snyder, Benjamin and Palmer, 2004) in all English tasks. Supervised and semi-supervised techniques have tended to outperform the knowledge-based methods as they use machine learning, which to an extent can identify the semantic structure of a sentence which knowledge-based methods fail to. Pal and Saha (2015) also suggest that while precision is high for knowledge-based approaches, supervised approaches are best for languages with rich amounts of data. In the case of Hindi and Hinglish code mixed data, however, supervised approaches will only do so well due to some level of data scarcity. This prompted us to employ knowledge-based methods for our specific problem statement. With regards to Hindi, Singh et al. (2013) carried out WSD by computing similarity based on semantics. They were able to achieve a commendable accuracy of about 60% on 20 polysemous Hindi nouns. Sinha et al. (2004) also carried out a detailed evaluation of ambiguous Hindi words and evaluated accuracies of particular words grouped on the basis of domains. Gautam and Sharma (2016) used an interesting approach wherein they made use of bigrams and trigrams to disambiguate 15 commonly used Verb Hindi words. They achieved the highest precision of about 53% on bigram words. All these papers leveraged the Hindi WordNet. Through our model, we have tried to focus on Hinglish code mixed as well as Hindi data. In the case of WSD for Hinglish code mixed data, the only extra step is the transliteration of this Hinglish data to Devanagari Hindi post which we carry on with our usual algorithm as is described in the methodology section.

3. Methodology

A pipeline was created to ensure our model could handle both Hinglish code-mixed as well as Hindi Devanagari data. Apart from carrying out WSD on Devanagari Hindi, we also leveraged pre-existing tools for spell correction, POS tagging, etc. The following sections describe the algorithm used for WSD and modifications made to it to further improve accuracy.

3.1. Lesk Algorithm

Lesk algorithm is a knowledge-based algorithm for WSD. It is based on the assumption that words in a given neighborhood will tend to share the same topic. Simplified lesk algorithm is used to compare the dictionary definition of an ambiguous word with the terms contained in its neighborhood and take an overlap of them. The highest overlap is then processed as the correct meaning. The pseudo-code is shown in algorithm 1 along with the flow diagram in Figure 1 and Figure2.

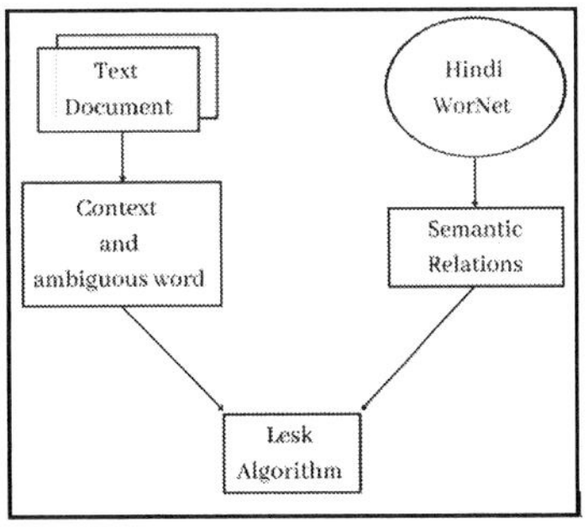

Figure 1: Traditional Lesk algorithm

```
function LESK (word, sentence) returns best sense of
word
        best sense <- most frequent use for word
        max_overlap <- 0
        context <- set of words in sentence
        for each sense in sense of word do
                signature <- set of words in the gloss
and examples of sense
                overlap <- COMPUTEOVERLAP
                (signature, context)
                if overlap > max_overlap then
                        max_overlap <- overlap
                        best_sense <- sense
end return (best_sense)
```

Figure 2: Traditional Lesk algorithm

3.2. Custom Lesk Algorithm

In addition to the traditional Lesk algorithm, we employed a modified Lesk algorithm that made use of a helper dataset, tailored specifically for our task of disambiguating the most commonly used Hindi words. An intersection was taken with the input sentence and the keywords in the helper dataset to find which meaning for a particular word had the highest overlap. This was then compared to the initial lesk overlap, the highest overlap was then chosen as the meaning of the ambiguous word. As opposed to the Lesk algorithm that required the POS tags[3] for words to be disambiguated, our custom algorithm leverages the synsets present in the Hindi WordNet to predict the meanings. The pseudo-code is as follows along with the flow diagram in Figure 4.

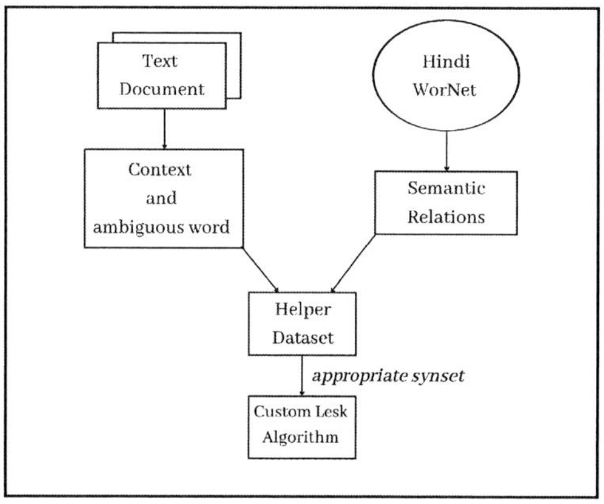

Figure 3: Custom Lesk algorithm

```
function LESK (word, sentence) returns best sense of word
        best sense <- most frequent use for word
        max_overlap <- 0
        context <- set of words in sentence
        intersection, synset_no, meaning =
EXTRAOVERLAP (word, sentence)
        for each sense in sense of word do
                signature <- set of words in the gloss
and examples of sense
                overlap <- COMPUTEOVERLAP
                (signature, context)
                if overlap > max_overlap then
                        max_overlap <- overlap

        if intersection > max_overlap and
intersection > 0 do
                best_sense <- word.synset_no
end return (best_sense)
```

Figure 4: Custom Lesk algorithm

3.3. Library Design and Features

The hindiwsd package is essentially a pipeline that will carry out the following tasks- Hinglish to Hindi transliteration Spell correction of Hindi text POS tagging of Hindi text Word Sense Disambiguation of Hindi text with the help of IndoWordNet Enhanced disambiguation using custom Lesk algorithm and custom dataset

A user can give input either as a Hinglish sentence or as a Hindi sentence to the wordsense function (see snippet 3.3). The wordsense function prints

```
>>> from hindiwsd import hindi_wsd
>>> print(hindi_wsd.wordsense("aaj achha din hai")) #Hinglish
>>> print (hindi_wsd.wordsense("आज अच्छा दिन है")) #Hindi
```

out each word of the sentence along with its disambiguated word meaning if the respective Hindi word is present in the IndoWordNet.

3.3.1. Library Design

The hindiwsd package is built on top of a few scripts taken from other pre-existing libraries with modifications made to them to make them compatible with hindiwsd and modules written by the authors. With the help of pre-existing libraries, we were able to ensure the dependable functionality of the pipeline as a whole and provide a well-compiled multi-faceted model to be used for Hindi and Hinglish WSD. The pipeline along with the working of the key features has been explained in the Features section.

3.3.2. Features

The input can either be a Hindi sentence in its Devanagari form or a Hinglish code mixed sentence. In any case, the sentence is then converted to Devanagari Hindi using the indic-transliteration tool[4]. After this, spell correction is performed using Spello[5]. The resultant sentence is then passed through a POS tagger and the tags are then condensed and converted into 4 simple tags, i.e., noun, adjective, verb, and adverb. This is done in order to be able to use pyiwn (Panjwani et al., 2018) and access the IndoWordNets synsets. Figure 5 shows the pipeline that the data flows through.

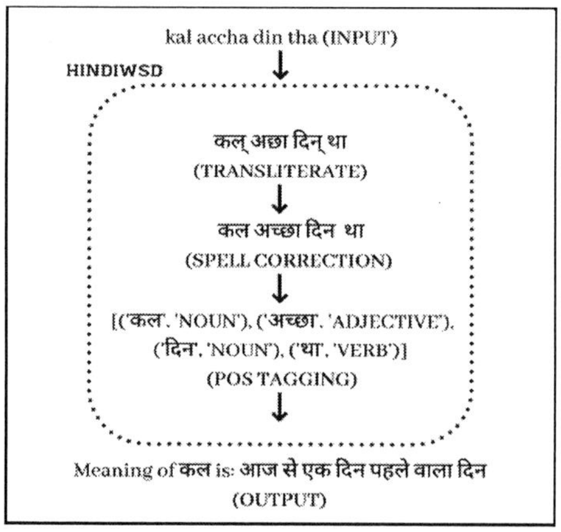

Figure 5: Pipeline for Hindi WSD

[3]https://nptel.ac.in/courses/106101007

[4]https://github.com/indic-transliteration/indic_transliteration_py

[5]https://github.com/hellohaptik/spello

3.3.3. Hinglish to Hindi Transliteration using indic-transliteration

The indic-transliteration package helps convert the Hinglish code-mixed data to Hindi by making use of dictionaries along with rules specified for the conversion of each set of letters in a word from Latin script to Devanagari Hindi.

3.3.4. Spell correction using spello

The spello package makes use of two spell correction models, namely, Phoneme which uses the Soundex algorithm[6], and Symspell[7]. The Phoneme model makes use of the Soundex algorithm and suggests spellings based on phonetics. The Symspell model uses edit distances to suggest spell corrections. Spello combines both these models and provides accurate spell correction.

3.3.5. POS tagging with indic_tagger

The indic_tagger package[8] is a state-of-the-art POS tagger and chunker for Indian languages. We made use of the pre-trained CRF model for chunking[9] and POS tagging. In order to make the tags compatible and useful for the Lesk algorithm, we carried out a mapping of the numerous model generated tags to 4 tags, i.e., noun, adjective, verb, and adverb to make the tags useful for Lesk algorithm. The POS mappings are shown in Figure 6

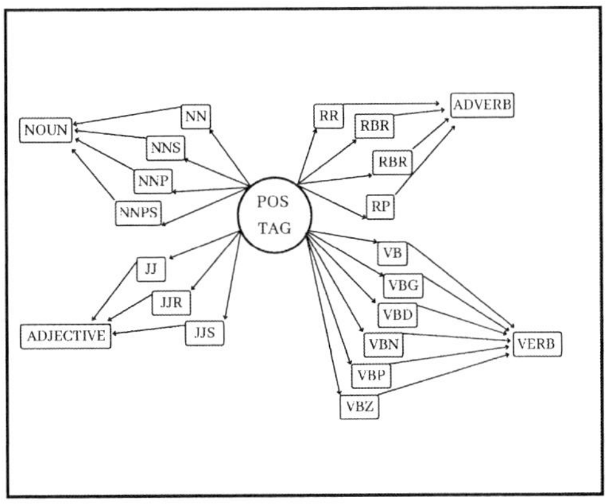

Figure 6: POS Mappings

3.3.6. Improved word sense disambiguation with pyiwn

The pyiwn package is an API developed to access the IndoWordNet. Using pyiwn, we were able to access the synsets[10], glosses, examples, and lexico-semantic relations[11] between synsets. We were able to perform the Lesk algorithm on our data successfully. Apart from this, as mentioned earlier, a helper dataset was developed for the most commonly used Hindi words to further aid our custom Lesk algorithm and make WSD more robust.

4. Helper Dataset

The Helper dataset is a small dataset that was manually curated by us for the purpose of enhancing Lesk algorithm. It contains 20 of the more commonly used ambiguous Hindi words and words which occur frequently with those particular words. Due to time constraints and limited manpower, we curated the dataset to only hold the two most frequent meanings of an ambiguous word despite there being more. The dataset was structured in a way such that for each meaning of a word, we provide two sets of keywords generated from random sentences consisting of the ambiguous word. See 7 for a better understanding. In the example in

Word	Sentence
पता	मेरा नाम नहीं लगेगा सब बारे उसके घटना चलती चला है मुझे उसे हमें चले यह लगाने कैसे चलता लगाते लगा
पता	क्या जगह घर दफ्तर पते पहुंच वहां जाना जा मालुम पूछना

Figure 7: Helper dataset example

table 1, we try to showcase the meaning of the word पता in different sentences where the context is different. In the first row the word means got to know, whereas, in the second row, it means address. To a native speaker, this is rather straightforward to identify with the help of the context, that is, the surrounding or supporting words in the sentence.

5. Results

Table 2 represents the results that we obtained when we tested a word for a particular meaning. The synset column in the table signifies the particular meaning of the word as indicated in the IndoWordNet. The test set contains sentences for each meaning along with the ambiguous word in question. Along with the synset number, the meaning corresponding to that particular synset is shown in the meaning column. Finally, the results of the traditional and modified Lesk algorithms are displayed.

Figure 8 shows words and their respective meanings along with the results obtained for both Lesk

[6] https://en.wikipedia.org/w/index.php?title=Soundex&oldid=1055316589

[7] https://github.com/wolfgarbe/SymSpell

[8] https://github.com/avineshpvs/indic_tagger

[9] https://www.analyticsvidhya.com/blog/2021/10/what-is-chunking-in-natural-language-processing/

[10] https://www.nltk.org/howto/wordnet.html

[11] https://en.wikipedia.org/w/index.php?title=Lexical_semantics&oldid=1041088037

Word	Synset	Meaning	Lesk	Modified Lesk
कल	2	आज के बाद आने वाला पहला दिन	1	1
कल	0	आज से एक दिन पहले वाला दिन	1	1
सोना	2	लेटकर शरीर और मस्तिष्क को विश्राम देने वाली निद्रा की अवस्था में होना	0	1
सोना	0	एक बहुमूल्य पीली धातु जिसके गहने आदि बनते हैं	1	1
कर	2	वह नियत धन आदि जो किसी व्यक्ति या किसी संपत्ति, व्यापार आदि के काम में से कोई अधिकारिकी अपने लिए लेती है	0	1
कर	N	हाथ	0	1
चाल	4	कामयाबी पाने के लिए चालाकीपूर्वक लगाई जाने वाली युक्ति	0	0
चाल	2	व्यवहार की वह प्रकृति जो लगातार दोहराव से प्राप्त होती है	1	1

Figure 8: Results for a few common Hindi words and their meanings

algorithms that were used. The comparison makes it evident that our modified Lesk algorithm outperforms the normal Lesk algorithm. This was what we expected as our helper dataset was tailored to help improve disambiguation for commonly used Hindi words.

Accuracy = Correctly predicted samples / Total predicted samples (1) Table 3 shows the final re-

	Lesk	Modified Lesk
Accuracy (2 meanings of 20 most common Hindi words)	34.21%	71.05%

sults measured using accuracy as the performance metric This also shows that instead of maybe approaching WSD as a broad task, one can break it down into smaller, more specific, and meaningful subtasks, allowing for better accuracy and greater utility.

6. Conclusion and Further Work

Creating a WSD model for a language with a scarce amount of resources is a cumbersome task. In this paper, we have tried our best to limit our problem statement and focus on a task with real-world applications, hence we chose to go with common words and dictionary-based methods while also coming up with utilities that can aid further research in this domain. The Lesk algorithm is not the most efficient way to perform WSD since it is incapable of understanding context or even the semantics involved. However, this algorithm is easy to use, quick to make predictions and can be used to target specific subtasks even within WSD as was demonstrated in this paper. Due to limited resources, we did not feel it would be the best approach to employ supervised methods. Further work can involve increasing the size of the dataset and maybe involving machine translation systems (Appicharla et al., 2021).

7. Bibliographical References

Appicharla Ramakrishna & Gupta, Kamal & Ekbal, Asif & Bhattacharyya, Pushpak, (2021). IITP-MT at CALCS2021: English to Hinglish Neural Machine Translation using Unsupervised Synthetic Code-Mixed Parallel Corpus. 31-35. 10.18653/v1/2021.calcs-1.5.

Banerjee, Satanjeev & Pedersen, Ted. (2002). An Adapted Lesk Algorithm for Word Sense Disambiguation Using WordNet. Computational Linguistics and Intelligent Text Processing. 2276. 136-145. 10.1007/3-540-45715-1_11.

Chandra Bhal Singh Gautam and Dilip Kumar Sharma. (2016). Hindi Word Sense Disambiguation Using Lesk Approach on Bigram and Trigram Words. *In Proceedings of the International Conference on Advances in Information Communication Technology & Computing (AICTC '16).* Association for Computing Machinery, New York, NY, USA, Article 81, 1–5.

Michael Lesk. (1986). Automatic sense disambiguation using machine readable dictionaries: how to tell a pine cone from an ice cream cone. *In Proceedings of the 5th annual international conference on Systems documentation (SIGDOC '86).* Association for Computing Machinery, New York, NY, USA, 24–26.

Mihalcea, Rada, 1974- & Faruque, Ehsanul. SenseLearner: Minimally Supervised Word Sense Disambiguation for All Words in Open Text, paper, (2004); [Stroudsburg, Pennsylvania], University of North Texas Libraries, UNT Digital Library.

Pal, Alok Ranjan and Diganta Saha.(2015). "Word sense disambiguation: a survey." ArXiv abs/1508.01346: n. pag

8. Language Resource References

Bhattacharyya, Pushpak, Prabhakar Pande, and Laxmi Lupu. (2008). Hindi WordNet LDC2008L02. Web Download. Philadelphia: Linguistic Data Consortium.

George A. Miller. (1995). WordNet: a lexical database for English. Commun. ACM 38, 11 (Nov. 1995), 39–41.

Pushpak Bhattacharyya. 2010. IndoWordNet In *Proceedings of the Seventh International Conference on Language Resources and Evaluation (LREC'10).*

Proceedings of the WILDRE-6 Workshop @LREC2020, pages 24–28
Marseille, 20 June 2022

Pāṇinian Phonological Changes: Computation and Development of Online Access System

Sanju, Subhash Chandra
Ph.D. Research Scholar, Assistant Professor
Department of Sanskrit, University of Delhi
New Delhi-110007, India
sanjunandal77@gmail.com, schandra@sanskrit.du.ac.in.

Abstract

Pāṇini used the term saṃhitā for phonological changes. Any Sound change which alters phonemes in a particular language is called Phonological Change. It arises when two sounds are pronounced in a language with uninterrupted speed, then those letters are affected by each other due to Articulatory, Acoustic and Auditory principles in language. The pronunciation of two sounds that are in extreme proximity, affects each other and changes them. In simple words, this phenomenon is known as sandhi. Sanskrit is considered one of the oldest languages in the world. It has produced one of the most huge literary text corpora in the world. The tradition of Sanskrit began in the Vedic period. Pāṇini's Aṣṭādhyāyī (AD) is a complete grammar of Sanskrit. It also covers Sanskrit sounds and phonology. Phonological changes are a natural phenomenon in any language during speech but in Sanskrit, it is highly reflected. Sanskrit corpora contain numerous long words. It looks like a single sentence due to sandhi between multiple words. The process of phonological changes occurred based on certain rules of pronunciation and it is codified by the Pāṇini in AD. Pāṇini has codified these rules systemically but the computation of these rules is a challenging task. Therefore, the objective of the paper is to compute the rules and demonstrate an online access system for Sanskrit sandhi. The system also generates the whole process of phonological changes based on Pāṇinian Rules. It also plays a very effective role in Digital classroom teaching, boosting teaching skills and the learning process.

Keywords : Phonological Changes, Computation and Development of Online Access, Sandhi, Pāṇinian, Aṣṭādhyāyī (AD), Digital classroom teaching, Sanskrit Grammar, Derivational Process etc.

1. Background

The most prominent feature of ancient Indian linguistic culture was its concern for maintaining the accuracy of the spoken word. It was speech, spoken word, and not written letters based on Sanskrit grammar. The spoken language is considered the basis of the actual Sanskrit language. All speculations and practices are concerned with the oral methodology. Sanskrit is a compounding, morphologically and phonetically strong language. Sanskrit texts contain numerous words which are composed by the combination of two or more words using the last letter from the first word and the first letter from the second word. The last letter of the first word and the first letter of the second word sometimes change during the pronunciations. This process is generally known as Phonological Changes. Any sound change which alters the number or distribution of phonemes in a particular language is called Phonological Change. Because whenever two letters are pronounced in a language with uninterrupted speed, then those letters are affected by each other. These two letters or sounds may merge to give a single sound, one of the two sounds may get changed or reduplicated before combining with the other, or even get elided. A new sound may also be appended in between. This linguistic variation is reckoned as Phonetic Change or Sandhi. Sound Changes in Pronunciation are majorly due to the frequency of words which are motivated by physiological factors. Sound change takes place due to Articulatory, Acoustic and Auditory principles in language. The pronunciation of two sounds that are in extreme proximity, affects each other and changes them. These variations are known in Sanskrit as Sandhi. Sandhi refers to "put together". Sandhi is the coalescence of two letters in immediate contact. It means when two sounds combine, they influence each other's sound structure, resulting in different variant pronunciations for these sounds. Sandhi word is itself made up of two components *"sam + dhi"*. Sam means "together" and *dhi* refers to "placement or location". It is conjoined to depict the meaning of place together or merged. Sandhi takes place according to certain rules codified by the *Pāṇini* and are explained formally in his grammar known as *Aṣṭādhyāyī* (AD). *Pāṇini's* AD is also based on the sound of Spoken Sanskrit. But the word Sandhi does not appear in any of the AD *sūtras* (Bhardwaj, Gantayat, Chaturvedi, Garg, & Agarwal, 2018). There are certain *sūtras* that are governed by a condition known as *saṃhitā* which as defined in *sūtra "paraḥ sannikarṣaḥ saṃhitā"* (1.4.109) means "closest proximity of letters". These *sūtras* talk about the changes that occur when two letters are in "immediate proximity". The process of Sandhi is fundamental to the Sanskrit language as it enables the formation of new and more complex words using simple words. Any computational tool for processing Sanskrit must to be able to merge words according to the rules of Sandhi. The accuracy of any such tool critically depends on the eradication of errors in the Sandhi processing. The AD is formulated in a morphologically, syntactically and lexically regimented form of Sanskrit (Kiparsky, 1995). AD includes generative phonology of a depth and exhaustiveness to which no modern generative phonology has even come close, which is moreover integrated with a fully panned out generative syntax and morphology, in a system of 4000 formalized rules based on very specific and elaborate principles of Sanskrit linguistic description (Joshi & Kiparsky, 1977). NASA scientist Rick Briggs (1985) has attracted public attention to his artificial intelligence research and has accepted the techniques used to present knowledge to the methods used in the implementation of rules used in *Pāṇinian* grammar (Chandra, 2021). In modern grammar, *Pāṇinian grammar* is comprehensive, scientific, and organized equivalent to working of a computer program. Nevertheless, despite the vast literature on the Sanskrit language, the amount of digital medium of Sanskrit is scanty in comparison to other language literature. In the field of Sanskrit research, constantly state-of-the-art techniques and tools are being developed which are helpful in e-learning. In order to fulfill this goal, the

Pāṇinian rule and example-based hybrid approach is adopted to create the online access system.

2. Problem, Solution and Objective

Along with the progress, and changes in information technology, society has had a profound impact on the education system. It provides an opportunity to develop new flexible learning an environment that was not possible before. In the age of digitalization and technology, the Sanskrit field is engrossed in a conflicting sphere where Sanskrit language and literature have gigantic literary corpora but we have an extreme scarcity of Sanskrit electronic tools to aid the teaching and learning process of Sanskrit texts. So that this Indian knowledge tradition is available online in digital form and is accessible to all the enthusiasts. Presently, it is part of the curriculum of all major Indian universities and affiliated colleges conducting Sanskrit courses and teaching grammar topics based on *Siddhāntakaumudī* or *Laghusiddhāntakaumudī*. Also, Sandhi and its Derivational Process is a part of the *Vayakaranasiddhāntakaumudī* and *Laghusiddhāntakaumudī* but there is no such digital medium or any tools available which discuss the derivations in detail. The development of any such digital online process would aid learners in garnering knowledge of the Sanskrit Sandhi derivational process. Although there are a handful of tools available that does the task of sandhi in capacious to depicting the entire derivational process. Also, Sanskrit has *kādambarī, vāsavadattā* etc. text there are huge uses of sandhi padas having enormous sandhi terms which appear to be like a whole sentence. To grasp the content and have an informed understanding of this linguistically advanced text, it is necessary that researchers, laureates, and scholars develop the grammatical skills of sandhi. But the lack of efficient tools harms the learning process and therefore, the progress is also much dilated.

The only solution to the aforementioned problems is to build an electronic system for the Sanskrit Sandhi Siddhi process. With the help of tools, learners will easily access to learn sandhi and understand Sanskrit text.

Therefore, the main objective of this paper is to develop a web-based system for e-learning by computing *Pāṇini's* Phonological rules. Thus, we discuss a structure for computer representation of the *Pāṇinian* Phonological Changes in Sanskrit grammar. Sandhi tool is an easy as well as an interesting medium that renders an entirely new dimension in the field of Education, Speech Technology and adds unique prospects to the traditional approach of Sanskrit Teachings. As result, it will boost the teaching skills and the learning process. This tool will prove very helpful for those who wish to grasp Sandhi in grammatical tradition. Simultaneously, other topics of Sanskrit can also be made easily comprehensible with the help of this tool.

3. Phonological Changes in Sanskrit

Phonetic change occurs when two sounds in proximity are pronounced and make changes. In this process, internal and external oral factors of the mouth affect the pronunciation of sounds. In AD (दीक्षित, 2016) Pāṇini used the word *Saṃhitā* (परः सन्निकर्षः संहिता-1.4.109) to depict phonological changes. There are three possible potential combinations leading to the formation of sandhi such as; *svara* sandhi, *vyañjana* sandhi and *visarga* sandhi. When a vowel affects the second vowel and changes it to another sound, called *svara* sandhi. Similarly, a consonant followed by a consonant is defined as *vyañjana* sandhi *(saṃhitā)* and the combination of a vowel and visarga followed by a vowel or consonant is called *visarga* sandhi (*saṃhitā*). *Pāṇini* uses the term *saṃhitā* only to connotate the vowel-vowel combinations (Zwicky and Arnold, 1965). Other rules are just called consonant-consonant changes. Visarga sandhi elucidated under *Pāṇini's* AD is nothing but changes associated with a final or in a word and is grouped by *Pāṇini* with other consonant changes. *Visarga* rules are generally expressed as changes that occur when a particular vowel or group of vowels is followed by *visarga* which in turn is followed by various letters. The internal sandhi and external sandhi are other useful classifications are also done by the scholars. Internal Sandhi refers to the sandhi amongst case endings, verbal affixes, prefixes and suffixes which results in the formation of a word as *saṁ* + *krita* = *saṁskrita*. External Sandhi is what occurs between words, whether they form a compound or not (Chakraborty, 2021) as *sūrya* + *udayam* = *sūryodayam*. Due to this classification, sandhi has five types: *svara* sandhi, *prakṛtibhāva* sandhi, *vyañjana* sandhi, *visarga* sandhi, *svādi* sandhi (आचार्य, 2019). These are not additional sandhi but the incorporation of major *sandhis*. *Prakṛtibhāva* sandhi is part of *svara* sandhi and *svādi* sandhi is a part of visarga sandhi. These additional types are due to internal and external conditions of sandhi. Thus, Sandhi is mainly three types.

4. Digital Access and Sanskrit Sandhi

Information technology affects all aspects of human activities and therefore, exerts a similar influence in the education sector as well. When a learner is able to take responsibility for their own learning, it would result in an increased demand for education and magnify the need for more digital learning equipment and e-tools. E-learning is commonly referred to as the intentional use of networked information and communications technology in teaching and learning. Digital Access for education and learning can be described as using a digital medium or electronic media and technologies such as the internet, intranet, extranet, satellite broadcasts, audio/videotape, interactive television and video-conferencing, to delivery instructional content and to create, foster and facilitate learning experiences. In contemporary times, when globalization and the sector of information technology are at their peak, the entire world is connected by a click of a button, the global news is generated and exchanged through web mediums, yet, any instant e-learning system for important grammatical content such as *sandhi, subanta, tiṅanta, kṛdanta, samāsa etc* are unavailable to the digital world.

Sandhi as previously discussed is an eminent topic of Sanskrit linguistics and a part of major curriculum content in every university having a linguistics and Indic department. The system being deliberated in this research paper is a digital platform enduring the potential for global access to the derivational process of sandhi along with its exegesis and detailed description.

Sanskrit Sandhi is an issue on which almost all the institutions working on computational linguistics in Sanskrit and other primitive languages are continuously performing research and making significant advancements. The most prominent of these institutions are The Computational Linguistics R&D at the School of Sanskrit and Indic Studies (J.N.U), Department of Sanskrit, University of Hyderabad and Technology Development for Indian Languages (TDIL, 2021). These institutes have continuously created computational tools by performing various researches on the basis of Computational Sanskrit. Along with many tools manufactured by these institutes, two sandhi-related tools- Sandhi Generator and Sandhi splitter are also available. Both the systems developed by Jawaharlal Nehru University are based on *Laghusiddhāntakaumudī.* Sandhi Generator System (Mishra & Jha, 2009) makes a Sandhi between two *padas* or *varnas* on the basis of Panini's Sandhi rule. And Sandhi Splitter System (Kumar and Jha 2007) identifies the syntactic term given in the input form and makes a possible break of it and also presents the sandhi *sūtra*, on the basis of which the Sandhi term is formed. Department of Sanskrit (UOH) Under the guidance of Prof. Amba Kulkarni (Kulkarni 2021), two tools related to the Sandhi- *sandhi* and *sandhi-vicchedikā* are based on *Vayakaranasiddhāntakaumudī.* The first tool treats on the basis of input in the form of two words. And the second Sandhi breaks the word. The department declares 96%-98% fair results of these sandhi tools. Similarly, Sandhi and Sandhi splitter tools have also been manufactured by Technology Development for Indian Languages (TDIL). This system also presents its AD sequence along with the Sandhi *Sūtra*. Many Sanskrit tools are available on the portal (www.sanskritworld.in) a web portal for Computational Sanskrit created by Dr. Dhaval Patel (2022). There is also a sandhi tool in Tools. Input form for Sandhi, this tool by taking *pada* + *pada* or *prātipadika* + *pada* and identifying the Sandhi on the basis of input presents Sandhi form, Sandhi *sūtra, vārtika* and their work, AD's *sūtra.* The Sandhi splitter system is being manufactured by the Karnataka Sanskrit University. This system was developed by Amba Kulkarni (*Samskrit* Studies Department, University of Hyderabad), P. Ramanuja (Karantaka *saṃskṛta* University) and Nicolas Reimen, Karantaka *Saṃskṛta* University. The system is currently under development. This work is being developed to split the Sandhi. A Sandhikosh: A Benchmark Corpus for Evaluating Sanskrit Sandhi Tools has been developed by the Indian Institute of Technology, Delhi and IBM Research in collaboration with Shubham Bhardwaj and his colleagues (2018) in which five different departments- *aṣṭādhyāyī* Corpus, *Bhagvad_Gita* by making Corpus, Rule-based Corpus and Literature Corpus, UoH Corpus, data collection of about 14000 Sandhi words has been made. Under the guidance of Pro. Gérard Hute (2013), the INRIA (French Institute for Research in Computer Science and Automation) developed the sandhi tool called the Sandhi Engine. It is the only system in the systems of the Sandhi that explains the internal and external distinction between the Sandhi. Similarly, on another website, Green Message: The Evergreen Messages of Spirituality, Sanskrit and Nature (Message 2021), there are two systems for Sanskrit Sandhi, Sanskrit Sandhi Rules and Sanskrit Sandhi Tool. The first system presents three options to the user, vowel, consonant, and visarga. This system exhibits the collection of disparate Sandhi rules and presents an example-based Sandhi between whichever characters is favored. It further elucidates the Sanskrit Sandhi Tool gives the dissection, i.e on giving two different terms, Sandhi, the name of the Sandhi and the Sandhi Rules by identifying the Sandhi in the result. Sanskrit Dictionary (2022) website has prepared some online tools. In which there is a Sanskrit Sandhi Calculator and a Sandhi Game called *'Sandhi Invaders'*. This calculator accepts two characters or words as input. by identifying the inputs like syllables, syllable positions, changed characters, and the rule by which the Sandhi is It has happened, presents that AD *Sūtra*. The 'Sandhi Invaders' is a typing game, in which 572 Sandhi rules have been arranged in a particular order. It's a simple and interesting way to learn facts of the sandhi generation. In this sequence, many computer tools have been developed in the field of Computational Linguistics since 2014 by the Department of Sanskrit, University of Delhi. *Sasūtra* Sandhi Generator related to Sanskrit Sandhi was built by this department which works with the perfect example and rule method and it is the only system of sandhi that presents the complete derivational process along with making the sandhi.

5. Computation Process of Pāṇinīan Rules for Sandhi

Pāṇini has encoded the rules in AD and presented them very briefly just like in a computer program the data is different. A relatively small part of these underlying principles is described in the rules of *Pāṇini* AD. To understand them, first of all, we have to decode these rules. These rules can be computed very easily. The *śivasūtras,* enumerate a catalog of sounds (*varṇasamāmnāya*) in fourteen classes. *Pāṇini* uses abbreviatory labels termed pratyahara to describe phonological classes. This *pratyahara* are interpreted in the context of an ancillary text of the AD (Malcolm, 2007). For example- If we take the formula '*iko yaṇaci*' (इको यणचि- 6.1.77) (आचार्य, 2019) for the sandhi of *yaṇ*. To understand this formula, first of all, the passage (separate each of the words) is done. By separating, we get a total of three words *ikaḥ, yaṇ* and *aci*. Now division is seen in this these words *ikaḥ* has the sixth declension (*vibhakti*), the *yaṇ* has the first *vibhakti* and Achi has the seventh *vibhakti*. In order to understand the meaning of these words, *Pāṇini* has given the rules that the word in which the sixth declension will be there, the word with the first declension will be in its place, and the word with the seventh declension will be after (*nimitta*). In this way the general meaning of this *sūtra* is - In place of *ik*, there will be *yaṇ* after *ac*. Now these three words are *ik, yaṇ* and *ac* technical words, to understand this we have to go to the sound module of *Pāṇini`s* AD. This will give us the detail of all these three technical terms. *ik* to *i/ī, u/ū, ṛ/ṝ, lṛ* and *yaṇ* to *y, v, r, l* and *ac* to *a/ā, i/ī, u/ū, ṛ/ṝ, lṛ, e, o, ai, au.* There is a sense of letters like *ai, au* (all vowels) etc. There is also an exception to this *sūtra*, there will be a long sandhi in the same tone. In this way, the meaning of this *sūtra* is *i/ī, u/ū, ṛ/ṝ, lṛ* after any dissimilar vowel, then y (य्) in place of *i/ī, v*,(व्) in place of *u/ū*, r (र्) in place of ṛ/ṝ and in place of lṛ, the order becomes l (ल्). This process is easy to compute. Its format can be seen in Table no-1.

SR	Rec Nn.	End w1	Start w2	Rem W1	Rem W2	Addstr
1	1	इ (*i*)	अ (*ā*)	इ (*i*)	अ (*a*)	य (*ya*)
2	1	इ (*i*)	आ (*ā*)	इ (*i*)	आ (*ā*)	या (*yā*)

3	1	इ (*i*)	उ (*u*)	इ (*i*)	उ (*u*)	यु (*yu*)

Table 1: Computational Rules for Sandhi Recognition and Analysis

The rules database and AD *Sūtrapath* database for the *Rupasiddhi* process have been created in a specific format. In this way, the Sandhi *Sūtras* have been computed using the method given by *Pāṇini.*

6. Used Research Methodology

The basis of the computational rules is the sandhi *prakaraṇa* analyzed in the *Vayakaranasiddhāntakaumudī.* This system was developed on the basis of about 131 Sandhi *Sūtras* and 39 *vārtikas* of *kātyāyana* related to the sandhi. It has been developed on the basis of the Rule and the Example-Based Hybrid Approach. For the general procedure, the formulas are kept under the example method and in special cases, the formulas are kept under the rule method.

Rules and examples in two databases have been created to identify the sandhi. There are total of 4194 computational rules have been kept in the computational format by expanding the *Pāṇinian* rules related to the Sandhi. From this database, the identification of the sandhi between two characters, the analysis and the sandhi is done.

Pāṇini's rule and example-based hybrid method have been used in the development of web-based computing systems for the sandhi. Just as *Pāṇini* has presented two types of rules in his AD, which are called General Rules and Exceptional Rules. Similarly, in this system also the sandhi is obtained with the help of a rule-based method for general rules and an example database for exceptions. Simultaneously, computational linguistics and web technology methods have been used. The Research Methodology can be understood in figure 1.

7. Computational Platform and Techniques

This sandhi system is Web based system. There are mainly two main components to develop any Web based system-first front end and second back end. Front-end can be said to be all the visible aspects of the website that the user can see and experience. In technical language, the term 'client-side' is used for the front-end. The front end mainly consists of web pages. For this system, we used an HTML page, and code of CSS and JavaScript have been included in the HTML code to make it attractive and useful. Back-end is where all work is done in the background. It makes all decisions about how and when to present the information. The programming language Python has been used for web development. The Python-supported Flask server is used for the server and the MySQL database and text files have been used for the database.

8. Components of the System

There are mainly three components in this system-

- The first component identifies the sandhi on the basis of user provided terms and makes a Sandhi.
- On the basis of the second identity, codified changes of sandhi.
- On the basis of the third sandhi, it shows the complete Derivational process of making a sandhi word with the *Pāṇini's Sūtras* and *kātyāyana's vārtikas.*

This can be understood through figure no-1.

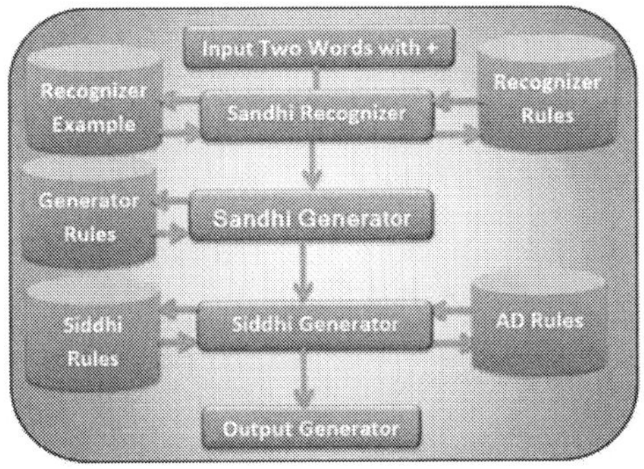

Figure 1: Diagram of the system.

The first webpage of this system is the user interface. The user interface is the point through which a user interacts with a computer, website, or application. The user interface of the presented system is developed in HTML with the help of a Form-based user interface. When submitted by the user by entering his input in Devanagari Unicode (two words with "+" sign) in a text area available in the interface. So that given gets refined and comes to the component called Sandhi Identifier. This component identifies the sandhi with the help of base sandhi identification rules based on the given input. After that, on the basis of the identification, the Sandhi Generator module does the work with the help of rules and an example database and generates a code for the accomplishment process, and sends it to the next step. The Sandhi Siddhi Generator module generates the Siddhi codes from the code obtained from the Sandhi Generator with the help of the *rūpasiddhi* database. Again, this siddhi code is sent to the AD database, where *Pāṇini* converts the code from the rules and communicates it to the output generator. The Output Generator converts the string obtained from the previous element i.e Sandhi Siddhi Generator into text. After that, by creating an automatic table, replaces that text in its rows and columns. As a result, all the information about the derivational process is displayed to the user in the same webpage result.

9. Result and Discussion

With the help of this interface, the user can type any two words in Unicode incorporating a "+" sign between them in Devanagari and click on the submit button for *sasūtrasandhi.* The result is generated on the webpage on the basis of the input provided in UTF-8 in Devanagari script, the Derivational process of sandhi is displayed on a webpage in tabular form. In the result obtained, each *sūtras* and *vārtikas* used in the process of sandhi are hyperlinked. On which, when the cursor is moved, the meaning of that *sūtras* and *vārtikas,* its complete explanation appears on a new webpage. This system is a completely user-friendly system and is easy to use. Through the use of this system, any student can easily use it in his studies and faculties in their teaching pedagogies. This web-based system is completely dependent on the rules of the procedure discussed in the *Vayakaranasiddhāntakaumudī*.

This system can be easily accessed anywhere at the user's convenience with the use of the internet. In the Sandhi system, no dictionary has been used for the Siddhi process, but the basis of the entire Siddhi process is examples and rules and methods. By looking at the position of the sandhi, this system identifies the automatic sandhi in a few moments and at the same time, it also verifies how many sandhi forms are formed in the case of a particular sandhi. On the basis of the given input, this system automatically analyzes the sandhi along with the identification of the sandhi between the given words, which the AD's sandhi rule is derived from. User-supplied words, saṃhitā/sandhi words, sandhi identity, siddhi codes are obtained in this analysis form. Based on the analysis provided by this system, all the sandhi forms have been made. Presents all the information of accomplishment like *sūtras*, *vārtikas*, rules, definitions etc. in text form with hyperlinked meaning and explanation in the form of the automatic table of all those forms. This system is a very helpful resource for people who are curious about the sandhi and the form of the sandhi. By using this system the seeker can not only learn the sandhi himself. Rather, it can also be used as teaching material in the classroom for the teaching of sandhi.

This system achieves the then sandhi and *rūpasiddhi*. As a result, this web-based style affects teaching as well as attracts students' attention to the reading process. The use of the book is of limited consequence. Whereas the use of the system is of unlimited consequence. This system is available online 24*7. Therefore, it can be used without compulsion at any time in reading and learning. Therefore, this system will prove to be very effective in e-learning.

10. Future Directions of the Research

This online sandhi system has been designed according to the *Vayakaranasiddhāntakaumudī*. This system gives sandhi and its Derivational Process between any two words or two varṇa. This system will play a very effective role in Digital classroom teaching, boosting teaching skills and the learning process. In the context of information technology, this research will encourage innovation in future Sanskrit research works. This research will prove to be helpful in future research work on other topics of Sanskrit grammar process like *subanta, tiṅanta, ṇijanta, yaṅanta, sanādyanta, samāsa, taddhita* etc. With the help of this system, the development of *Sasūtrarupasiddhi* Sandhi Splitter system can be done which will prove to be very important in the world of Sanskrit literature. Presently this system has been made in the Hindi version only. After that, it can also be developed for another language versions such as Sanskrit, English, Bangla, Tamil, Telugu etc. And speech technology can also be used for input-output in this.

11. Bibliographical References

Bhardwaj, S., Gantayat, N., Chaturvedi, N., Garg, R., & Agarwal, S. (2018). *SandhiKosh: A Benchmark Corpus for Evaluating Sanskrit Sandhi Tools*. Proceedings of the Eleventh International Conference on Language Resources and Evaluation (LREC 2018). Miyazaki, Japan: European Language Resources Association (ELRA).

Briggs, R. (1985). *Knowledge Representation in Sanskrit and Artificial Intelligence*. AI magazine,6(1), 32. https://doi.org/10.1609/aimag.v6il.466.

Chakraborty, D. S. (2021, feb 7). *The Role of Specific Grammar for Interpretation in Sanskrit*. Journal of Research in Humanities and Social Science, 9(2), 107-187. Retrieved from www.questjournals.org

Joshi, S. D., & Kiparsky, P. (1977). *Siddha and Asiddha in Pāṇinian Phonology*. In D. Dinnsen, Current Approaches to Phonological Theory. Bloomington, Indiana USA: Indiana University Press.

Kiparsky, P. (1995). *Concise History of the Language Sciences (Pāinian Linguistics)*. (E. KOERNER, & R. ASHER, Eds.) Pergamon. Retrieved from https://doi.org/10.1016/B978-0-08-042580-1.50012-X.

Kulkarni, A. (2021). *संसाधनी (A Sanskrit Computational Toolkit)*. University of Hyderabad. http://sanskrit.uohyd.ac.in/scl/.

Kumar, S., & Jha, G. (2007). *Sandhi Splitter and Analyzer for Sanskrit (with special reference to aC sandhi)*. New Delhi: Special Centre for Sanskrit Studies, Jawaharlal Nehru University.

Malcolm, D. H. (2007). *From Paninian Sandhi to Finite State Calculus*. First International Sanskrit Computational Linguistics Symposium (pp. 13-22). Rocquencourt, France: INRIA Paris.

Message, G. (2021). *Green Message*. Retrieved January 24, 2022, from https://greenmesg.org

Mishra, D., & Jha, G. N. (2009). *Issues and Challenges in Computational Processing of Vya–jana Sandhi*. New Delhi: Special Centre for Sanskrit Studies, Jawaharlal Nehru University.

Patel, D. (2022). *Sanskrit World*. Retrieved January 24, 2022, from https://www.sanskritworld.in/sanskrittool/sandhi.html

TDIL. (2021). http://tdil-dc.in/san/sandhi/index_dit.html .

Zwicky, J., & Arnold, M. (1965). *Topics in Sanskrit phonology*. princeton University: Massachusetts Institute of Technology. Retrieved from https://dspace.mit.edu/handle/1721.1/13015

आचार्य, ग. (2019). *वैयाकरणसिद्धान्तकौमुदी*. दिल्ली: चौखम्बा संस्कृत प्रतिष्ठान.

चन्द्र, सु. (2021). *भाषासंगणन*. दिल्ली: विशाल कौशिक प्रिंटर्स.

दीक्षित, प. (2016). *अष्टाध्यायीसूत्रपाठः*. दिल्ली: संस्कृतभारती.

सोमलेखा. (2014). *पाणिनीय शिक्षा*. दिल्ली: चौखम्बा संस्कृत प्रतिष्ठान.

Proceedings of the WILDRE-6 Workshop @LREC2020, pages 29–34
Marseille, 20 June 2022

L3Cube-MahaNER: A Marathi Named Entity Recognition Dataset and BERT models

Parth Patil [*1,3], **Aparna Ranade**[*1,3], **Maithili Sabane**[*1,3], **Onkar Litake**[*1,3], **Raviraj Joshi** [2,3]
[1] Pune Institute of Computer Technology, [2] Indian Institute of Technology Madras, [3] L3Cube Pune
[1,3] Pune, Maharashtra India, [2] Chennai, Tamilnadu India,
{parthpatil8399,aparna.ar217,msabane12}@gmail.com
onkarlitake@ieee.org, ravirajoshi@gmail.com

Abstract

Named Entity Recognition (NER) is a basic NLP task and finds major applications in conversational and search systems. It helps us identify key entities in a sentence used for the downstream application. NER or similar slot filling systems for popular languages have been heavily used in commercial applications. In this work, we focus on Marathi, an Indian language, spoken prominently by the people of Maharashtra state. Marathi is a low resource language and still lacks useful NER resources. We present L3Cube-MahaNER, the first major gold standard named entity recognition dataset in Marathi. We also describe the manual annotation guidelines followed during the process. In the end, we benchmark the dataset on different CNN, LSTM, and Transformer based models like mBERT, XLM-RoBERTa, IndicBERT, MahaBERT, etc. The MahaBERT provides the best performance among all the models. The data and models are available at https://github.com/l3cube-pune/MarathiNLP .

Keywords: Named Entity Recognition, NER, Marathi Dataset, Transformers

1. Introduction

A principal technique of information extraction is Named Entity Recognition. It is an integral part of natural language processing systems. The technique involves the identification and categorization of the named entity (Marrero et al., 2013; Lample et al., 2016). These categories include entities like people's names, locations, numerical values, and temporal values. NER has a myriad of applications like customer service, text summarization, etc. Through the years, a large amount of work has been done for Named Entity Recognition in the English language (Yadav and Bethard, 2018). The work is very mature and the functionality comes out of the box with NLP libraries like NLTK (Bird et al., 2009) and spacy (Honnibal and Montani, 2017). In contrast, limited work is done in the Indic languages like Hindi and Marathi (Kale and Govilkar, 2017). (Patil et al., 2016) addresses the problems faced by Indian languages like the presence of abbreviations, ambiguities in named entity categories, different dialects, spelling variations, and the presence of foreign words. (Shah, 2016) elaborates on these issues along with others like the lack of well-annotated data, fewer resources, and tools, etc. Furthermore, the existing resources for NER in Marathi released in (Murthy et al., 2018) titled IIT Bombay Marathi NER Corpus has only 3588 train sentences and 3 target named entities. Also, about 39 percent of sentences in this dataset contain O tags only further reducing the number of useful tokens. Moreover, many datasets aren't available publicly or contain fewer sample sentences. We aim to build a much bigger Marathi NER corpora with a variety of labels currently missing in the literature. The FIRE 2010 dataset is a comparable dataset with 27,177 sentences but is not publicly available. Although, text classification in Hindi and Marathi has recently received some attention (Joshi et al., 2019; Kulkarni et al., 2022; Kulkarni et al., 2021; Velankar et al., 2021), however the same is not true for NER.

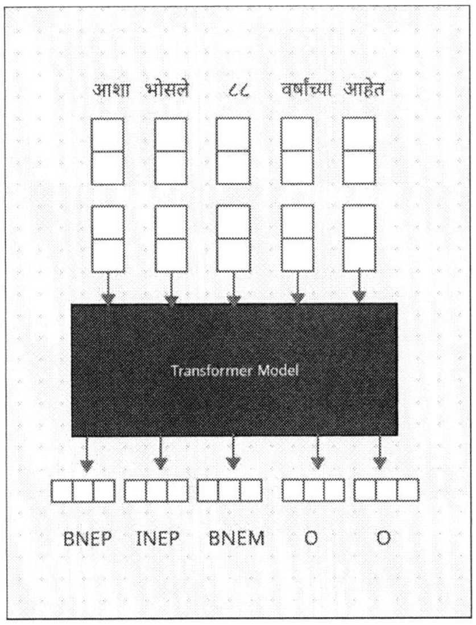

Figure 1: Model Architecture

In this paper, we present our dataset L3Cube-MahaNER. This dataset has been manually annotated and compiled in-house. It is a large dataset annotated

[*] Equal contribution of the authors.

according to the IOB, non-IOB, and binary entity notation for Marathi NER. It contains 25,000 manually tagged sentences categorized according to the eight entity classes. The original sentences have been taken from a news domain corpus (Joshi, 2022a) and the average length of these sentences is 9 words. These entities annotated in the dataset include names of locations, organizations, people, and numeric quantities like time, measure, and other entities like dates and designations. The paper also describes the dataset statistics and the guidelines that have been followed while tagging these sentences.

We also present the results of deep-learning models like Convolutional Neural Network (CNN), Long-Short Time Memory (LSTM), biLSTM, and Transformer models like mBERT (Devlin et al., 2019a), IndicBERT (Kakwani et al., 2020), XLM-RoBERTa, RoBERTa-Marathi, MahaBERT (Joshi, 2022a), MahaROBERTa, MahaALBERT that have been trained on the L3Cube-MahaNER dataset. We experiment on all major multi-lingual and Marathi BERT models to establish a benchmark for future comparisons. The dataset and resources will be publicly shared on Github.

2. Related Work

Named Entity Recognition is a concept that originated at the Message Understanding Conferences (Grishman and Sundheim, 1996) in 1995. Machine learning techniques and linguistic techniques were the two major techniques used to perform NER. Handmade rules (Abdallah et al., 2012) developed by experienced linguists were used in the linguistic techniques. These systems, which included gazetteers, dictionaries, and lexicalized grammar, demonstrated good accuracy levels in English. However, these strategies had the disadvantage of being difficult to transfer to other languages or professions. Decision Trees (Paliouras et al., 2000), Conditional Random Field, Maximum Entropy Model (Bender et al., 2003), Hidden Markov Model, and Support Vector Machine were included in machine learning techniques. To attain better competence, these supervised learning algorithms make use of massive volumes of NE annotated data.

A comparative study by training the models on the same data using Support Vector Machine (SVM) and Conditional Random Field(CRF) was carried out by (Krishnarao et al., 2009). It was concluded that the CRF model was superior. A more effective hybrid system consisting of the Hidden Markov Model, a combination of handmade rules and MaxEnt was introduced by (Srihari, 2000) for performing NER. Deep learning models were then utilized to complete the NER problem as technology progressed. CNN (Albawi et al., 2017), LSTM (Hochreiter and Schmidhuber, 1997), biLSTM (Yang and Xu, 2020), and Transformers were among the most popular models.

NER for Indian languages is a comparatively difficult task due to a lack of capitalization, spelling variances, and uncertainty in the meaning of words. The structure of the language is likewise difficult to grasp. Furthermore, the lack of a well-ordered labeled dataset makes advanced approaches such as deep learning methods difficult to deploy. (Bhattacharjee et al., 2019) has described various problems faced while implementing NER for Indian languages.

(Murthy et al., 2018) introduced Marathi annotated dataset named IIT Bombay Marathi NER Corpus for Named Entity Recognition consisting of 5591 sentences and 108359 tags. They considered 3 main categories named Location, Person, and Organization for training the character-based model on the dataset. They made use of multilingual learning to jointly train models for multiple languages, which in turn helps in improving the NER performance of one of the languages.

(Pan et al., 2017) in 2017 released a dataset named WikiAnn NER Corpus consisting of 14,978 sentences and 3 tags labeled namely Organization, Person, and Location. It is however a silver-standard dataset for 282 different languages including Marathi. This project aims to create a cross-lingual name tagging and linking framework for Wikipedia's 282 languages.

3. Compilation of dataset

3.1. Data Collection

Our dataset consists of 25,000 sentences in the Marathi language. We have used the base sentences from the L3Cube-MahaCorpus (Joshi, 2022a), which is a monolingual Marathi dataset majorly from the news domain. The sentences in the dataset are in the Marathi language with minimal appearance of English words and numerics as present in the original news. However, while annotating the dataset, these English words have not been considered as a part of the named entity categories. Furthermore, the dataset does not preserve the context of the news, such as the publication profiles, regions, and so on.

3.2. Dataset Annotation

We have manually tagged the entire dataset into eight named entity classes. These classes include Person (NEP), Location(NEL), Organization(NEO), Measure(NEM), Time(NETI), Date(NED), and Designation(ED). While tagging the sentences, we established an annotation guideline to ensure consistency. The first 200 sentences were tagged together to further establish consistency among four annotators proficient in Marathi reading and writing. Post this the tagging was performed in parallel except for ambiguous sentences which were separately handled. Firstly, the sentences were relieved of any contextual associations. Then, the approach for the contents of the named entity classes was decided as follows. Proper nouns involving persons' names are tagged as NEP and places are tagged as NEL. All kinds of organizations like companies, councils, political parties, and government departments are

Link to the dataset

Dataset	Sentence Count	Tag Count
Train	21500	27300
Test	2000	2472
Validation	1500	1847

Table 1: Count of sentences and tags in the dataset.

Tags	Train	Test	Validation
NEM	7052	620	488
NEP	6910	611	457
NEL	4949	447	329
NEO	4176	385	268
NED	2466	244	182
ED	1003	92	75
NETI	744	73	48

Table 2: Count of individual tags of L3Cube-MahaNER.

tagged as NEO. Numeric quantities of all kinds are tagged as NEM concerning the context. Furthermore, temporal values like time are tagged as NETI, and dates are tagged as NED. Apart from that, individual titles and designations, which precede proper nouns in the sentences are tagged as ED. Despite maintaining these guidelines, some entities had ambiguous meanings and were difficult to tag. In these circumstances, we resolved the intricacies unanimously by taking a vote amongst the annotators. The sentences were tagged according to the predominant vote.

3.3. Dataset Statistics

For more clarity, some example sentences with tagged entities are mentioned in Table 6.

4. Experimental Techniques

4.1. Model Architectures

The deep learning models are trained using large labeled datasets and the neural network architectures learn features from the data effectively, without the need for feature extraction to be done manually.

Tags	Train	Test	Validation
B-NEM	5824	523	404
I-NEM	1228	97	84
B-NEP	4775	428	322
I-NEP	2135	183	135
B-NEL	4461	407	293
I-NEL	488	40	36
B-NEO	2741	256	178
I-NEO	1435	129	90
B-NED	1937	191	141
I-NED	529	53	41
B-ED	838	74	61
I-ED	165	18	14
B-NETI	633	63	43
I-NETI	111	10	5

Table 3: Count of individual tags of L3Cube-MahaNER.

Similarly, the transformer aims to address sequence-to-sequence problems while also resolving long-range relationships in natural language processing. The transformer model contains a "self-attention" mechanism that examines the relationship between all of the words in a phrase. It provides differential weightings to indicate which phrase components are most significant in determining how a word should be read. Thus the transformer identifies the context that assigns each word in the sentence its meaning. The training time also is lowered as the feature enhances parallelization.

CNN: This model uses a single 1D convolution over the 300-dimensional word embeddings. These embeddings are fed into a Conv1D layer having 512 filters and a filter size of 3. The output at each timestep is subjected to a dense layer of size 8. The dense layer size is equal to the size of the output labels. There are 8 output labels for non-IOB notation and 15 output labels for IOB notation. The activation function used is relu. All the models have the same optimizer and loss functions. The optimizer used is RMSPROP. The embedding layer for all the word-based models is initialized using fast text word embeddings.

LSTM: This model uses a single LSTM layer to process the 300-dimensional word embeddings. The LSTM layer has 512 hidden units followed by a dense layer similar to the CNN model.

biLSTM: It is analogous to the CNN model with the single 1D convolution substituted by a biLSTM layer. An embedding vector of dimension 300 is used in this model and the biLSTM has 512 hidden units. A batch size of 16 is used.

BERT: BERT (Devlin et al., 2019b) is a Google-developed transformer-based approach for NLP pre-training that was inspired by pre-training contextual representations. It's a deep bidirectional model, which means it's trained on both sides of a token's context. BERT's most notable feature is that it can be fine-tuned by adding a few output layers.

mBERT: mBERT (Pires et al., 2019), which stands for multilingual BERT is the next step in constructing models that understand the meaning of words in context. A deep learning model was built on 104 languages by concurrently encoding all of their information on mBERT.

ALBERT: ALBERT (Lan et al., 2020) is a transformer design based on BERT that requires many fewer parameters than the current state-of-the-art model BERT. These models can train around 1.7 times quicker than BERT models and have greater data

Model	F1	Precision	Recall	Accuracy
mBERT	82.82	82.63	83.01	96.75
Indic BERT	84.66	84.10	85.22	97.09
XLM-RoBERTa	84.19	83.42	84.97	97.12
RoBERTa-Marathi	81.93	81.58	82.29	96.67
MahaBERT	84.81	84.55	85.07	97.10
MahaRoBERTa	**85.30**	**84.27**	**86.36**	**97.18**
MahaAlBERT	84.50	84.54	84.45	96.98
CNN	72.2	81.0	66.6	97.16
LSTM	70.0	77.1	64.8	94.46
biLSTM	73.7	77.2	77.6	94.99

Table 4: F1 score(macro), precision and recall of various transformer and normal models for IOB notation using the Marathi dataset.

Model	F1	Precision	Recall	Accuracy
mBERT	85.3	82.83	97.94	96.92
Indic BERT	86.56	85.86	87.27	97.15
XLM-RoBERTa	85.69	84.21	87.22	97.07
RoBERTa-Marathi	83.86	82.22	85.57	96.92
MahaBERT	**86.80**	**84.62**	**89.09**	**97.15**
MahaRoBERTa	86.60	84.30	89.04	97.24
MahaAlBERT	85.96	84.32	87.66	97.32
CNN	79.5	82.1	77.4	97.28
LSTM	74.9	84.1	68.5	94.89
biLSTM	80.4	83.3	77.6	94.99

Table 5: F1 score(macro), precision and recall of various transformer and normal models for non-IOB notation using the Marathi dataset.

throughput than BERT models. IndicBERT is a multilingual ALBERT model that includes 12 main Indian languages and was trained on large-scale datasets. Many public models, such as mBERT and XLM-R, have more parameters than IndicBERT, although the latter performs exceptionally well on a wide range of tasks.

RoBERTa: RoBERTa (Liu et al., 2019) is an unsupervised transformers model that has been trained on a huge corpus of English data. This means it was trained exclusively on raw texts, with no human labeling, and then utilized an automated approach to generate labels and inputs from those texts. The multilingual model XLM-RoBERTa has been trained in 100 languages. Unlike certain XLM multilingual models, it does not require lang tensors to detect which language is being used. It can also deduce the correct language from the supplied ids.

MahaBERT: MahaBERT (Joshi, 2022b) is a 752 million token multilingual BERT model fine-tuned using L3Cube-MahaCorpus as well as other Marathi monolingual datasets that are available publicly.

MahaROBERTA: MahaROBERTA (Joshi, 2022b)is a MarathiRoBERTa model that is based on a multilingual RoBERTa (xlm-roberta-base) framework that has been fine-tuned using L3Cube-MahaCorpus and other publicly released Marathi monolingual corpora.

MahaALBERT: MahaALBERT (Joshi, 2022b) is an AlBERT-based Marathi monolingual model trained using L3Cube-MahaCorpus as well as other Marathi monolingual datasets available publicly.

5. Results

In this study, we have experimented with various model architectures like CNN, LSTM, biLSTM, and transformers like BERT, and RoBERTa to perform named entity recognition on our dataset. This section presents the F1 scores attained by training these models on our dataset for IOB and non-IOB notations. The results have been reported in Table 4 and Table 5 respectively. Among the CNN and LSTM-based models, the biLSTM model with the trainable word embeddings gives the best results on the L3Cube-MahaNER dataset for IOB as well as non-IOB notations. Moreover, for the transformers-based models, it is observed that the Ma-

Sentence	English translation	Tag
कोलकाता आणि दक्षिण भारतातूनही सुपारी नागपुरात येत	Arecanuts also come to Nagpur from Kolkata and South India	NEL O NEL NEL O NEL
या हल्ल्यात काश्मीर पोलिसांच्या एका जवानाने तर सीआरपीएफच्या दोन जवानांनी आपले प्राण	One Kashmir policeman and two CRPF personnel were killed in the attack	O O NEO NEO NEM O O NEO NEM O O O O
दरम्यान राज्यातील सरकारच्या स्थैर्यावर नारायण राणे यांनी याआधीही प्रश्नचिन्ह उप	Meanwhile, Narayan Rane has already questioned the stability of the state government	O NEP NEP O O O O O O
विरोधी पक्षनेते देवेंद्र फडणवीस यांनीही हे सरकार अंतर्विरोधातून कोसळेल असा दावा के	Leader of Opposition Devendra Fadnavis also claimed that this government will collapse due to contradictions	O ED NEP NEP O O O O O O O O O

Table 6: Sample Tagged Sentences

haRoBERTa model yields the best results for IOB and MahaBERT provides the best results for non-IOB notations. The LSTM and the RoBERTa-Marathi models report the lowest scores among all models for both.

6. Conclusion

In this paper, we hold forth on the problem of scarcity of annotated corpora and hence present L3Cube-MahaNER which is a large dataset for Marathi Named Entity, containing 25000 distinct sentences. We achieved the results using IOB and non-IOB notations on deep learning models such as CNN, LSTM, biLSTM, and transformers in BERT as listed above, to set the basis for future work. We observed the highest accuracy on MahaRoBERTa for IOB notations and model MahaBERT for non-IOB notations. We believe that our corpus will play a pivotal role in expanding conversational AI for the Marathi Language.

7. Bibliographical References

Abdallah, S., Shaalan, K., and Shoaib, M. (2012). Integrating rule-based system with classification for arabic named entity recognition. volume 7181, pages 311–322, 03.

Albawi, S., Mohammed, T. A., and Al-Zawi, S. (2017). Understanding of a convolutional neural network. In *2017 International Conference on Engineering and Technology (ICET)*, pages 1–6.

Bender, O., Och, F. J., and Ney, H. (2003). Maximum entropy models for named entity recognition.

Multicase BERT
Indic BERT
Xlm-roberta
Roberta-Marathi
Roberta-Hindi
indic-transformers-hi-roberta
MahaBERT
MahaRoBERTa
MahaAlBERT

In *Proceedings of the Seventh Conference on Natural Language Learning at HLT-NAACL 2003*, pages 148–151.

Bhattacharjee, K., S, S. K., Mehta, S., Kumar, A., Mehta, R., Pandya, D., Chaudhari, P., and Verma, D. (2019). Named entity recognition: A survey for indian languages. In *2019 2nd International Conference on Intelligent Computing, Instrumentation and Control Technologies (ICICICT)*, volume 1, pages 217–220.

Bird, S., Klein, E., and Loper, E. (2009). *Natural language processing with Python: analyzing text with the natural language toolkit.* " O'Reilly Media, Inc.".

Devlin, J., Chang, M.-W., Lee, K., and Toutanova, K. (2019a). Bert: Pre-training of deep bidirectional transformers for language understanding.

Devlin, J., Chang, M.-W., Lee, K., and Toutanova, K. (2019b). Bert: Pre-training of deep bidirectional transformers for language understanding.

Grishman, R. and Sundheim, B. (1996). Message Understanding Conference- 6: A brief history. In *COLING 1996 Volume 1: The 16th International Conference on Computational Linguistics.*

Hochreiter, S. and Schmidhuber, J. (1997). Long short-term memory. *Neural Computation*, 9:1735–1780.

Honnibal, M. and Montani, I. (2017). spaCy 2: Natural language understanding with Bloom embeddings, convolutional neural networks and incremental parsing. To appear.

Joshi, R., Goel, P., and Joshi, R. (2019). Deep learning for hindi text classification: A comparison. In *International Conference on Intelligent Human Computer Interaction*, pages 94–101. Springer.

Joshi, R. (2022a). L3cube-mahacorpus and mahabert: Marathi monolingual corpus, marathi bert language models, and resources. *arXiv preprint arXiv:2202.01159*.

Joshi, R. (2022b). L3cube-mahacorpus and mahabert: Marathi monolingual corpus, marathi bert language models, and resources.

Kakwani, D., Kunchukuttan, A., Golla, S., N.C., G., Bhattacharyya, A., Khapra, M. M., and Kumar, P. (2020). IndicNLPSuite: Monolingual corpora, evaluation benchmarks and pre-trained multilingual language models for Indian languages. In *Findings of the Association for Computational Linguistics: EMNLP 2020*, pages 4948–4961, Online, November. Association for Computational Linguistics.

Kale, S. and Govilkar, S. (2017). Survey of named entity recognition techniques for various indian regional languages. *International Journal of Computer Applications*, 164(4):37–43.

Krishnarao, A. A., Gahlot, H., Srinet, A., and Kushwaha, D. S. (2009). A comparative study of named entity recognition for hindi using sequential learning algorithms. In *2009 IEEE International Advance Computing Conference*, pages 1164–1169.

Kulkarni, A., Mandhane, M., Likhitkar, M., Kshirsagar, G., and Joshi, R. (2021). L3cubemahasent: A marathi tweet-based sentiment analysis dataset. *arXiv preprint arXiv:2103.11408*.

Kulkarni, A., Mandhane, M., Likhitkar, M., Kshirsagar, G., Jagdale, J., and Joshi, R. (2022). Experimental evaluation of deep learning models for marathi text classification. In *Proceedings of the 2nd International Conference on Recent Trends in Machine Learning, IoT, Smart Cities and Applications*, pages 605–613. Springer.

Lample, G., Ballesteros, M., Subramanian, S., Kawakami, K., and Dyer, C. (2016). Neural architectures for named entity recognition. In *Proceedings of NAACL-HLT*, pages 260–270.

Lan, Z., Chen, M., Goodman, S., Gimpel, K., Sharma, P., and Soricut, R. (2020). Albert: A lite bert for self-supervised learning of language representations.

Liu, Y., Ott, M., Goyal, N., Du, J., Joshi, M., Chen, D., Levy, O., Lewis, M., Zettlemoyer, L., and Stoyanov, V. (2019). Roberta: A robustly optimized bert pretraining approach.

Marrero, M., Urbano, J., Sánchez-Cuadrado, S., Morato, J., and Gómez-Berbís, J. M. (2013). Named entity recognition: fallacies, challenges and opportunities. *Computer Standards & Interfaces*, 35(5):482–489.

Murthy, R., Kunchukuttan, A., and Bhattacharyya, P. (2018). Judicious selection of training data in assisting language for multilingual neural NER. In *Proceedings of the 56th Annual Meeting of the Association for Computational Linguistics (Volume 2: Short Papers)*, pages 401–406.

Paliouras, G., Karkaletsis, V., Petasis, G., and Spyropoulos, C. D. (2000). Learning decision trees for named-entity recognition and classification. In *In ECAI Workshop on Machine Learning for Information Extraction*.

Pan, X., Zhang, B., May, J., Nothman, J., Knight, K., and Ji, H. (2017). Cross-lingual name tagging and linking for 282 languages. In *Proceedings of the 55th Annual Meeting of the Association for Computational Linguistics (Volume 1: Long Papers)*, pages 1946–1958, Vancouver, Canada, July. Association for Computational Linguistics.

Patil, N., Patil, A., and B.V, P. (2016). Issues and challenges in marathi named entity recognition. *International Journal on Natural Language Computing*, 5.

Pires, T., Schlinger, E., and Garrette, D. (2019). How multilingual is multilingual bert?

Shah, H. (2016). Study of named entity recognition for indian languages. *International Journal of Information Sciences and Techniques*, 6.

Srihari, R. (2000). A hybrid approach for named entity and sub-type tagging. In *Sixth Applied Natural Language Processing Conference*, pages 247–254, Seattle, Washington, USA, April. Association for Computational Linguistics.

Velankar, A., Patil, H., Gore, A., Salunke, S., and Joshi, R. (2021). Hate and offensive speech detection in hindi and marathi. *arXiv preprint arXiv:2110.12200*.

Yadav, V. and Bethard, S. (2018). A survey on recent advances in named entity recognition from deep learning models. In *Proceedings of the 27th International Conference on Computational Linguistics*, pages 2145–2158.

Yang, G. and Xu, H. (2020). A residual bilstm model for named entity recognition. *IEEE Access*, 8:227710–227718.

Proceedings of the WILDRE-6 Workshop @LREC2020, pages 35–41
Marseille, 20 June 2022

Identifying Emotions in Code Mixed Hindi—English Tweets

Sanket Sonu, Rejwanul Haque, Mohammed Hasanuzzaman, Paul Stynes, and Pramod Pathak
School of Computing
National College of Ireland
Mayor Street Lower, IFSC, Dublin 1, Ireland
x19206071@student.ncirl.ie, firstname.lastname@ncirl.ie

Abstract

Emotion detection (ED) in tweets is a text classification problem that is of interest to Natural Language Processing (NLP) researchers. Code-mixing (CM) is a process of mixing linguistic units such as words of two different languages. The CM languages are characteristically different from the languages whose linguistic units are used for mixing. Whilst NLP has been shown to be successful for low-resource languages, it becomes challenging to perform NLP tasks on CM languages. As for ED, it has been rarely investigated on CM languages such as Hindi—English due to the lack of training data that is required for today's data-driven classification algorithms. This research proposes a gold standard dataset for detecting emotions in CM Hindi–English tweets. This paper also presents our results about the investigation of the usefulness of our gold-standard dataset while testing a number of state-of-the-art classification algorithms. We found that the ED classifier built using SVM provided us the highest accuracy (75.17%) on the hold-out test set. This research would benefit the NLP community in detecting emotions from social media platforms in multilingual societies.

Keywords: Emotion Detection, BERT, Code-mixing

1. Introduction

People nowadays use social media more often; even they follow news channels on micro-blogging websites such as Twitter and Facebook. In fact, many users prefer to use such platforms and avoid traditional media platforms (e.g. television) for news. India is a country with a one and a half billion population. A significant portion of the population makes use of microblogs on daily basis for a variety of reasons, e.g. entertainment, learning, and motivation. Short comments posted by social media users on the micro-blogging websites may show certain kinds of emotions. This can be used by multinational companies and SMEs to check the opinions of the users for a variety of reasons, e.g. reviewing products (Onan, 2021), identifying buying intentions (Haque et al., 2019), recognising complaints about products or services (Preoţiuc-Pietro et al., 2019; Singh et al., 2020a; Singh et al., 2020b). Such hidden insights could be crucial for improving the quality of their products or services. Over and above, identification of emotions or sentiments could be used in improving the quality of output of other NLP models, e.g. machine translation (MT) (Kumari et al., 2021), text summarization (Abdi et al., 2018). In fact, ED is not a new area of NLP and being heavily investigated over a decade and on a variety of contents, e.g. tweets (Liew and Turtle, 2016), technology review (Garcia-Garcia et al., 2017), suicide notes (Desmet and Hoste, 2013). The bidirectional encoders using masked language models, e.g. bidirectional encoder representations from Transformers (BERT) (Devlin et al., 2018), multilingual BERT (mBERT) (Pires et al., 2019), produce state-of-the-art results in numerous NLP tasks. This transfer learning strategy is very effective when labelled data is not abundantly available especially in low-resource scenarios. To the best of our knowledge, none of the existing large-scale language models have been trained exclusively with code-mixed data. Therefore, the problem is that they do not perform well in the NLP tasks involving CM languages. Despite this problem, we considered a popular CM language for investigating emotion analysis, Hindi–English. Hindi is the most popular language in India, and it is spoken as a first language by nearly half a billion people worldwide and as a second language by some 120 million more. A large number of people use Hindi with English for speaking and writing. In social networking platforms, this has even become a normal trend that users write Hindi posts in scripts that are a mixture of Hindi and English linguistic units (e.g. words, syllables). Such code-mixed posts are hard to parse for a variety of reasons, e.g. the NLP preprocessors were traditionally trained on monolingual datasets, not on CM datasets. Moreover, the expression of interest of a social media user may be associated with the user's state of mind, emotion, or other phenomena. Hence, the different users can express their thoughts of interest in numerous ways. For an example, a Hindi word "tmhara" which means 'your' in English can be written in a variety of forms, e.g. "tmharaa", "tumhara", "tumara", "tmhare". To the best of our knowledge, there are no freely-available linguistic preprocessors and tools (syntactic or semantic) that can handle CM Hindi–English texts, e.g. word sense disambiguation, lemmatization, parsing, spelling corrections. This is another challenge that researchers face while they encounter CM languages for different NLP tasks.

In this work, we focused on creating a gold standard dataset for detecting emotions in CM Hindi–English social media texts. To the best of our knowledge, the paper that is closely related to ours is (Vijay et al., 2018), who investigated emotion detection from CM Hindi–English social media texts. More specifically, (Vijay et al., 2018) extracted tweets using Twitter's API and created a small data set that constitutes of 2,866 instances which were annotated into six emotions (Ekman, 1992): *'Happy'*, *'Sad'*, *'Angry'*, *'Fear'*, *'Disgust'*, or *'Surprise'*. For building their ED classifiers they used only three emotion classes. They considered those classes that are more prevalent in the dataset, i.e., *'Happy'*, *'Sad'*, *'Angry'*. Although the work of Vijay et al. (2018) is closely related to ours, our work differs from them in many ways and the key contributions of this work are: (i) we manually created a gold-standard dataset for detecting emotions in CM Hindi–English social media texts. Unlike (Vijay et al., 2018), this is nearly a class-balanced data set, and (ii) we achieved an F_1 score of 75.17% on our held-out test set with our best-performing ED classifier that was built using the SVM algorithm, which surpassed the performance of the best-performing models of Vijay et al. (2018) and Wadhawan and Aggarwal (2021).

2. Related Work

As discussed above, Vijay et al. (2018) investigated ED from CM Hindi–English social media texts. They created a small data set that has a class-imbalance issue. In order to avoid the class-imbalance problem in classification, they considered instances with the three most frequent classes for system building. Vijay et al. (2018) applied a number of preprocessing strategies including replacement of URLs, user names, emoticons with placeholders such as 'URL', 'USER', 'Emoticon', respectively. For building classifiers they extracted features using character n-grams, n-grams, emoticons, punctuation, repeating characters, negations, sentiment lexicons, upper case characters, and intensifiers. They were able to achieve a maximum of 58.2% accuracy when SVM is used. They demonstrated the performance of their classifiers by integrating the aforementioned features into their classification models. Their experiments showed that features derived from URLs, user names, emoticons, negations, lexicons do not help. More recently, Wadhawan and Aggarwal (2021) cited the problem of using the data created by Vijay et al. (2018) for building data-driven classifiers in detecting emotions in CM user-generated content. Instead, they created a self-annotated class-balanced Hindi–English CM dataset using Twitter tags like #happy, #sad, #angry, #fear, #disgust, #wow. In other words, they automatically annotated tweets using a list of collected searched #tags. For example, all tweets under the *#happy* tag were labelled as *'Happy'* emotion. They used different recurrent neural networks (RNNs) for building their classifiers, in particular with Bi-directional Long Short-Term Memory (LSTM) (Hochreiter and Schmidhuber, 1997). Additionally, they made use of three pre-trained LMs for classification, BERT, RoBERTa (Liu et al., 2019), ALBERT (Lan et al., 2019). They were able to achieve an accuracy of 71% on their test set when they used BERT.
We now turn our attention to the papers that looked into sentiment analysis in the social media sphere. The works of Tiwari and Sinha (2020) and Srividya and Sowjanya (2019) focused on sentiment detection in English Facebook posts. They collected Facebook posts and annotated the collected datasets into three sentiments, positive, negative, or neutral. As for training, they mainly considered the supervised learning algorithms that are commonly used for text data such as SVM and Naïve Bayes. They were able to achieve an accuracy in the range of 90% on their test data. There have been a plethora of works that studied this area of NLP considering both high-resource (e.g. English) or low-resource languages (e.g. Indic languages); we refer interested readers to some of the notable papers (Ahmad et al., 2019; Mukherjee, 2019; Singh, 2021). We also refer an excellent initiative to promote this line of NLP research through introducing a shared task (Sentiment Analysis of Code-Mixed Tweets) (Patwa et al., 2020).

3. Corpus Creation and Annotation

The data set created by Vijay et al. (2018) contains a list of 2,866 instances, each of which is manually tagged into one of the following six sentiments *'Happy', 'Sad', 'Angry', 'Fear', 'Disgust', or 'Surprise'*. They made their data set available online for the NLP community. We followed their annotation scheme for creating a robust and balanced dataset. First, we collected tweets using Twitter's official API – Tweepy.[1] Since our aim is to collect CM Hindi–English tweets, we set the language parameter of API to 'Hindi'. We used a list of #tags in order to collect tweets that are expected to be CM Hindi–English texts; some of them are *happy, smile, birthday, badhai ho, Sad, darr, mujhe darr lag rha, Surprise, amazing*. This crawling process provided us with a raw dataset that contains 102,809 CM Hindi–English tweets. In this regard, as pointed out in Section 2, Wadhawan and Aggarwal (2021) automatically created a CM Hindi–English data set using the strategy that we just described. However, the process of automatically annotating tweets by making use of #tags has an important drawback. Many tweets that were extracted with #tag *'happy'* may not be opinionated texts. In fact, some of them could belong to different emotion classes. As an example, consider a tweet "wow amazing. I can't even imagine, how can he be so happy?". This tweet was labelled as *'Happy'* since it was extracted using #tag. In reality, the tweet should belong to the *'Surprise'* emotion class. Since we wanted to create a balanced dataset for emotion detection in user-generated content and it would serve as a gold-standard dataset for this task, the dataset must

[1] https://www.tweepy.org/

not contain any noisy or anomalous examples. That is the reason why we carried out a systematic manual annotation task which is described below.
The tweets that we crawled contains a significant amount of unnecessary entries. For example, they are too short text, contain only URLs, links, #tags, images, Hindi script or English scripts. Such tweets were automatically discarded from the initial list of tweets. Then, we applied the following cleaning procedure in order to clean the tweets: (i) removing URL: links, email IDs, and URLs that were part of tweets were removed, (ii) removing #tags and @User_Names: #tags and @User_Names were removed. (iii) removing emoticons: all emoticons that were part of tweets were removed.[2] (iv) removing RT: all RT tags that were part of tweets were removed, and (v) removing noises: all the null values and special characters were removed from tweets.
As pointed out above, posts in micro-blogging websites usually are short and a word can take one of the numerous lexical variations of the word (e.g. "tmhara" as "tmharaa", "tumhara", "tumara", "tmhare"; cf. Section 1). This can easily be captured by continuous distributed vector representation of words using the Skip-gram model (also known as Word2Vec) (Mikolov et al., 2013) or similar algorithms. However, for this, we need to have a word-embedding model trained on CM Hindi-English corpus. To the best of our knowledge, there is no such freely available corpus to be used for this purpose. Alternatively, we created a list of the most frequently used (Hindi or CM Hindi–English) words on Twitter, which are written in multiple ways. We manually created a list of 365 words, and for each word all alternative variations were turned into their most widely used variation. We will see in the next section that this strategy helped in improving the performance of our ED classification models. We illustrate this with an example. Consider the following Hindi tweet "bro tm pagaal hoo", its literal English translation is "bro you are crazy". The Hindi word 'tum' may be written as 'tumm', 'tm', 'tuum'. In our case, this Hindi tweet is turned into "bro tum pagal ho". Additionally, if there is a tweet that has spelling mistakes, spelling errors are corrected. As an example, consider a Hindi tweet 'bro tm pagaalhoo gaeho" whose literal English translation is "You have become crazy". This tweet is modified or corrected as "bro tum pagal ho gaye ho". This is accomplished via manual inspection since such spelling mistakes cannot be detected using regular expressions.
In sum, we applied a noise cleaning method to the tweets. This cleaning process was carried out with a manual editor who has excellent English and Hindi skills and good knowledge of tweets. On completion of preprocessing and manual cleaning, we ended with a set of 7,150 tweets.

[2]In future, we aim to test emoji normalisation method (https://pypi.org/project/emoji/) too as they could interesting signal for detecting emotions.

3.1. Annotation

We label each of the collected clean tweets with either one of the 6 emotion categories (*'Happy', 'Sad', 'Anger', 'Fear', 'Disgust', 'Surprise'*) or the no emotion category. The manual annotation process is accomplished with a GUI that randomly displays a tweet from the set of 7,150 tweets. At the end of the annotation task, each tweet is associated with one tag. Since we have three annotators and three values are associated with each of the tweets of the set of 7,150 labeled tweets. The final class for a tweet is determined based on a majority voting strategy. There might be complete disagreement (i.e. each annotator tag it with different class) among the annotators. In that case, we do not consider that Tweet. On completion of the annotation task, we ended up with a set of 6,299 annotated Tweets. The inter-annotator agreement was computed using Fleiss' Kappa (Fleiss and Cohen, 1973) at tweet level. For each tweet, we count an agreement whenever three annotators agree with the annotation result. We found the kappa score to be high (i.e. 0.83) for the annotation task. This indicates that our tweet labeling task is to be excellent in quality.
In Table 1, we show two examples of CM Hindi–English tweets from our dataset. The first and second examples shown in Table 1 belong to *'Happy'* and *'Sad'* classes, respectively.

Table 1: CM Tweets from our gold-standard dataset.

CM Tweet	main bht khush hn Modi k decision se
Translation	I am happy with Modi's decision
CM Tweet	ipl kab se chalu hoga bhaiya so sad
Translation	When will IPL start brother so sad

4. Data Statistics

The CM Hindi-English dataset of Vijay et al. (2018) contains 2,866 tweets which are labeled with 6 emotions. From now on, we call this dataset Dataset 1. As mentioned in the above section, our CM Hindi–English dataset contains 6,299 tweets which were labeled with 7 emotion tags. From now on, this dataset is referred to as Dataset 2. Table 2 shows the data distribution, i.e., count of tweets in each emotion class. To build our classifiers, we used a combined dataset (i.e. our dataset with one created by Vijay et al. (2018)) that contains a total of 9,165 CM Hindi–English tweets. From now on, we call the combined dataset Final Dataset. As can be seen from Table 2, although numbers for "No emotion" and "Fear" are slightly high (1,892) and low (559), respectively, Final Dataset is nearly a class-balanced data set. In future, we aim to enrich this data set by increasing the number of Tweets in each class (e.g. "Fear").

5. Emotion Detection: Methodology, Results, and Discussion

In above, we discussed how we created a gold-standard dataset for detecting emotions in CM Hindi English

Labels	Dataset 1	Dataset 2	FD
No emotion	0	1,892	1,892
Happy	595	631	1,226
Sad	878	651	1,529
Angry	667	1,096	1,763
Fear	85	474	559
Disgust	291	856	1,147
Surprise	182	867	1,049

Table 2: Data Distribution

social media texts. We tested the usefulness of this dataset by employing a number of classification algorithms on it. This section details the building of our ED classification models and presents evaluation results.

5.1. Experimental Setups

The recurrent neural network, in particular with LSTM hidden units, has been proved to be an effective model for many classification tasks in NLP. In addition to LSTM, we used SVM, Logistic Regression, Random Forest algorithms for building our classifiers. As discussed in Section 2, Wadhawan and Aggarwal (2021) fine-tuned BERT on an automatically created CM Hindi–English dataset and achieved an accuracy of 71% on their test set. We also tested how BERT would perform on our data set. In order to obtain an optimal set of hyperparameters for SVM, Logistic Regression, and Random Forest, we used a simple grid search algorithm[3] based on a 5-fold cross-validation strategy. For building our classifiers we tried with a range of hyperparameters and a number of their combinations for training our neural-network-based classifiers, LSTM and BERT. We list the optimal set of hyperparameters for each of the classification algorithms: (i) *SVM*: kernel = ['rbf ','linear','poly','sigmoid'], gamma = [1, 0.1, 0.01], and C = [0.1, 1, 10, 100], (ii) *Logistic Regression*: C = [0.1, 1, 20, 40, 60, 80, 100], solver = ['lbfgs', 'liblinear'], (iii) *Random Forest*: n_estimators = [80,85,90,95,100], max_depth = [20,30,None], criterion = ['gini','entropy'], (iv) *LSTM*: epochs = 2, batch size = 64, embedding dim = 100, SpatialDropout1D = 0.4, Memory, unit = 250, LSTM layer dropout = 0.2 and recurrent dropout = 0, Dense layer activation = 'softmax', loss='categorical crossentropy', and optimizer = 'adam', and validation split = 0.1 and (v) *BERT*: epochs = 3, dropout = 0.2, Dense layer activation ='softmax', loss='categorical crossentropy', and optimizer = 'adam'.

We applied four different types of preprocessing modules to our dataset: (i) *punctuation*: This preprocessing module removes all the punctuation's from the dataset, (ii) *stop-words*: We used a list of 1,036 Hindi–English stop-words, (Rana, accessed on 1st Oct 2021). These stop-words are removed from the corpus, (iii) *numbers*: This module removes all the numeric entities from the corpus, and (iv) *repeating characters*: the repeating characters are removed from the corpus (e.g. *'happyyyyy' is changed to 'happy'*).

Each of our classification models were tested on the following setups: (a) setup 1: Removing Punctuation: All the models are trained and tested after removing punctuations from the corpus, (b) setup 2: Removing Stop words: All the models are trained and tested after removing stop words from the corpus, (c) setup 3: Removing Numbers: All the models are trained and tested after removing numbers from the corpus, (d) setup 4: Removing Repeating Characters: All the models are trained and tested after removing repeating characters, (e) setup 5: setups 1–4 All the models are trained and tested after removing punctuation, stop-words, numbers, and repeating words, and (f) setup 6: Keeping all above features: All the models are trained and tested without eliminating any of the above special features.

5.2. Feature Extraction

We followed the standard methods to convert texts (tweets) into numerical vectors so that it is understandable by machine learning models. For this, we applied a popular bag-of-words strategy with two different weightings: word frequency counts (WFC), term-frequency inverse-document-frequency (TF-IDF). We found that classifiers trained on TF-IDF weighted data outperformed the one that was trained on WFC weighted. Therefore, we used the TF-IDF weighting in our training setup. As for measuring TF-IDF weights, we considered both 1-gram and 2-gram word occurrences. Additionally, we also experimented with converting text data into dense vectors using Doc2Vec.[4] We tested three different algorithms available in Doc2Vec: distributed bag-of-words (DBOW), distributed memory (DM), concatenation of DBOW and DM (DBOW+DM).

5.3. Results

For evaluation we split our data set into two parts, i.e. 80% instances used for training and 20% instances were used for evaluation. In order to measure classifier's performance on the test set, we used a widely-used evaluation metric: accuracy.

Table 3 presents performance of our classifiers for TF-IDF features (1- and 2-grams). As can be seen from Table 3, SVM with TF-IDF unigrams weighting provided us an accuracy of 75.17% when none of the special features were eliminated from the dataset (Setup 6). This turned out to be our best-performing ED classifier.

We picked the best-performing model (SVM; cf. Setup 6 of Table 3), and show confusion matrix and classification performance in terms of precision, recall and $F1$ in Tables 4 and 5. We can see from Tables 4 and 5 that our ED SVM model performs consistently across the

[3] `https://scikit-learn.org/stable/modules/generated/sklearn.model_selection.GridSearchCV.html`

[4] `https://radimrehurek.com/gensim/auto_examples/tutorials/run_doc2vec_lee.html`

	Models for TF-IDF (1-gram)			
Setups	**SVM**	**LR**	**RF**	**LSTM**
1	75.12%	73.37%	73.32%	71.03%
2	72.83%	72.77%	74.24%	68.47%
3	75.12%	73.32%	72.94%	71.96%
4	75.06%	73.37%	73.75%	68.14%
5	72.88%	73.15%	74.74%	69.78%
6	75.17%	73.43%	73.48%	71.79%
	Models for TF-IDF (2-gram)			
Setups	**SVM**	**LR**	**RF**	**LSTM**
1	74.03%	74.30%	71.24%	71.36%
2	74.03%	74.41%	73.64%	69.34%
3	74.03%	74.79%	72.34%	73.05%
4	73.97%	74.57%	71.35%	68.19%
5	73.64%	74.41%	72.83%	69.18%
6	73.97%	74.30%	72.23%	72.23%

Table 3: Performance of our ED classifiers (accuracy).

all emotion classes and produces excellent precision, recall, and F_1 on the evaluation test set.

	Confusion Matrix						
Labels	**0**	**1**	**2**	**3**	**4**	**5**	**6**
NE - 0	323	2	5	19	3	1	8
Happy - 1	43	171	13	14	0	1	0
Sad - 2	53	11	219	24	0	1	2
Angry - 3	58	5	13	259	0	7	4
Fear - 4	14	3	6	6	70	3	2
Disgust - 5	35	3	4	21	1	175	0
Surprise - 6	45	4	4	14	2	1	161

Table 4: Confusion Matrix of SVM with TF-IDF(*1*-gram) weighting without removing any of the special features (Setup 6). NE: No Emotions.

Labels	Precision	Recall	F1-score	Support
0	0.57	0.89	0.69	361
1	0.86	0.71	0.78	242
2	0.83	0.71	0.76	310
3	0.73	0.75	0.74	346
4	0.92	0.67	0.78	104
5	0.93	0.73	0.82	239
6	0.91	0.70	0.79	231
accuracy			0.75	1833
macro avg	0.82	0.74	0.76	1833
weighted avg	0.79	0.75	0.76	1833

Table 5: Performance of SVM with TF-IDF(*1*-gram) weighting without removing any of the special features (Setup 6).

In Table 6, we present the performance of our classification models when features were extracted using the "Doc2Vec" word embedding method. As can be seen from Table 6, none of the features (DBOW, DM, DBOW+DM) is effective, the classification models performed quite poorly as they produce accuracy in the range of 28–45%. As in (Wadhawan and Aggarwal, 2021), we fine-tuned BERT on our data set in order to see how it would perform on a small-sized CM data. We found that BERT's accuracy is quite low (nearly 20%) on our held-out test set.

	Models for Doc2Vec – DBOW		
Setups	**SVM**	**LR**	**RF**
1	29.84%	28.69%	27.82%
2	36.33%	35.35%	35.51%
3	29.18%	28.75%	28.91%
4	29.89%	28.53%	28.96%
5	34.47%	34.58 %	34.58%
6	29.51%	28.09%	28.80%
	Models for Doc2Vec – DM		
Setups	**SVM**	**LR**	**RF**
1	33%	34.04%	25.25%
2	32.46%	31.96%	27.71%
3	33.06%	32.73%	23.94%
4	33.82%	34.64%	24.22%
5	31.96%	33.06 %	29.51%
6	32.18%	32.67%	24.05%
	Models for Doc2Vec – (DBOW+DM)		
Setups	**SVM**	**LR**	**RF**
1	37.97%	38.62%	30.44%
2	43.97%	44.62%	40.48%
3	35.62%	37.20%	28.15%
4	38.35%	38.62%	29.78%
5	41.89%	42.22 %	38.78%
6	38.89%	39.77%	31.42%

Table 6: Performance of classification models building using word-embeddings generated by Doc2Vec.

6. Conclusions and Future Work

In this paper, we presented our experiments on emotion detection in code-mixed Hindi–English social media text. Since there was no publicly available balanced data set for this task, we created a moderate-sized gold-standard balanced dataset. For this, we crawled CM Hindi–English tweets from the most popular micro-blogging website, Twitter. Our data preparation process included a number of steps including cleaning, transformation, and annotation. Next, we investigated usefulness of our dataset and used a number of state-of-the-art classification algorithms for building emotion detection classifiers. We carried out a wide range of experiments in order to find the setup that would work best for this dataset. We obtained an accuracy of 75.17% on our hold-out test set with our best-performing ED classifier that was built using the SVM algorithm. Our best-performing ED classifier outperformed the best-performing models presented in Wadhawan and Aggarwal (2021) and Vijay et al. (2018) with large margins.

In future, we aim to test multi-stage fine-tuning strategy on BERT (Xie et al., 2020) for this task, where in the first stage we will fine-tune BERT on automatically extracted self-annotated data as in Wadhawan and Aggarwal (2021), and in the second stage we will fine-tune the model obtained in first stage on our data set.

7. Bibliographical References

Abdi, A., Shamsuddin, S. M., Hasan, S., and Piran, J. (2018). Machine learning-based multi-documents sentiment-oriented summarization using linguistic treatment. *Expert Systems with Applications*, 109:66–85.

Ahmad, G. I., Singla, J., and Nikita, N. (2019). Review on sentiment analysis of indian languages with a special focus on code mixed indian languages. In *2019 International Conference on Automation, Computational and Technology Management (ICACTM)*, pages 352–356.

Desmet, B. and Hoste, V. (2013). Emotion detection in suicide notes. *Expert Systems with Applications*, 40(16):6351–6358.

Devlin, J., Chang, M.-W., Lee, K., and Toutanova, K. (2018). Bert: Pre-training of deep bidirectional transformers for language understanding. *arXiv preprint arXiv:1810.04805*.

Ekman, P. (1992). Are there basic emotions?

Fleiss, J. L. and Cohen, J. (1973). The equivalence of weighted kappa and the intraclass correlation coefficient as measures of reliability. *Educational and Psychological Measurement*, 33(3):613–619.

Garcia-Garcia, J. M., Penichet, V. M., and Lozano, M. D. (2017). Emotion detection: a technology review. In *Proceedings of the XVIII international conference on human computer interaction*, pages 1–8.

Haque, R., Ramadurai, A., Hasanuzzaman, M., and Way, A. (2019). Mining purchase intent in twitter. In *Proceedings of CICLing 2019, the 20th International Conference on Computational Linguistics and Intelligent Text Processing*, La Rochelle, France.

Hochreiter, S. and Schmidhuber, J. (1997). Long short-term memory. *Neural computation*, 9(8):1735–1780.

Kumari, D., Ekbal, A., Haque, R., Bhattacharyya, P., and Way, A. (2021). Reinforced nmt for sentiment and content preservation in low-resource scenario. *ACM Transactions on Asian and Low-Resource Language Information Processing*, 20(4):1–27.

Lan, Z., Chen, M., Goodman, S., Gimpel, K., Sharma, P., and Soricut, R. (2019). Albert: A lite bert for self-supervised learning of language representations. *arXiv preprint arXiv:1909.11942*.

Liew, J. S. Y. and Turtle, H. R. (2016). Exploring fine-grained emotion detection in tweets. In *Proceedings of the NAACL Student Research Workshop*, pages 73–80.

Liu, Y., Ott, M., Goyal, N., Du, J., Joshi, M., Chen, D., Levy, O., Lewis, M., Zettlemoyer, L., and Stoyanov, V. (2019). Roberta: A robustly optimized bert pretraining approach. *arXiv preprint arXiv:1907.11692*.

Mikolov, T., Sutskever, I., Chen, K., Corrado, G., and Dean, J. (2013). Distributed representations of words and phrases and their compositionality. *CoRR*, abs/1310.4546.

Mukherjee, S. (2019). Deep learning technique for sentiment analysis of hindi-english code-mixed text using late fusion of character and word features. In *2019 IEEE 16th India Council International Conference (INDICON)*, pages 1–4.

Onan, A. (2021). Sentiment analysis on product reviews based on weighted word embeddings and deep neural networks. *Concurrency and Computation: Practice and Experience*, 33(23):e5909.

Patwa, P., Aguilar, G., Kar, S., Pandey, S., PYKL, S., Gambäck, B., Chakraborty, T., Solorio, T., and Das, A. (2020). Semeval-2020 task 9: Overview of sentiment analysis of code-mixed tweets. *CoRR*, abs/2008.04277.

Pires, T., Schlinger, E., and Garrette, D. (2019). How multilingual is multilingual bert? *arXiv preprint arXiv:1906.01502*.

Preoţiuc-Pietro, D., Gaman, M., and Aletras, N. (2019). Automatically identifying complaints in social media. In *Proceedings of the 57th Annual Meeting of the Association for Computational Linguistics*, pages 5008–5019, Florence, Italy.

Rana, S. (accessed on 1st Oct 2021). Hinglishnlp. `https://github.com/TrigonaMinima/HinglishNLP/blob/master/data/assets/stop_hinglish`.

Singh, R. P., Haque, R., Hasanuzzaman, M., and Way, A. (2020a). Identifying complaints from product reviews: A case study on hindi. In *Proceedings of the Irish Conference on Artificial Intelligence and Cognitive Science (AICS 2020)*, Dublin, Ireland.

Singh, R. P., Haque, R., Hasanuzzaman, M., and Way, A. (2020b). Identifying complaints from product reviews in low-resource scenarios via neural machine translation. In *Proceedings of ICON 2020: 17th International Conference on Natural Language Processing*, Patna, India.

Singh, D. (2021). Detection of emotions in hindi-english code mixed text data. *CoRR*, abs/2105.09226.

Srividya, K. and Sowjanya, A. M. (2019). Sentiment analysis of face book statuses.

Tiwari, S. and Sinha, A. (2020). Sentiment analysis of facebook data using machine learning. *International Journal of Innovative Research in Applied Sciences and Engineering*, 4:2456–8910, 10.

Vijay, D., Bohra, A., Singh, V., Akhtar, S. S., and Shrivastava, M. (2018). Corpus creation and emotion prediction for hindi-english code-mixed social media text. pages 128–135, 01.

Wadhawan, A. and Aggarwal, A. (2021). Towards emotion recognition in hindi-english code-mixed data: A transformer based approach.

Xie, Y., Yang, W., Tan, L., Xiong, K., Yuan, N. J., Huai, B., Li, M., and Lin, J. (2020). Distant supervision for multi-stage fine-tuning in retrieval-based question answering. In *Proceedings of The Web Conference 2020*, pages 2934–2940.

Proceedings of the WILDRE-6 Workshop @LREC2020, pages 42–47
Marseille, 20 June 2022

Digital Accessibility and Information Mining of Dharmaśāstric Knowledge Traditions

Arooshi Nigam, Subhash Chandra
Department of Sanskrit, University of Delhi
New Delhi-110007, India
arooshinigam@gmail.com, schandra@sanskrit.du.ac.in.

Abstract

The heritage of Dharmaśāstra (DS) carries extensive cultural history and encapsulates the treatises of Ancient Indian Social Institutions (SI). DS is reckoned as an epitome of the primitive Indian knowledge tradition as it incorporates a variety of genres for sciences and arts such as family law and legislation, civilization, ritualistic procedures, environment, economics, commerce and finance studies, management, mathematical and medical sciences etc. SI represents a distinct tradition of civilization formation, society development and community living. The texts of the DS are primarily written in the Sanskrit language and due to its expansive subject stream, it is later translated into various other languages globally. With the ingress of internet, development of advanced digital technologies and IT boom, information is accessed and exchanged via digital platforms. DS texts are studied not only by Sanskrit scholars but also referred by historians, sociologists, political scientists, economists, law enthusiasts and linguists worldwide. Despite its eminence, there is a major setback in digitizing and online information mining for DS texts. The major objective of the paper is to digitize and develop an instant referencing system to amplify the digital accessibility of DS texts. This will act as an effective and immediate learning tool for researchers who are keen on intensive studying of DS concepts.

Keywords: Information Extraction (IE), Online Indexing, Information Technology (IT), Heritage Computing, Cultural Tradition, Dharmaśāstra (DS), Manusmṛti (MS), Social Institutions (SI)

1. Background and Introduction

Ancient Bharata, a pseudonym for India, was a storehouse of indigenous knowledge tradition of various sciences and technology. The opulent knowledge system was documented in the Sanskrit language in the form of compendiums known as *śāstras*. Sanskrit is the classical language of Bharata. It is a language of learned treatises and an exquisite amalgamation of both arts and sciences. Indeed, Sanskrit as a language or a subject field is primitive in nature but scholars from all around the globe reckon Sanskrit as a lingua franca. As a language, it is used in an extremely limited and very specific context, yet, the socio-cultural value of the language retains its significance in the modern Indian milieu. Since the beginning, Bharata has achieved advancement in every aspect of intellectual traditions. The knowledge traditions of ancient Bharat have been cumulative and continuously expanding. It is intensively cohesive of many different fields of studies in ancient Indian texts ranging from the *Vedas*, *Brāhmaṇa*, *Upaniṣada*, *Dharmaśāstra* (DS), the six-fold Indian Philosophical tradition and so forth. Biswas and Banerjee (2016) highlighted the significance of Sanskrit texts such as *Caraka* and *Suśruta's* compendiums on medicine, *Āryabhaṭṭa's* work on mathematics, *Bhāskara's* astronomy, *Kauṭilya's* politics and administration and *Pāṇinī's* grammar by depicting the advanced scientific perspectives dexterously elucidated in them. They proclaimed these primitive texts as landmarks for the modern development of science and logic.

DS is a genre of Sanskrit compendium exclusively privé to dharma and an idiosyncratic writing style of Sanskrit texts depicting the Indian knowledge tradition. The term DS is composed using two words "*dharma*" and "*śāstra*". The word *dharma* originated from the "*dhṛ*" verb root in Sanskrit, which means to uphold, support or sustain, or to nourish, whereas, the word "*Sāstra*" derives from the root "*śas anuśiṣṭau*" with "*ṣṭrana*" suffix added to it. It literally means "which has been instructed and rescripted". It is one of the genres of Sanskrit texts devoted entirely to the ancient Indian tradition of social management through prescribed duties for every individual (Banerjee, 1999). It represents dharma as a right way of living (Dubey, 2012). They are part of Vedic literature. Vedas are considered to be the ancient text and the most credible source of DS. The four Vedas namely; *ṛgveda*, *Yajurveda*, *Sāmaveda*, and *Atharvaveda*, are considered the root of our ancient Indian religious and cultural prescriptions. In India, there is an exciting blend of scientific perspectives, artistic traditions, and philosophical perceptions. There is a multiplicity of ideas, manifold thoughts, disparate languages, substantial cultural heritage, exceedingly rich literature, sociological milieu, economic and political conditions, internal and external Epistemology (Phillips, 2014). Sociologist Bogardus (1924) defines Social Institutions (SI) as a structure of society that is organized to meet the needs of people through well-established procedures. It ensures the smooth functioning of the social structure, provides an established mechanism for positive growth and foundation for an organized society. SI organizes, directs and executes the multifarious activities required to fulfill the basic human needs which are essential for the proper working of society. India has been paramount in the field of primitive arts, ancient traditions, prescribed rituals and primordial scientific technologies. The DS texts are the oldest sources of the social phenomena, political scenarios, economic conditions, ethical norms and religious living of the primitive Indian society. The following section will briefly introduce various knowledge traditions and scientific perspectives conglomerated as Sanskrit literary heritage. These dimensions are as follows:

2. Research Problem and Objective

DS texts have been studied and continuously iterated by scholars globally. The traditional concepts and literary heritage of DS have often seen a literary revival and now the world is striving forward in the direction of exploring scientific nuances and technological perspectives in the primitive DS. The major key texts of DS encapsulate a wide range of subjects. To intensify our knowledge of traditions, culture, history and heritage, as well as to rehabilitate the prior wisdom on ancient scientific aspects, DS texts need to be read and studied thoroughly by the sanskritists, sociologists, experts of management sciences, political scientists, economists, legal experts, *āyurveda ācāryas* and various science experts. The opulent knowledge base in Sanskrit has been a source of attraction for both Indians as well as western intellectuals. In recent years, there has been a tremendous body of work which is being conducted on various scientific fields in lieu of DS such as computational linguistics (CL) and spatial data mining, medical sciences, military and mathematical sciences, environmental sciences, management studies, economics and commerce, legal prescriptions etc. The philosophical influence of Sanskrit is evidently visible in the field of psychological studies health and physiological sciences. The ancient asceticism and healing traditions of Sanskrit scriptures have found their way into modern health and clinical sciences. This paper focuses on the various different dimensions and scientific perspectives from Sanskrit literature, specifically DS. It further elucidates the impact of Sanskrit studies on the global platform in the field of world science.

Therefore, the accessibility of Sanskrit resources is of utmost importance in India and also in the world for the extensive knowledge discourse of Sanskrit. In the contemporary era of globalization, with the worldwide influx of internet and digital innovations, the entire universe has witnessed a major IT-boom. The entire world is connected by a click of a button, people of one city are associated with the citizens of another continent, every individual today, is a world citizen, the world news is generated, accessible and received through web consortiums, traditional classroom teaching methodologies and lecture-based pedagogies have pivoted to digital learning and electronic tools, primitive physical athenaeums have transformed into digital libraries, yet its cataclysmic that hitherto we do not have any instant information retrieval system or online indexing apparatus based on DS texts, where desired information appertained to this specific knowledge field can be attained. In today's era of IT and Globalization, when there is a continuous surge in demand for educational materials to be made available online the availability of Sanskrit texts in the form of e-content is extremely scarce. The major objective of the system is to develop a Web-based Search Mechanism and an IE Mechanism for DS texts.

3. Dharmaśāstric Knowledge Tradition

In this section, the focus is devoted on the brief discussion on all the major fields of DS knowledge tradition. DS are the prominent sources of dharma. Dharma is the most fundamental tool in shaping various streams of Indian Knowledge System. It is essential for better understanding of Indian spirituality and scriptures as well as the most important uniting force of ancient Bharata. India developed its own distinct systems of ethics and values. The exercise of reasoning and the practice of argument was recorded in the early texts of India. It became the basis of a very well-known tradition of *śāstrārtha;* an open enquiry and debate to investigate the truth. This tradition in DS was connected with the subject of ontology, epistemology and dialectics. The classical systems of Indian philosophy such as; *vedāṃtā*, *nyāya* and *sāṃkhya* in continuation with *mīmāṃsā*, *vaiśeṣika* and Yoga, including Buddhism, Jainism and atheistic schools, is the major constituent of DS knowledge tradition. Other knowledge traditions such as, arts and aesthetics, theory of emotion, drama, poetry, music, folk culture, paintings, language, grammar and literature are the primitive knowledge traditions propounded in the DS. Though the elementary focus of DS is on traditional contents yet it is considered constructive in the following areas of discussion.

3.1 Society Management through Varṇāśrama System

Varṇa is considered as the classifications of the major responsibilities held by the individuals of the society in Ancient India. It basically manages the society through appropriate distributions of the duties to everyone ensuring their rights and safeguarding the interests of every individual in the society (Chaubey, 2005). In ancient Indian civilization, to make human life civilized, cultured and well-planned, *varṇaāśrama* system was introduced. The society was divided into four major *varṇas*: *brāhmaṇa*, *kṣatriya, vaiśya* and *śūdra* on the basis of the citizens bearing the corresponding social responsibilities. *Āśrama* is an important institution of Hindu social organization which is intimately associated with *varṇa*. The life of every human being is believed to be of training and self-governance. During this phase of training, humans supposedly pass through four stages. Just like the ancient Indian society was distributed into four *varṇas*. Similarly, an individual's life was divided in four stages known as *āśrama* system. According to the DS, an ideal life span of a human is a minimum of a 100 years. This period of 100 years is divided in equal parts of four. These were given the name of *āśrama*. It includes *brahmacaryā* (training and education period), *gṛhastha* (household), *vānaprastha* (retirement) and *saṃnyāsa* (life of renunciation). The concept of *āśrama* system in accordance with dharma is also very popular in ancient scriptures (Jayapalan, 2001). According to the AS, the strict observance of the duties of the four *varṇa* and *āśrama* system 'leads us to heaven' and bestows eternal bliss (Chander, 2015). The principle of *puruśārtha* is introduced to fulfil the human needs through dharma in ancient Indian society. The psychological-moral basis of the *āśramas* system is *puruṣārthas* namely the dharma-artha-*kāma-mokṣa* which helps in organizing and operating the individual's life through *āśramas. Āśramas* are considered to have a close relationship with *puruṣārthas*. The various efforts that a human undertakes to achieve his desires, is known as a *puruśārtha*. It makes a person aware of his ultimate goals and inspires him to perform their fundamental duties. Thus, *āśramas* and *puruṣārthas* are intimately associated with each other.

3.2 Society Management through Politics and Ruling

The concept of good governance in the ancient Hindu system is based on brahmanical notion of '*yogakṣema*' which means the wellbeing of people. The administrative system of ancient India can be traced back to Hindu jurisprudence texts, which describes the characteristics of a global society and the legal system. Distinct concepts and system of polity and governance developed in India over time and democratic mechanisms were put in place to restrict or channel the ruler's powers. In all the scriptures like *Manusmṛti* (MS), *Yājñavalkya* and *Arthaśāstra* (AS), *rājadharma* has been a very crucial topic. Major topics which come under *rājadharma* are the concept of state and nation, concept of religion, art of governance, duties of ruler, democracy or public happiness (Nath, 2019), social philosophy of fundamental rights, art and science of governance, electoral reforms, national unity, religious minorities and secularism, *yogakṣema* and *paṃcāyatī rāja* etc. These topics are all included in *smṛtis* (Sankhder, 2003). AS, deals extensively with law and order, political and bureaucratic accountability, elaborate legal framework, human resource management and prevention of corruption. Traditional Indian culture and administration have laid emphasis on peaceful and harmonious social order, delivery of justice, checking corruption, citizen participation, maintaining a balanced environment and collective welfare. Similar issues are described in MS, *Yājñavalkyasmṛti*, *Atrismṛti* etc. MS and AS are two prime examples of the DS which deals with state policy and theory of punishment, so that the society does not deviate from the dharma.

3.3 Management and Economics

For every society, the vital task is to arrange and maintain the provision of food, clothing, and shelter for its members. Business management, finance psychology, accounting all are imperative for a country's economic condition. *Kauṭilya* in his prestigious text AS highlighted the relevance of economics and management science for the contemporary society. Its main subjects are economy, state, science of business management, financial management during Maurya period, education and training for effective governance, marketing strategy, management of political economy for contemporary society as described by Manu and *Kauṭilya* etc (Chamola, 2007). It deals with diverse economic affairs such as commerce, accounts and coinage (Irani and Silver 1995). Saputra and Anggiriawan (2021) explores the concepts of Accounting, Auditing and Corruption from *Kauṭilya's* point of view and also suggests ways to prevent corporate corruption and tax evasion as per the guidelines of AS. Donald (2017) imparted knowledge on business ethics, capitalism, livelihood, government, means of existence, trade and merchant world, production, commerce, ancient Indian economy and commercial exchanges on the basis of scriptures like *Mahābhārata*, MS, *Nāradasmṛti*, AS etc. therefore, to understand the proper way of conducting trade and commerce, the study of ancient scriptures is necessary for students engaged in the field of commerce, business studies, financial management, economics etc.

3.4 Cleanliness and Environmental Awareness

The social scientists of the ancient period were fully aware of the importance of environment. Cleanliness, sanitation, purification of mind, body, soul and the various social rules and methodologies related to it are discussed in DS key texts. Cleanliness of the surroundings and the hygiene of the body has always been the priority. Protection of natural resources such as water, land, forests as well as, the preservation of water sources such as rivers, lakes, ponds etc. has been of major concern in the DS texts. Throwing of waste and filth in these natural water resources were declared as punishable offenses. This indicates that the primitive sages were extremely aware of the necessity of various natural resource and cautious of the complications of the scarcity of the water. The DSs always deliberated on the issues such as how much water to be used for various essential needs like bathing, cleaning utensils and clothes, drinking and various other purposes such as sweeping the floors, in agriculture, gardening etc., how to keep our water sources pristine, which type of water is fit and suitable for consumption. Similarly, the concept of sanitation and method of defecation is widely propagated in DS. It throws light on subjects like the importance of yoga and exercises, the benefits of a nutritious, healthy and balanced diet, the direction in which the defecation spot must be constructed. MS promotes sustainable community living and harmony with the environment and ecology (Bobade, 2019). DSs presented a unique perception on viable environmental perspectives. It explores new approaches and dimensions to enhance the knowledge on ancient aspects of environmental science, natural healing techniques, conservation, climatology, preservation measures of natural resources.

3.5 Health Care and Management

Ancient India is considered to be the emanation of many advanced sciences. All the ancient civilizations of the world have developed their own specific medicinal systems, but the ancient Indian system of medicine is considered to be the most systematic and the most holistic system, both in its ideas and remedial measures. Apart from the sacraments, the management of human health has also been done under the *āśrama* system in MS. In old age, it is natural for the physical and mental health of man to deteriorate. Texts like *yogadarśana*, *upaniṣada*, *āyurveda* etc., disperses the importance of yoga and yoga asanas for elderly people. *Acārya* Manu manages the human health in two ways; first is by the division of *saṃskāras* and the second is through *āśrama* system. *Saṃskāras* are a central concept in the field of social science. They play an important role in the society. DS elucidates *saṃskāras* as the basis for a man to live a better life. *Saṃskāras* are a religious medium which sanctify the body, mind and intellect. DS corroborated the *saṃskāras* as a foundation for neonatal health, child's immunity development and elementary nutrition. The Indian health system emphasizes on lifestyle changes, purification treatments, spiritual and mental health, positive attitude, season specific diet, exercise and yoga for healthy living (Tiwari and Pandey, 2013).

4. Data Mining and Indian Dharmaśāstric Knowledge Traditions

Information or data mining is a process used to search and extract desired information from big data. It can be implied by analyzing data patterns or using a set of rules of data using one or more software. It involves efficacious data collection and specific patterns or conceptual tagging. Information Mining is also known as Information Extraction or Data mining process. It is the process of searching large-scale documents or unstructured text to mine relevant information, ideas and content. Sanskrit has the biggest literary tradition. Many texts are also available on the web. So mining the specific information from these texts are very essential. Therefore, an online web-based system is being developed to access the content and extract information from DS texts. The information of various DS knowledge traditions embedded in MS is to be extracted. The Sanskrit texts are enormously huge and contain opulent information on knowledge traditions. But the access to authentic information from the humongous database is a very challenging task.

Concept mining is the process of searching documents or unstructured text for ideas and topics. Similar to text mining and data mining, concept mining involves creating a mining model and applying artificial intelligence (AI) to it. However, concept mining focuses on finding intent and deep-rooted meaning rather than extracting explicit information. Text mining is the process of extracting important information and knowledge from unstructured text. This was first proposed by Feldman and Dagan (1955). Till date, not much work has been done in this area of information mining and data extraction for Sanskrit literature.

In Bharata, the leading institutes working in the area of computational Sanskrit are School of Sanskrit and Indic Studies, Jawaharlal Nehru University, New Delhi[1], The Department of Sanskrit Studies, University of Hyderabad[2] and Department of Sanskrit, University of Delhi[3]. They have been carried R&D in the field of information mining and searching for Sanskrit such as online indexing and instant search or immediate referencing system for AS[4], *Amarakośa*[5] (Khandoliyan 2012), *Mahābhārata*[6] (Mani 2010), *Nirukta, Vedāṃta*[7], *Maṃkhakośa*[8], *Śrīmadbhagavadgītā*[9], *Āyurveda*[10], *Medinīkośa*[11] and *Bṛhadāraṇyakopaniṣad*[12], manuscripts catalogue[13]. Sinha and Jha (2020) have presented exemplary work in the field of text summarization for Sanskrit.

The Online Multilingual *Amarakośa* system is based on the archaic text *Amarakośa*, the Sanskrit thesaurus ascribed to *Amarasiṁha*. It is developed using RDBMS techniques. The system facilitates storing up to 50 synonyms with category, gender, number information and detailed glosses, with cross-referencing among synonyms, search capability in the supported Indian languages and ontology display. Any word found in the text of *Amarakośa* can be searched online[14] using this system (Khandoliyan 2012). Likewise, *purāṇas* are reckoned as eminent texts in the Indian knowledge system. Digitization and online search for *Purāṇa* is a major contribution to the field (Anju and Chandra 2017) of Sanskrit CL. *Sāṃkhya-yoga* technical terms database and online search are also important to work in the field of digitization and search (Anju and Chandra 2018).

Despite the recent development in the field of Sanskrit CL, there is no work in sight where the information can be searched from the DS texts. The only way of accessing and studying the MS as of today is using the print medium. But the MS in the format of hardcopies, pose some gruesome challenges as these books are not very durable and instant search is definitely out of question. To study a particular concept the whole book needs to be read or studied. This is very time consuming and yet not accurate. It might also have typing, printing and editing errors. Apart from these, the print medium has physical inhibitions such as it is not feasible to carry the books around and there is surety of the availability of books at all times. To surpass the aforementioned shortcomings, the digital platform incubated with the technology of online indexing and concept tagging gives rise to the information mining techniques. It helps the researchers to immediate search the particular concept they wish to study. If scholar wishes to pursue a deliberation for the concept of *āśrama* in MS. The single word input will provide a tabular list of outcomes related to *āśramas*. Therefore, the system provides immediate, appropriate and reliable intelligence information to the scholars and enable them to quantify the direction, enhance their assessment of the subject theme and provide objectives for the further research work.

5. Data, Data Collection and Research Methodology

In computational terminology, a database is an organized collection of data stored and accessed electronically. Small databases can be stored on a file system while large databases are hosted on computer clusters or popularly known as cloud storage. Digital Databases are a set of computerized collection used to record and store information digitally and accessible through the computer program for specific purposes. These are comprehensive, sometimes exhaustive, collection of computer files or computer records pertaining to a specific subject. Thus, 2703 verses in 12 chapters of MS were collected and digitized in text file in Devanagari script. MS of *Kauṇḍinnyāyana* (2014) and *Viśuddha Manusmṛti* of Prof. Surendra Kumar (1996) are selected as the primary texts of MS for data Collection. Shivraj Acharya *Kauṇḍinnyāyana* (2014), Pravin Pralayankar (2010) and Surendra Kumar (1996) has been considered for Hindi translations. Likewise, for English translation Buhler (2004) has been considered. The exegesis of all the "*ślokas*" has been done on the basis of *Medhātithi's Manubhāṣya* (Jha 2016) and *Kullukabhaṭṭa's Manavarthamuktāvali (Kauṇḍinnyāyana* 2014). Other eminent key texts in this field are http://sanskrit.jnu.ac.in/omacs/index.jsp MS authored by Rajvir Shastri (2000) and Pt. Rameshwar Bhatt (2015). MS With *Manavarthamuktāvali* composed by Rakesh Shastri (2005) and Conceptualizations in the *Manusmṛti* by Parnasabari Bhattacharya (1996). Data of original *śloka* and translations were preserved in separate text files in the UTF-8 *Devanagari* format. Later the data shall be kept in proper designated database.

[1] http://sanskrit.du.ac.in
[2] https://sanskrit.uohyd.ac.in/scl/
[3] https://cl.sanskrit.du.ac.in
[4]http://sanskrit.jnu.ac.in/student_projects/lexicon.jsp?lexicon=artha
[5] http://sanskrit.jnu.ac.in/amara/index.jsp
[6] http://sanskrit.jnu.ac.in/mb/index.jsp
[7] http://sanskrit.jnu.ac.in/vedanta/index.jsp
[8]http://sanskrit.jnu.ac.in/student_projects/lexicon.jsp?lexicon=mankha
[9] http://sanskrit.jnu.ac.in/sbg/index.jsp
[10] http://sanskrit.jnu.ac.in/ayurveda/index.jsp
[11]http://sanskrit.jnu.ac.in/student_projects/lexicon.jsp?lexicon=medini
[12] http://sanskrit.jnu.ac.in/vedanta/busearch.jsp
[13] http://sanskrit.jnu.ac.in/omacs/index.jsp
[14] http://sanskrit.jnu.ac.in/amara/index.jsp

The MS instant referencing system is an input-output generating system. It takes input from the user and generates the corresponding output. The researcher can give the input in either roman or Devanagari based upon his or her language convenience. The Quantitative methodology is used for data collection, analysiss and digitization. The objective of quantitative research methodology is to observe, collect and build databases. Information extraction methodology, web technology and web searching methods have been primarily used to data mining. Based on this tagging information those verses are mined where the direct searched word doesn't appear.
Once the input is provided, multiple exiguous programs work simultaneously to give the output such as; the pre-processor runs the initial query at back end syncing it with the digital information indexer. The script validator checks the input language, concept indexer matches the tags of the respective verses with the given input query, meaning generator furnishes the exegesis of the *ślokas*, then the following query is searched one by one from different databases and corresponding result is generated by the output generator. The generated result is formatted according to the users query input and then displayed on the clients end. Thus, this system is a cohesive mechanism working with the help of multifarious digital components. The major components are User Interface, Preprocessor, Information extractor, Information generator, Meaning generator, concept generator, script validator and output generator.

5.1 Digital Platform

The online indexing and concept mining system for MS is a web-based system. A user interface has also been developed for the purpose of searching for the user to interact and submit their query. The system facilitates two kinds of input options and furnishes analysed output in the corresponding format. The first input mechanism is 'Direct Search' where the user can enter any keyword in Devanagarī UTF-8 or in Roman IAST and receive all the references, translations and exegesis from the MS of the input word. The second input option is a 'Dropdown Menu' facility where one can just select the keyword from the list of pre-created concepts of MS and quickly obtain accurate information related to it. Clicking on an indexed word, the system displays the details with the *śloka* in which it occurs. The user interface accepts the input given by the user, pre-processes it and produces the corresponding output on the same page.

Accessibility and Information Mining for MS is a web based online system. A web-based system contains two major parts: Front-End and Back-End. Front-end is developed using HTML (Hyper Text Markup Language) along with CSS (Cascading Style Sheets) and JS (Java script). The back-end contains programming language, databases and servers. For this, the programming language Python is used, data is stored in Text files and Flask is used as server which is supported by Python.

6. Features of the System for MS

The web-based system is designed in such a manner that it has an interactive data search, which gives the system a very user-friendly and easy-to-navigate approach. The system can mine the information from MS in Multiscript (Devanagari and Roman). It also provides the options of keyword searching, concept or Phrase searching for the feasibility of the user through a dropdown menu. The system exhibits output in the searched scripts and translations in English and Hindi also be produced. It is web-based, hence widely accessible. The system produces information in two ways, one is instant indexing and the second is concept mining. In some cases, instant indexing does not produce complete information. It is unable to generate those *ślokas* where the searched word isn't visible directly in the verse. In this case, concept mining works.

Conceptual searching is a special feature of this system. Therefore, Information retrieval is quick and error-free. The feature of referencing index is very useful as it provides the researcher with accurate reference numbers of all the *ślokas* of MS. Downloading option of the results as a text file/ pdf is also available.

7. Result and Discussions

The system is developed by the Computational linguistics R&D, department of the Sanskrit University of Delhi. It is designed in such a way that it is able to produce output analogous to the user's query. As previously discussed, since, the system accepts input in the two major scripts namely; Devanagari and roman (IAST), the result is also generated in the corresponding script. The multitude of DS concepts, disparate *ślokas*, or words in MS can be easily searched using information mining, online indexing and tagging techniques. Thus, the system dispenses keyword, concept and phrasal searching using the online indexing modules. The result engendered by the system includes complete information regarding the searched query. It includes the *mūla* (original) *ślokas* along with its complete accurate reference. The referencing index exhibits the serial number of the chapter, followed by the verse number of that particular *śloka*. Each *śloka* is hyperlinked to determine the word meanings and complete exegesis. On projecting the cursor over the *śloka*, a bilingual explanation of that verse appears. By clicking on the particular *śloka*, the interpretation of that verse will be automatically obtained in Hindi and in English. Getting complete information of any concept with original *ślokas*, its bilingual translations and interpretation prove the utility of the developed system.

8. Conclusion and Future Directions of Research

Although this system is currently under development, the prototype of this system has been developed and is under the testing phase. This system will make a significant impact on Sanskrit studies and DS on the global platform in the field of science and technology. Digitization of MS and making its availability online can play a very important role to protect and access the knowledge tradition as described in DS texts. The extent of global access to these texts can be increased and the critically correct knowledge of the subject be made available to everyone. In the future, it is planned to digitize the other major texts of DS like *Nāradasmṛti Yājñavalkya Smṛti Arthaśāstra* etc. And all the concepts mentioned in these *smṛti* can be searched online using this system. The input-output methods of this system can also be made multilingual such as; Punjabi,

Sanskrit, Bangla, Telugu, Tamil, Kannada etc. It is further planned to tag scientific concepts namely; environment, military, third gender, management, medical sciences, commerce, economics etc. as propounded in MS. It will prove to be very useful for teachers, students and especially for researchers in the field of Sanskrit and e-learning, as at present, there are no efficient online tools developed to access Indian knowledge tradition.

9. Bibliographical References

Anju, and Subhash Chandra. 2017. "Puranic Search: An Instant Search System for Puranas." *Language in India.*

Anju, and Subhash Chandra. 2018. "sāṃkhya-yoga darśana paribhāṣā ḍeṭābesa evaṃ Onalāina khoja." *Research Review International Journal of Multidisciplinary* 3 (11): 890-894.

Banerji, Suresh Chandra (1999). A Brief History of Dharmaśāstra. Abhinav Publications.

Bhattacharya, P. (1996). Conceptualizations in the Manusmriti. Manohar Publishers.

Bhatt. R. (2015). Manusmriti. Chaukhamba Sanskrit Pratishthan.

Biswas, S., & Banerjee, D. (2016). The Dead Language Sanskrit is not actually dead. Journal Of Education and Development, 6(12), 90-97.

Bobade, Anita P. 2019. Significance of Indian Philosophy, Tradition, Culture and Indian Management Science (bhāratīyavyavasthāpanaśāstra)." International Journal of Hinduism & Philosophy 1 (1): 24-29.

Bogardus, E. S. (1924). Fundamentals of social psychology. Century Company.

Buhler, George. 2004. The Laws of Manu. New Delhi: Cosmo Publication.

Chamola S.D. (2007). Kautilya Arthshastra and the Science of Management: Relevance for the Contemporary Society. Hope India Publications.

Chander, R. (2015). Arthśastra: A Replica of Social Dynamism in Ancient India . *International Journal of Innovative Research and Advanced Studies, 2*(4), 78-83.

Chaubey, S. (2005). Vedoṃ meṃ dharma kī avadhāraṇā. *PhD thesis*. Faizabad, India: Dr Rāma Manohara Lohiyā Avadha Viśvavidyālaya.

Donald, J.D.R, (2017). The Dharma of Business: Commercial Law in Medieval In-dia. Random House Publishers India Pvt. Ltd.

Dubey, V. K. (2012). Vedang Shiksha Sahitya me Vyasshhhiksha ek Parisheelan. *Doctorate thesis.* Faizabad, Uttar Pradesh, India: Dr. Rammanohar Lohia Avadh University.

Feldman, R., & Dagan, I. (1995). Knowledge Discovery in Textual Databases (KDT). *KDD, 95*, 112-117.

Irani, K.D. & Silver, M. (1995). Social Justice in the Ancient World. Greenwood Press.

Jayapalan, N. (2001). *Indian Society and Social Institutions.* New Delhi, India: Atlantic Publishers and Distributors.

Jha, Ganganath. 2016. Manusmriti with the 'manubhāṣya of medhātithi'. New Delhi: Motilal Banarasidas.

Kauṇḍinnyāyana, Shivraj A. 2014. manusmṛti. Varanasi: Chaukhamba Vidyabhavan.

Khandoliyan, Baldev Ram, Rajneesh Kumar Pandey, Archana Tiwari, and Girish Nath Jha. "Text encoding and search for Āyurvedic texts: An interconnected lexical database." *Adaptation of Language Resources and Tools for Processing Cultural Heritage Objects*: 2.

Kumar, Surendra. 1996. viśuddha-manusmṛti. New Delhi: Aarsh Sahitya Prachar Trust.

Mani, Diwakar. 2010. "RDBMS Based Lexical Resource for Indian Heritage: The Case of Mahābhārata." In International Sanskrit Computational Linguistics Symposium, pp. 137-149. Springer, Berlin, Heidelberg.

Nath, R. (2019). Good Governance and Ancient Indian Administration. Bihar Journal of Public Administration, 276.

Phillips, Stephen H. 2014. Epistemology in classical India: The knowledge sources of the Nyaya school. UK: Routledge.

Pralayankar, Pravin. 2010. manusmṛti. New Delhi)'New Bharatiya Book Corporation.

Sankhder, M. M. (2003). Democratic Politics and Governance in India. Deep and Deep Publications.

Saputra, K. A. K., & Anggiriawan, P. B. (2021). Accounting, Auditing and Corruption in Kautilya's Arthasastra Perspective and Psychogenetic Hindu: A Theoritical Review. South East Asia Journal of Contemporary Business, Economics and Law, 24(2), 67-72.

Śāstrī, R. (2000). Manusmṛti: Hindībhāṣya, prakṣiptaślokānusandhānanirdeśa evaṃ "anuśīlana" nāmaka samīkṣāsahita, śāstrīyapramāṇoṃ se alaṅkṛ ta tathā Manusmṛ tisambandhī ālocanātmaka adhyayana se yukta. Ārṣa Sāhitya Pracāra Ṭrasṭa.

Shastri, R. (2005). Manusmriti With Manvartha Muktavali. Vidya Nidhi Prakashan.

Tiwari, S. C., & Pandey, N. M. (2013). The Indian concepts of lifestyle and mental health in old age. Indian Journal of Psychiatry, 55(Suppl 2), S288.

Proceedings of the WILDRE-6 Workshop @LREC2020, pages 48–54
Marseille, 20 June 2022

Language Resource Building and English-to-Mizo Neural Machine Translation Encountering Tonal Words

Vanlalmuansangi Khenglawt[1], Sahinur Rahman Laskar[2], Santanu Pal[3], Partha Pakray[2], Ajoy Kumar Khan[1]
Department of Computer Engineering, Mizoram University, Mizoram, (India)[1]
Department of Computer Science and Engineering, National Institute of Technology, Silchar (India)[2]
Wipro Limited, Bengaluru (India)[3]
mzut208@mzu.edu.in, sahinurlaskar.nits@gmail.com, santanu.pal2@wipro.com,
partha@cse.nits.ac.in, ajoyiitg@gmail.com

Abstract

Multilingual country like India has an enormous linguistic diversity and has an increasing demand towards developing language resources such that it will outreach in various natural language processing applications like machine translation. Low-resource language translation possesses challenges in the field of machine translation. The challenges include the availability of corpus and differences in linguistic information. This paper investigates a low-resource language pair, English-to-Mizo exploring neural machine translation by contributing an Indian language resource, i.e., English-Mizo corpus. In this work, we explore one of the main challenges to tackling tonal words existing in the Mizo language, as they add to the complexity on top of low-resource challenges for any natural language processing task. Our approach improves translation accuracy by encountering tonal words of Mizo and achieved a state-of-the-art result in English-to-Mizo translation.

Keywords: English-Mizo, Tonal, NMT

1. Introduction

Neural machine translation (NMT) has attained a promising approach in machine translation (MT) because of its context analysis ability and deal with long-range dependency problems (Bahdanau et al., 2015; Vaswani et al., 2017). However, it needs a sufficient amount of training data, which is a challenging task for the low-resource language pair translation (Koehn and Knowles, 2017). In this work, NMT is used to deal with a low-resource language pair: English—Mizo. To the best of our knowledge, there is a lack of publicly available English–Mizo corpus suitable for MT work. Therefore, very few contributions are applicable, specifically for the English–Mizo NMT task. Mizo is popularly known as a tonal language, which means a word with various tones can express different meanings (further details available in Section 2). The distinct tone markers are used in Mizo to represent the tonal word contextually. Based on our primary investigation, the translation of English–Mizo MT suffers in handling these tonal words and their corresponding context. Table 1 shows an example where the baseline predicted sentence could not capture accurate tone markers (marked as 'bold'). Without tone markers, the meaning of the predicted sentence is ambiguous, corresponding to the source sentence. It can mean either "What is the price?" or "What did he catch?", but with a specific tonal marker, it is defined as the exact meaning of the sentence i.e "What did he catch?". As a result, the contextual meaning is not clear. To tackle this problem, we propose an approach for encountering context-specific tonal words to improve the predicted sentence during the post-processing step (see Section 5).

Source / Target	Predicted
What did he catch? (Source)	Eng nge a man? (baseline)
Èng nge a m**á**n? (Target)	**È**ng nge a m**á**n? (Current Objective)

Table 1: Example of predicted sentence (tone markers are marked as bold)

The major contributions are:

- Created an Indian language resource, namely, English–Mizo corpus that covers both parallel and monolingual data of Mizo. It will be publicly available here:`https://github.com/cnlp-nits/English-Mizo-Corpus`.
- Explored different NMT models and achieved a state-of-the-art result in English–Mizo translation.
- Proposed an approach of encountering context-specific tonal words for English-to-Mizo translation. To the best of our knowledge, we are the first to tackle this problem in English–Mizo translation.

2. Mizo Tonal Language

Along with English, Mizo[1] is the official language of the Indian state of Mizoram, and it is also known

[1] `https://en.wikipedia.org/wiki/Mizo_language`

Types of tone	Tone Marker (e)
High tone	é
Low tone	è
Rising tone	ĕ
Falling tone	ê

Table 2: Variation of tones with a tone marker

as Lushai which belongs to the Tibeto-Burman family of languages. According to Census-2011, there are 6,50,605[2] Mizo speakers, and they are known as Mizo/Lushai people. Although the writing system of the Mizo language is based on the Roman script like English, both languages are very different from each other. Generally, the word order of Mizo is Object–Subject–Verb (OSV), but in particular situations, it follows Subject–Verb–Object (SVO) like English. Apart from this, Mizo (Majumder et al., 2018; Pakray et al., 2015; Bentham et al., 2016) is quite different from English in linguistic aspects. Mizo language can be termed as a tonal language as the tone determines the lexical meaning of words. A total of eight tones are available in Mizo, wherein four tones are long tones and the remaining four are short tones. The use of diacritics is not standardized in Mizo tonal words. However, the tone markers or intonations are highlighted in the vowels (a, aw, e, i, o, u) with diacritics by some publisher[3] (Pakray et al., 2015). The main variation of tones in Mizo are high, low, rising and falling (Chhangte, 1993; Dutta et al., 2017; Gogoi et al., 2020). To indicate a distinct tone variation, a unique tone marker is employed, as shown in Table 2. As the tonal word alone can imply a different meaning, without the use of a tone marker, the tonal variation of a word will be determined by the context of the sentence. Therefore, an indication of proper tone marker is immensely imperative to determine the lexical denotation of the word. For example, as shown in Table 3, based on the tone, the Mizo word *'kang'* can have different connotations in English. *'Kang'* can be translated as *'fry'*, *'dried up'*, *'above the ground'* and *'burn'* with a tone of 'high', 'low', 'rising' and 'falling' respectively. The Mizo language can be categorized under the language group, which has words with diacritics (Náplava et al., 2018). Since the tonal words are represented by the tone markers (Pakray et al., 2015). However, it is observed that Mizo words with tone markers are less frequent than those without tone markers[4], unlike Vietnamese (Náplava et al., 2018), Yorùbá (Adelani et al., 2021) and Arabic language (Fadel et al., 2019).

3. Related Work

There is limited work in the area of MT on the English–Mizo language pair (Pathak et al., 2018; Lalrempuii and Soni, 2020; Lalrempuii et al., 2021). It

[2]https://bit.ly/3xA8AKj
[3]https://vanglaini.org/
[4]https://vanglaini.org/

Tone	Sentences
High	*'Kắng' - 'fry/fried'* *Mizo: Vawksa ka **kắng** a.* *English: **I fried** a pork.*
Low	*'Kàng'- 'dried up'* *Mizo: Ruahtui a tlem avangin lui tui pawh a **kàng** ral zo tawh.* *English: Due to less rainfall, the river **dried** up.*
Rising	*'Kăng' - 'above the ground'* *Mizo: I zuang **kăng** sang thei khawp mai.* *English: You can jump **above the ground** quite high.*
Falling	*'Kâng' - 'burn'* *Mizo: Tui sa in a inti **kâng**.* *English: **I burnt** myself with hot water.*

Table 3: Example sentences of different tones

is mainly due to the lack of availability of resources, as the Mizo language is a low resource language. In (Pathak et al., 2018), a parallel corpus of English-Mizo language pairs is prepared (29,973 train data) and performed a comparison between RNN based NMT and Phrase-based MT. Also, (Lalrempuii et al., 2021; Lalrempuii and Soni, 2020) investigated English-Mizo pair using several attention-based NMT models, including RNN, BRNN and transformer. Although researchers have explored the English-Mizo pair for the MT system, there are research gaps that are identified as follows:

- There is no standard English–Mizo corpus available publicly.
- None of them have tackled the linguistic challenges like tonal words of Mizo for English-to-Mizo translation.
- Although automatic translations like Google and Microsoft cover various languages worldwide, but lack the support of the Mizo language.

In this work, we have created an English–Mizo corpus and investigated with BERT-fused NMT (Zhu et al., 2020) using a bidirectional translation approach with synthetic parallel corpus (Niu et al., 2018; Sennrich et al., 2016). Also, we proposed a post-processing step for English-to-Mizo translation by focusing on tonal words.

4. Corpus Preparation

There is no standard or publicly available corpus for English–Mizo (En-Mz) corpus. Thus, we have prepared parallel data and Mizo monolingual data from different possible online resources. Online resources

Type	Sentences	Tokens	
		En	Mz
Train	118,035	1,314,131	1,468,044
Validation	2,000	52,320	55,316
Test	1,200	10,168	11,943

Table 4: Statistics for train, valid and test set

include, Bible[5], online dictionary (Glosbe)[6] and Government websites[7] [8]. We have prepared 121,235 numbers of parallel sentences that include 44,168 Mizo sentences having tonal words. The parallel corpus contains 118,895 sentences from online sources (98.06%) and manually[9] prepared 2,340 sentences (1.93%). The difference between online parallel sentences and manually prepared sentences is that online parallel sentences include both with and without tonal sentences, whereas manually prepared sentences only include tonal words to enhance the number of parallel sentences with tonal words. The manually prepared parallel sentences cover the general domain sentences, as shown in Table 10. Moreover, monolingual Mizo data of 2,061,068 sentences are prepared from various webpages, blogs and textbooks. To collect data from online sources, we have used web crawling[10] techniques. To allow for replication over different/several web pages, each element's `xpath` is formatted/encoded with a degree of generalization. It aided in crawling and retrieving information from a vast number of web pages. Before splitting a parallel corpus, we remove duplicates and noise (web-link (URLs), too many special characters, blank lines). Also, we verified by hiring a linguistic expert who possesses linguistic knowledge of both languages. The data statistics of the train, valid and test set, are shown in Table 4. During the split, we have considered parallel sentences having tonal words for validation and test data. The test and validation set include 98% and 2% sentences from online and manually prepared sentences and also, the train set includes 1.92% of and 98.07% sentences from manually prepared and online sources. The corpus covers domains: Bible, Government notices/messages, dictionaries, and general domains. The percentage of tonal words presents in the train, validation, and test set are 11.20%, 10.50%, and 10.30%.

5. Approach

Our approach consists of three phases, as shown in Figure 1. Initially, for the first phase, we extracted Mz tonal sentences from the monolingual data of Mz. Then, the extracted Mz tonal sentences are used to generate En synthetic sentences by utilizing the backward NMT model (Mz-to-En). In this case, we used the conventional transformer model (Vaswani et al., 2017). We removed blank lines, under-translated sentences (single or double words) from En synthetic sentences, and the corresponding Mz tonal sentences. Thus, we prepared 33,021 synthetic parallel sentences, as given in Table 5. In the second phase, the synthetic parallel corpus is augmented with the original parallel corpus. Then we followed the technique of (Niu et al., 2018) by augmenting the swapped sentences (Mz-to-En). We added artificial tokens at the beginning of the source sentences to recognize the target sentences (such as <2mz> for Mizo and <2en> for English target sentences) and trained with BERT-fused NMT (Zhu et al., 2020) for the forward (En-to-Mz) translation. BERT-fused NMT is utilized for leveraging the pre-trained model of English. We investigated different configurations, namely, unidirectional and bidirectional parallel corpus (trained on En-to-Mz and Mz-to-En simultaneously). BERT processes an input sequence by first transforming it into representations. Through the BERT-encoder attention module, each NMT encoder layer processes each of the representations from the BERT module. Besides, each NMT encoder layer's self-attention continues to process the previous NMT encoder layer's representations. Finally, it generates fused representations through the encoder layers feed-forward network by merging both the output of BERT-encoder attention and the self-attention. The decoder works similarly; the BERT-decoder attention is introduced to each NMT decoder layer. The obtained trained model is used to predict the target sentences. Lastly, to improve the translation accuracy of encountering tonal words, we propose an example-based post-processing step.

Example-based post-processing: For the post-processing step, we created an example-based dictionary by following these steps.

- We extracted keywords having tonal words from monolingual data of Mizo using a language-independent keyword extraction tool known as YAKE (Campos et al., 2020), considering maximum n-gram size$=3$.
- We discarded the uni-gram words from the extracted keywords. Since, the uni-gram words are not able to represent the context-specific tonal words.
- We created an example-based dictionary ($K_z||K_y$). Here, K_y denotes extracted keywords and K_z is prepared by removing the tonal markers from K_y.

The example-based dictionary is utilized for the post-processing of the predicted sentences. We searched each keyword of K_z in the predicted sentences and if it is found then replace it with the keyword of K_y. The reason behind using the post-processing step is that if

[5] https://www.bible.com/
[6] https://glosbe.com/en/lus
[7] https://finance.mizoram.gov.in/
[8] https://dipr.mizoram.gov.in/
[9] consumes manual effort and then verified by the hired linguistic expert
[10] https://scrapy.org/

Sentences	Tokens	
	En	Mz
33,021	5,49,822	6,08,586

Table 5: Synthetic parallel data statistics

the trained model is unable to capture the appropriate tone marker in the translation process, then the post-processing step attempts to correct the concerned tone marker using an example-based dictionary. We used an example-based dictionary because the tonal word is contextually dependent on the pre-or post-word of the concerned tonal word. In summary, the proposed approach is based on the BERT-fused NMT (transformer model), bidirectional data augmentation with synthetic parallel corpus, and an example-based post-processing step.

6. Experiment and Result and Analysis

We performed preliminary experiments for both En-to-Mz and Mz-to-En translations using RNN (Bahdanau et al., 2015), transformer model (Vaswani et al., 2017) with sub-word segmentation technique i.e., byte pair encoding (BPE) (considered 32k merge operations). The results of the preliminary experiment are reported in Table 6. The quantitative results are evaluated in terms of automatic evaluation metric, bilingual evaluation understudy (BLEU)[11] (Papineni et al., 2002) and also with human evaluation (HE) (Pathak et al., 2018) on randomly selected 100 sample sentences by hiring a linguistic expert. We followed default configurations of OpenNMT-py[12] toolkit to implement RNN and transformer model. The Adam optimizer with a learning rate of 0.001, drop-outs of 0.3 (in case of RNN) and 0.1 (in case of transformer) are used in the training process. Also, followed default configurations of Fairseq[13] toolkit to implement BERT-fused NMT (Zhu et al., 2020). For En-to-Mz translation, the comparative results are reported in Table 7 and 8, where our approach (M8) attains a higher score. To examine the effectiveness of our approach in terms of encountering tonal words, a comparative analysis is presented in Figure 2. Although our approach encounters a higher frequency of tonal words than conventional transformer (Vaswani et al., 2017) and BERT-fused transformer (Zhu et al., 2020) models, far away from the frequency of tonal words in reference test sentences. Further, to inspect qualitative analysis of encountering tonal words, a few examples are presented in Table 9. It is observed that the conventional transformer (M1) and BERT-fused transformer (M2) models are unable to encounter tone markers in the tonal words of the predicted sentences. However, with the post-processing approach M3,M5 and M8 generate tonal words with appropriate

[11] Utilized multi-bleu.perl script

[12] https://github.com/OpenNMT/OpenNMT-py

[13] https://github.com/bert-nmt/bert-nmt

Translation	Model	BLEU
En-to-Mz	RNN	16.98
	Transformer	17.86
Mz-to-En	RNN	15.46
	Transformer	16.52

Table 6: BLEU scores of preliminary experiments

Model	BLEU
M1 (UPC)	17.86
M2 (UPC)	18.39
M2 + PP (M3)	21.90
M2 + SPC (M4)	20.55
M4 + PP (M5)	23.82
M2 (BPC) (M6)	22.80
M6 + SPC (M7)	24.33
M7 + PP (M8)	**28.59**

Table 7: Comparative results (BLEU scores) of different models for En-to-Mz translation, M1: Transformer, M2: BERT-fused Transformer, SPC: Synthetic Parallel Corpus, PP: Post-processing, UPC: Unidirectional Parallel Corpus, BPC: Bidirectional Parallel Corpus

tonal markers, which are marked as 'bold.' By capturing tone markers in tonal words, our approach significantly represents the contextual meaning of the sentences as compared to other models.

Model	Adequacy	Fluency	Overall Rating
M1	2.58	2.76	2.67
M2	3.40	3.92	3.66
M3	3.76	4.54	4.15
M4	3.26	4.47	3.86
M5	3.92	4.68	4.30
M6	3.65	4.52	4.08
M7	3.32	4.64	3.98
M8	4.14	5.24	4.69

Table 8: Human evaluation scores of different models for En-to-Mz translation

7. Conclusion and Future Work

In this work, our goal is to prepare an Indian language resource, i.e., English–Mizo corpus and investigate En-to-Mz translation by encountering tonal words by exploring different NMT models on the developed dataset. We will release the English-Mizo corpus, to be publicly available. Our approach is based on BERT-fused NMT with bidirectional data augmentation with synthetic parallel corpus and an example-based post-processing step. We attained better translation accuracy than a conventional transformer and BERT-fused NMT. In the future, we will increase the dataset size, domain-wise translation, and do more experiments to improve the translational accuracy of encountering tonal words.

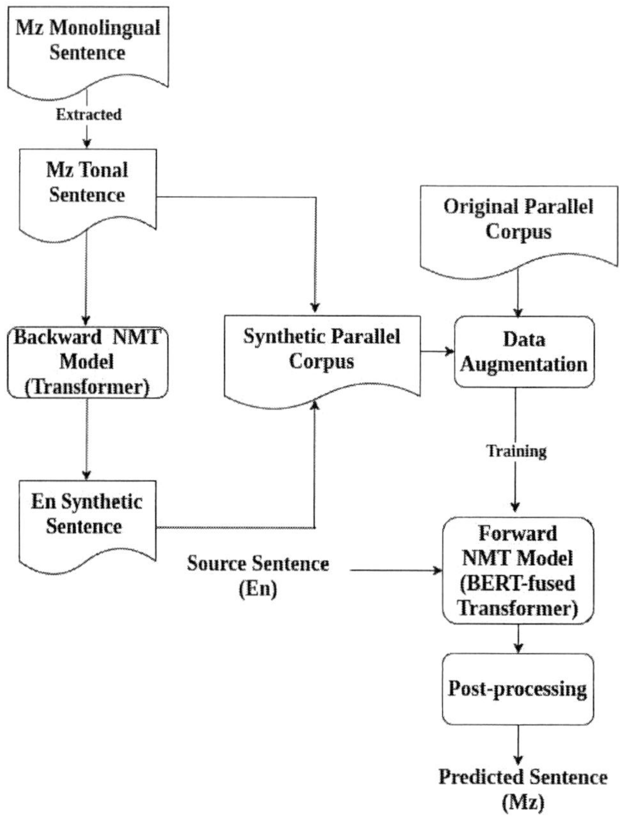

Figure 1: English-to-Mizo NMT System

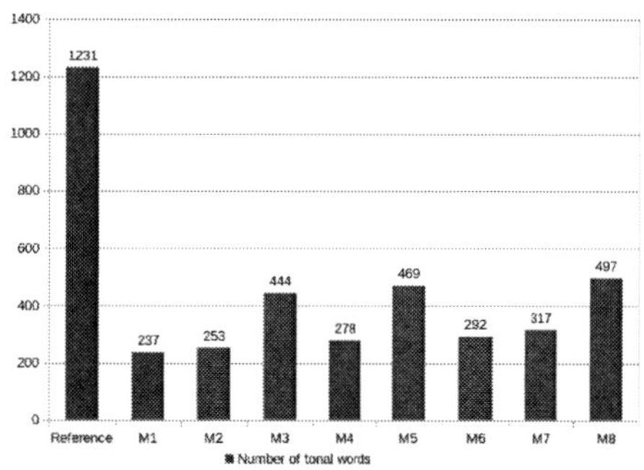

Figure 2: Comparative analysis on tonal frequency of words. Reference: Mizo target sentences (test data)

Source / Target	Predicted
It is nice. (En) A thà lutùk. (Mz)	A tha lutuk. (M1) A tha lutuk. (M2) **A thà lutùk.** (M3) A thà khawp mai . (M4) **A thà khawp mài .**(M5) A tha lutuk. (M6) A tha lutuk. (M7) **A thà lutùk .**(M8)
Don't tell lie. (En) Dáwt sáwi suh. (Mz)	Dawt sawi suh. (M1) Dawt sawi duh suh . (M2) **Dáwt sáwi duh suh .** (M3) Dawt sawi suh . (M4) **Dáwt sáwi suh .** (M5) Dáwt sawi suh . (M6) Dáwt sawi suh .(M7) **Dáwt sáwi suh .** (M8)

Table 9: Output examples of different models for En-to-Mz translation

Acknowledgement We want to thank the Center for Natural Language Processing (CNLP), the Artificial Intelligence (AI) Lab, and the Department of Computer Science and Engineering at the National Institute of Technology, Silchar, India, for providing the requisite support and infrastructure to execute this work.

8. Bibliographical References

Adelani, D. I., Ruiter, D., Alabi, J. O., Adebonojo, D., Ayeni, A., Adeyemi, M., Awokoya, A., and España-Bonet, C. (2021). The effect of domain and diacrit-

Table 10: Example of parallel sentences

English	Mizo	Source
Every grain offering of a priest shall be wholly burned.	Puithiam chhangphut thilhlan apiang chu **hâl** ral vek **tûr** a ni.	Glosbe
What burdens can advanced age impose on a person?	Kum upatnain mi chungah eng phurrit nge a thlen theih?	Glosbe
Joseph was already in Egypt.	Josefa chu Egypt ramah chuan lo awm tawh a.	Bible
Each with his household go to Jacob.	Mi tin mahni **chhûngte** ṭheuh **nên** Jakoba hnênah chuan an kal a.	Bible
Farmers are the backbone of our economy and our state.	Anni hi kan economy innghahna an ni a.	Government Website
This is a day for all of us to celebrate and honour our nation and our sovereignty.	He ni hi sawrkar ropui, mipui rorelna sawrkar kan neih theihna ni a ni a.	Government Website
I will be with you no more.	In hnênah hian ka **áwm dâwn** tawh lo a ni.	Manually
Now therefore you are cursed.	**Chuvângin**, **ânchhedawng** in lo nih **tâk** hi.	Manually

ics in yoruba-english neural machine translation. In *Proceedings of the 18th Biennial Machine Translation Summit - Volume 1: Research Track, MTSummit 2021 Virtual, August 16-20, 2021*, pages 61–75. Association for Machine Translation in the Americas.

Bahdanau, D., Cho, K., and Bengio, Y. (2015). Neural machine translation by jointly learning to align and translate. In Yoshua Bengio et al., editors, *3rd International Conference on Learning Representations, ICLR 2015, May 7-9, 2015, Conference Track Proceedings*, pages 1–15, San Diego, CA, USA. arXiv.

Bentham, J., Pakray, P., Majumder, G., Lalbiaknia, S., and Gelbukh, A. (2016). Identification of rules for recognition of named entity classes in mizo language. In *2016 Fifteenth Mexican International Conference on Artificial Intelligence (MICAI)*, pages 8–13. IEEE.

Campos, R., Mangaravite, V., Pasquali, A., Jorge, A., Nunes, C., and Jatowt, A. (2020). Yake! keyword extraction from single documents using multiple local features. *Inf. Sci.*, 509:257–289.

Chhangte, L. (1993). *Mizo syntax*. Ph.D. thesis, University of Oregon.

Dutta, I., S., I., Gogoi, P., and Sarmah, P. (2017). Nature of Contrast and Coarticulation: Evidence from Mizo Tones and Assamese Vowel Harmony. In *Proc. Interspeech 2017*, pages 224–228.

Fadel, A., Tuffaha, I., Al-Jawarneh, B., and Al-Ayyoub, M. (2019). Neural arabic text diacritization: State of the art results and a novel approach for machine translation. In *Proceedings of the 6th Workshop on Asian Translation, WAT@EMNLP-IJCNLP 2019, Hong Kong, China, November 4, 2019*, pages 215–225. Association for Computational Linguistics.

Gogoi, P., Dey, A., Lalhminghlui, W., Sarmah, P., and Prasanna, S. R. M. (2020). Lexical tone recognition in mizo using acoustic-prosodic features. In *Proceedings of the 12th Language Resources and Evaluation Conference*, pages 6458–6461, Marseille, France, May. European Language Resources Association.

Koehn, P. and Knowles, R. (2017). Six challenges for neural machine translation. In *Proceedings of the First Workshop on Neural Machine Translation*, pages 28–39, Vancouver, August. Association for Computational Linguistics.

Lalrempuii, C. and Soni, B. (2020). Attention-based english to mizo neural machine translation. In *Machine Learning, Image Processing, Network Security and Data Sciences*, pages 193–203, Singapore. Springer Singapore.

Lalrempuii, C., Soni, B., and Pakray, P. (2021). An improved english-to-mizo neural machine translation. *ACM Trans. Asian Low-Resour. Lang. Inf. Process.*, 20(4), May.

Majumder, G., Pakray, P., Khiangte, Z., and Gelbukh, A. (2018). Multiword expressions (mwe) for mizo language: Literature survey. In Alexander Gelbukh, editor, *Computational Linguistics and Intelligent Text Processing*, pages 623–635, Cham. Springer International Publishing.

Náplava, J., Straka, M., Straňák, P., and Hajič, J. (2018). Diacritics restoration using neural networks. In *Proceedings of the Eleventh International Conference on Language Resources and Evaluation (LREC 2018)*, Miyazaki, Japan, May. European Language Resources Association (ELRA).

Niu, X., Denkowski, M. J., and Carpuat, M. (2018). Bi-directional neural machine translation with synthetic parallel data. In Alexandra Birch, et al., editors, *Proceedings of the 2nd Workshop on Neural Machine Translation and Generation, NMT@ACL 2018, Melbourne, Australia, July 20, 2018*, pages 84–91. Association for Computational Linguistics.

Pakray, P., Pal, A., Majumder, G., and Gelbukh, A. (2015). Resource building and parts-of-speech (pos) tagging for the mizo language. In *2015 Fourteenth Mexican International Conference on Artificial Intelligence (MICAI)*, pages 3–7.

Papineni, K., Roukos, S., Ward, T., and Zhu, W.-J. (2002). Bleu: A method for automatic evaluation of machine translation. In *Proceedings of the 40th Annual Meeting on Association for Computational Linguistics*, ACL '02, pages 311–318, Stroudsburg, PA,

USA. Association for Computational Linguistics.

Pathak, A., Pakray, P., and Bentham, J. (2018). English–mizo machine translation using neural and statistical approaches. *Neural Computing and Applications*, 30:1–17, Jun.

Sennrich, R., Haddow, B., and Birch, A. (2016). Improving neural machine translation models with monolingual data. In *Proceedings of the 54th Annual Meeting of the Association for Computational Linguistics (Volume 1: Long Papers)*, pages 86–96, Berlin, Germany, August. Association for Computational Linguistics.

Vaswani, A., Shazeer, N., Parmar, N., Uszkoreit, J., Jones, L., Gomez, A. N., Kaiser, L., and Polosukhin, I. (2017). Attention is all you need. *CoRR*, abs/1706.03762.

Zhu, J., Xia, Y., Wu, L., He, D., Qin, T., Zhou, W., Li, H., and Liu, T. (2020). Incorporating BERT into neural machine translation. In *8th International Conference on Learning Representations, ICLR 2020, Addis Ababa, Ethiopia, April 26-30, 2020*. OpenReview.net.

Proceedings of the WILDRE-6 Workshop @LREC2020, pages 55–59
Marseille, 20 June 2022

Classification of Multiword Expressions in Malayalam

Treesa Anjaly Cyriac, Sobha Lalitha Devi
AU-KBC Research Centre, MIT Campus of Anna University, Chennai, India
treesaanjaly07@gmail.com, sobha@au-kbc.org

Abstract

Multiword expression is an interesting concept in languages and the MWEs of a language are not easy for a non-native speaker to understand. It includes lexicalized phrases, idioms, collocations etc. Data on multiwords are helpful in language processing. 'Multiword expressions in Malayalam' is a less studied area. The boundary between multiword expressions and other compositions is fuzzy. Not all the multiword expressions adhere to all the properties of MWEs. In this paper, we are trying to explore multiwords in Malayalam and to classify them as per the three idiosyncrasies: semantic idiosyncrasy, syntactic idiosyncrasy, and statistic idiosyncrasy. Though these are already identified, they are not being studied in Malayalam. The classification and features are given and are studied using Malayalam multiwords. Through this study, we identified how the linguistic features of Malayalam such as agglutination influence its multiword expressions in terms of pronunciation and spelling. Malayalam has a set of code-mixed multiword expressions which is also addressed in this study.

Keywords: Multiword expressions, NLP applications, idioms, Malayalam, Dravidian language, linguistic idiosyncrasy, MWE, Machine Translation, lexicalized expressions

1. Introduction

According to Sag et al. (2002), multiword expressions are "idiosyncratic interpretations that cross word boundaries". They show semantic, statistic, and syntactic idiosyncrasy. Multiword expressions are word sequences that act as a single lexical unit. The meaning of the individual components does not contribute to the collective meaning of the expression. It is difficult for humans to understand the underlying meaning of such expressions. It is even more difficult for a machine to resolve these expressions. To tackle this problem we need more linguistic analysis of multiwords. Machine translation has been helpful for language learners, non-native speakers, and even translators. Solving linguistic barriers could be the beginning of productive collaborations and innovations. But using machine translation systems to solve the problem of MWEs is not fruitful often because they lack good input regarding multiwords. Available information about Malayalam MWEs is insufficient to come up with an effective translation system that addresses this linguistic concept which Sag. et al. called 'a pain in the neck of NLP'. Through this research, we are trying to study the properties and types of Malayalam MWEs which would help in improving machine translation systems.

Multiword disambiguation is very important for language processing. Most of the time, the translation system gives a literal translation of the individual words. For example, consider the Malayalam word (kathakaḻikkuka | lit. 'To end the story.') 'To kill/ to end/ to defeat.' If the input is 'kathakaḻikkuka' Google translate translates it as 'eat the story'. If the input is given without a space in between i.e. 'katha kaḻikkuka system translates it as 'tell the story'.

The paper is divided into seven main sections: The first section is the Introduction. The second section deals with relevant previous works which is followed by the Classification of MWEs. In the fourth section we discuss about the Types of Multiword Expressions and the Properties of MWEs in the fifth section. Findings are mentioned in the sixth section and the Conclusion in the seventh section. The examples used to substantiate the classification, types and properties are randomly taken from the language.

2. Related Work

We explored many previous studies and in this section we are trying to explain how their findings helped the present work.

Ivan Sag et al. (2002) classify MWEs into lexicalized phrases and institutionalized phrases and it gives further classification for lexicalized phrases. The paper also provided some analytic techniques for MWEs. They used the constraint based Head-driven Phrase Structure Grammar formalism. Rules and disambiguation strategies in the English- Malayalam Machine Aided Translation system (AnglaMalayalam) has been discussed in Vasudevan et al. (2016). According to the authors, the English- Malayalam Machine Aided Translation system based on AnglaBharati Technology which is discussed in this paper showed good results after introducing these rules.

Lahari Poddar (2016) presents some of the features and classifications of multiword expressions and different approaches towards their automatic extraction. The paper also presents numerous examples from Indian languages. Tanmoy Chakraborty (2011) presents a vast study on multiwords with main focus on Bengali MWEs. This paper also presents different types and properties of MWEs. The paper gives classification of MWEs in Bengali. The study modeled the syntax and semantics of Bengali MWEs based on the statistical approaches of substitutability, co-occurrence properties, semantic clustering and linguistic properties. Timothy Baldwin and Su Nam Kim (2010) shed light to the research issues relating to MWEs.

3. Classification of MWEs

Sag et al. (2002) classifies MWEs into lexicalized phrases and institutionalized phrases. Many other classifications come under these broad terms.

3.1 Lexicalized Phrases

Lexicalized phrases "have at least in part idiosyncratic syntax or pragmatics" (Sag et al., 2002). Lexicalized phrases are again classified as fixed, semi-fixed and syntactically flexible expressions.

3.1.1 Fixed Expressions

Fixed expressions are frozen expressions that do not undergo any morphosyntactic variations or internal modifications. They can be considered as words-with-spaces. Generally, they are transparent in meaning.

3.1.2 Semi-Fixed Expressions

In the case of semi-fixed expressions, word order and composition are strictly invariable. However, some lexical variations are possible. Semi-fixed expressions can be further classified into three subcategories:
Non-decomposable idioms: We cannot analyze or understand non-decomposable idioms from the words they are composed of. They are semantically opaque and do not undergo syntactic variability. But they can take inflections and reflexive form variations. Examples: (kuḷam thoṇṭuka| lit. 'To dig the pond.') 'To destroy.'
Compound Nominals: Compound nominals do not undergo syntactic variations. But they do inflect for number. Compound nominals such as (erivumpuḷiyum | lit. 'spicinessand sourness') 'Taste' are very frequent.
Proper Names/Named entities: Proper names aresyntactically highly idiosyncraticin nature.

1) mahatmagāndhi saṟvakalāśāla
Mahatma Gandhi University
2) trśūṟ pūram
Thrissur Pooram
A temple festival held in the district of Thrissur.

3.1.3 Syntactically Flexible Expressions

Unlike semi-fixed expressions or fixed expressions, syntactically flexible expressions allow a range of syntactic variations. Syntactically flexible expressions include:
Verb-Particle Constructions: These are the expressions that consist of a verb and one or more particles and they can be compositional or semantically idiosyncratic.

3) kaḷaññu kuḷikkuka
wasted bathe
lit. 'To waste and bath.'| 'To fritter.'
4) peṭṭpōvuka
happen to go
lit. 'Get into.' | 'To get trapped.'

Decomposable Idioms: Decomposable idioms are syntactically flexible to some extent. It is very difficult to predict the syntactic variations they undergo. (mūkkumkuttivīḻuka |lit. 'To fall upside-down.') 'Plummet.' is a decomposable idiom.
Light Verbs: Light-verb constructions are highly idiosyncratic. They undergo full syntactic variability. Expressions like (tīrumānam eṭukkuka | 'Take a decision.') are light verb constructions.

3.2 Institutionalized Phrases

Institutionalized phrases are syntactically and semantically compositional, but statistically idiosyncratic. They occur with high frequency and undergo full syntactic variability. Phrases such as (erivum puḻiyum| lit. 'spiciness and sourness') and (tekk vaṭakk naṭakkuka | lit.'walk south to north.') 'Walk/ live aimlessly.' are institutionalized phrases.

4. Types of Multiword Expressions

Multi-word expressions can be grouped into the following types: Reduplication, partial reduplication, semantic relationship, code-mixed multiwords, collocations and compound verbs.

4.1 Reduplication

Reduplication is a word-formation process by which the root or stem of a word, or a part of it, is repeated to produce meaning. Exampls : ḍumḍum (knoking sound), ōṭiyōṭi (ran continuously), jillampaṭapaṭa (the sound of a musical instrument, chenda), payyepayye (slowly) etc.

4.2 Partial Reduplication

In partial reduplication, the given word is partially replicated. Examples: vīṭvīṭāntaram (house to house), talaṅṅumvilaṅṅum (hither and thither) etc.

4.3 Semantic Relationship

There are expressions with some kind of semantic relationship existing between the constituent words.
Synonym: (sambalsamrddhi | lit. 'riches and abundance') 'prosperity', (āyuṟārōgyam | 'life and health') 'welfare' etc.
Antonym: (jīvan maraṇa) 'life or death situation', (dinarātṟaṅṅaḷ) 'days and nights', (sukhadukham) 'happiness and sadness' etc.
Sister Words: (veḷivum veḷḷiyāḻccayum | 'Sense and Friday')sanity', (bellum bṟeykkum | 'bell and breake') 'control', (kaṇṇum mūkkum | 'eye and nose') 'sense' etc.

4.4 Code-mixed Multiwords

Code mixed multiwords are very common in Malayalam. They are not just large in number, they occur very frequently too. Examples:

5) āyuṟārōgyam
lifehealth
lit. 'Life and health' | 'Welfare'
6) fyūspōyi
fuseleft
lit. 'The fuse tripped.' | 'Lost one's mind.'
7) ṭyūb-laiṟṟāyirikkuka
tube-light be
lit. 'To be a tube-light.'| 'To be obtuse.'
8) kḻikkākuka
click to get
lit.'Happen to click.' | 'To understand/ get liked by others/ to become successful.

In example (5), the word (āyuṟ | lit. 'life') is taken from Sanskrit. The first parts of (6), (7), and (8)are English words. Code-mixed multiwords are very often used among Malayalam speakers. Some of them can have multiple meanings. For instance, example (8) can be used in different contexts:

a. enikk onnum kl̲ikk āyilla
I anything click didn't happen
lit. 'Nothing clicked for me.' | 'I didn't understand anything.'

b. putiya kaṭa kl̲ikk āyi
new shop click became
lit. 'The new shop became click.' | 'The new shop became successful.'

4.5 Collocations

Collocations are word sequences that co-occur more often than would be expected by chance. Examples: (śuddhavāyu) 'fresh air', (iṭiyumminnalum) 'thunder and lightning', (vaṇṭiyumvaḷḷavum) 'transportation' etc.

4.6 Compound Verb

A compound verb is a series of words that acts as a single verb. One part of the sequence is a light verb that can take inflections of tense, mood, or aspect. The other part carries most of the semantics and hence the key. Examples: (*ōṭipōyi*), 'ran away', (*kēṭṭuninnu*) 'listened without responing', (*vann kaṇṭu*) 'visit', (*uṛaṅṅi pōyi*) 'fell asleep' etc.

5. Properties of MWEs

Non-compositionality and Non-literal translatability: Multiword expressions are semantically idiosyncratic. The meaning of the whole expression cannot be inferred from the meanings of its parts. Therefore word-for-word translation tends to generate unnatural, ungrammatical and, sometimes nonsensical results.

9) cukkān piṭikkuka
helm hold
lit. 'Hold the helm' | 'Take the helm.'

10) kaṭakkal kōṭāli vakkuka
At the root axe lay
lit. 'Lay axe at the root.' | 'Put at stake'

Non-compositionality is considered a prominent feature of multiword expressions. This also compliments the feature, non-literal translatability**.** Multiword expressions are idiomatic by definition. But this feature is not observed throughout all kinds of multiwords. Consider the expressions like 'iṭiyum minnalum' (thunder and lightning), 'vaṇṭiyum vaḷḷavum' (transportation) etc. Here, the constituent words bear a direct relation to the meaning of the expressions. Multiword expressions can have compositional or non-compositional semantics. Many MWEs, especially some collocations, do not stick to this property.

Ambiguity: An MWE is ambiguous when its compositional words can co-occur without forming an expression. Example: (kaikōṛkkuka | lit. 'Join hands.') 'Work together/ collaborate.', (gyāstīruka | lit. 'Run out of gas.') 'Getting tired.'etc. These expressions can act as an MWE or can take the literal meaning of the sequence. This selection is contextual.

Discontinuity: Parts of certain MWEs may get separated from each other by a/ some external element/s. Depending on the context the intervening word may change. This makes it difficult to identify multiword expressions from a sentence. For example, the expression (paṇipāḷi | lit. 'work slipped') 'Messed up' can occur as (paṇi pinneyum pāḷi | lit. 'work slipped again') 'Messed up again'. Another example is (gyāstīruka | lit. 'Run out of gas.') 'Getting tired.'.

11) gyās mul̲uvanum tīruka
gas completely run out
lit.'Completely run out of gas.' | 'Exhausted.'

Non-substitutability: Non-substitutability is a property that is relevant for most MWEs. According to this property, it is not possible to replace a part of an expression with a synonym or similar word. It often causes lexical rigidity. Examples:

12) kāṭ kayaṛi
forest climbed
lit. 'Went to the forest.'| 'To do something too much.'
*vanam kayaṛi
forest climbed

13) kaṇṇ maññaḷikkuka
eye turn yellow
lit. 'Eye turn yellow.' | 'Lose sight under the influence of something exciting.'
*nayanammaññaḷikkuka
eye turn yellow

14) uppum muḷakum
saltchilli
lit. 'Salt and chilli.' | 'Taste'

15) erivum puḷiyum
spiciness sourness
lit. 'spiciness and sourness' | 'Taste.'

16) uppum puḷiyum
salt sour
lit. 'salt and sourness' | 'Taste.'

17) arakkainōkkuka
half hand try
lit. 'Try half hand.' | 'To give something a try.

18) orukainōkkuka
one hand try
lit. 'Try one hand.' | To give something a try.

(mukham maññaḷikkuka | lit. 'Face turn pale') 'Feel embarrassed' is an error-free multiword we get by substituting one item of the expression (13) with another. Here, the meaning of the expression changes. In the case of (14) and (15), both the expressions represent the same concept. But here, the substitution of a part of the former by a part of the latter can happen. I.e. (16).Though it is less frequent than the others, it still conveys the same meaning. Similarly, (17) & (18) refer to the same concept. In these examples, the final part stays constant. The initial parts, *arakkai* & *orukai*, can be used interchangeably without causing any change in meaning. Non-substitutability is not a mandatory property multiword expressions should follow.

Frequency & Collocation: One of the typical properties of MWEs is that the constituent words tend to occur (together) more than expected. When compared to the chances of using a possible alternative, the frequency of co-occurrence of the component words of an MWE is larger. Examples: (kīḻmēl mar̲iññu | 'Fell bottom-up.') 'Turn upside down.', (kaṇṇil eṇṇayoḻiccirikkuka | lit. 'Poured oil in the eye.') 'Wait impatiently.',(bellum br̥eykkum | lit. 'Bell and brake.') 'control' etc.
Since the language speakers tend to use MWEs instead of explaining the concept, multiwords happen to occur frequently. Multiword expressions are stored in the mental lexicon of language speakers. They become habitual through frequent usage. Frequency can be considered as a reliable criterion for lexicalization, but it should not be a necessary one. Consider the following expression:

19) kōl oṭikkuka
stick to break
lit. 'Break the stick.' | 'To give up'.

This expression is rarely used in the language. And it seems to be a regional usage. Even though multiword expressions appear to be frequent in the language they do not adhere to the property of frequency.
Single lexical unit: Multiword expressions consist of a minimum of two words that cut across word boundaries and are complex than the individual units. Generally, MWEs do not cross the sentence boundaries and are treated as single lexical units. The component words do not act individually. Instead, they work together as a group and contribute meaning to the expression as a whole. They are stored as a single unit or a particular concept in the mental lexicon of the speaker.
Syntactic fixedness: MWEs are considered syntactically fixed expressions. However, in the opinion of many linguists, MWEs exhibit a continuum of syntactic fixedness.
Spelling: MWEs are widely seen as words with spaces. Defining multiword expressions as words with spaces is theoretically unsatisfactory. The speakers are not accurate all the time and spelling is not always consistent. Since Malayalam is an agglutinative language, there is a tendency to join words very often. For example,

20) tēcc oṭṭikkuka
iron out to paste
lit. 'Iron out and paste.' | 'To cheat.'
21) paṇi pāḷi
work slipped
lit. 'Work slipped.' | 'Messed up.'
22) kaṭiññāṇ iṭuka
bridle to put
lit. 'Put a bridle.' | 'Bring under control.',
23) kai kaṭattuka
hand to insert
lit. 'Insert the hand.' | 'To interfere'

Examples (20), (21), (22), and (23) can be written as tēccoṭṭikkuka, paṇipāḷi, kaṭiññāṇiṭuka, and kaikaṭattuka respectively. The native speakers show a tendency to pronounce them as a single word. This trend is seen in both written and spoken forms. This property makes them look like a compound word. Therefore, we struggle to define an explicit boundary between multiword expressions and compound words.
Unlike most compounds, we can insert external words (property of discontinuity) within some MWEs that look like compound words. For instance, (20) can be modified as (tēcc bhittiyil oṭṭikkuka | lit. 'Iron out and paste on the wall.') 'to cheat brutally'. But this is not a generic criterion. In the opinion of Bauer (2019), compounds are one type of MWE and since they overlap with other MWEs, it's not easy to define compounds.

6. Findings

From the studies we arrive at the following findings that make Malayalam multiwords different:
Agglutination: Multiwords may get agglutinated with the neighboring words or with the component words of the same expression itself.
Two-way rendering: Multiwords can be written together or separate, without any meaning change.
Code-mixed multiwords: Malayalam has a large set of code-mixed multiwords and many of them are high-frequency words.

7. Conclusion& Future Work

Green et al. (2011) point out that "MWE knowledge is useful, but MWEs are hard to identify." Types of word combinations lie in a spectrum. The boundary between multiword expressions and other compositions is fuzzy. Not all the multiword expressions adhere to all the properties of MWEs. The examples were given in this paper are randomly taken from the language.
Agglutination and two-way rendering of Malayalam multiwords are serious problems that require special attention. This information is very important for speech recognition systems to understand the dialogues by a native speaker.
Processing of multiword expressions requires contextual information. Otherwise, problems related to discontinuation and ambiguity could not be resolved.
Available data is very insufficient for the improvisation of translation systems and other NLP areas. Our future work includes preparing a glossary of Malayalam multiword expressions with wide coverage and sufficient linguistic knowledge.
Implementing computational models is also our future concern. Incorporating them in machine translation and other NLP areas could help the betterment of the system significantly.

8. References

Baldwin, T. and Kim, S. N. 2010. Multiword expressions, In N. Indurkhya and F. Damerau, (Eds.), *Handbook of Natural Language Processing, Second Edition.* CRC Press, Boca Raton, pages, 267-292.

Barreiro, A., Monti, J., Orliac, B., and Batista, F. 2013. When Multiwords go bad in machine translation. InMonti, J., Mitkov, R., Pastor, G. and Seretan, V., (Eds.), *Proceedings of the MT Summit Workshop Proceedings on Multi-word Units in Machine Trans-*

lation and Translation Technology, The European Association for Machine Translation, pages 26–33.

Bauer, L. 2019. Compounds and multi-word expressions in English. In B. Schlücker, editor, Complex lexical units. Berlin, Boston: De Gruyter, pages 45-68.

Chakraborty, T. 2011. Multiword Expressions. Master's thesis, Jadavpur University, May.

Hüning, M. and Schlücker, B. Multi-word expressions. 2015. Muller, Peter O., Ohnheiser, I., Olsen, S., and Rainer, (Eds.), Word Formation, An International Handbook of the Languages of Europe. Berlin: De Gruyter.

Kuiper, K. 2018. Multiword expressions and the Law of Exceptions. In M., Sailer, and S., Markantonatou, editors, *Multiword expressions: Insights from a multi-lingual perspective*. Berlin: Language Science Press, pages 121-141.

Poddar, L. 2016. Multilingual Multiword Expressions. Master's thesis, Indian Institute of Technology, Bombay.arXiv:1612.00246.

Rayson, P., Piao, S., Sharoff, S., Evert, S., and Moirón, B. 2010. Multiword expressions: hard going or plain sailing?. Lang Resources & Evaluation 44, 1-5.

Sag, I., Baldwin, T., Bond, F., Copestake, A., and Dan Flickinger.2002. Multiword expressions: A pain in the neck for NLP. In *Proceedings of the Third International Conference on Intelligent Text Processing and Computational Linguistics,* 1-15. Mexico City.

Vasudevan, J., Bhadran, V.K., and Raghunathan, A. 2016. Contextualizing multi-word expressions in English and Malayalam. *Proceedings of the International conference on Dravidian linguistics*, Hyderabad.

Proceedings of the WILDRE-6 Workshop @LREC2020, pages 60–67
Marseille, 20 June 2022

Bengali and Magahi PUD Treebank and Parser

Pritha Majumdar[1], Deepak Alok[1], Akanksha Bansal[1], Atul Kr. Ojha[2,1], John P. McCrae[2]
[1]Panlingua Language Processing LLP, India, [2]DSI, National University of Ireland Galway, Ireland
panlingua@outlook.com, {atulkumar.ojha, john.mccrae}@insight-centre.org

Abstract

This paper presents the development of the Parallel Universal Dependency (PUD) Treebank for two Indo-Aryan languages: Bengali and Magahi. A treebank of 1,000 sentences has been created using a parallel corpus of English and the UD framework. A preliminary set of sentences was annotated manually - 600 for Bengali and 200 for Magahi. The rest of the sentences were built using the Bengali and Magahi parser. The sentences have been translated and annotated manually by the authors, some of whom are also native speakers of the languages. The objective behind this work is to build a syntactically-annotated linguistic repository for the aforementioned languages, that can prove to be a useful resource for building further NLP tools. Additionally, Bengali and Magahi parsers were also created which is built on machine learning approach. The accuracy of the Bengali parser is 78.13% in the case of UPOS; 76.99% in the case of XPOS, 56.12% in the case of UAS; and 47.19% in the case of LAS. The accuracy of Magahi parser is 71.53% in the case of UPOS; 66.44% in the case of XPOS, 58.05% in the case of UAS; and 33.07% in the case of LAS. This paper also includes an illustration of the annotation schema followed, the findings of the Parallel Universal Dependency (PUD) treebank, and it's resulting linguistic analysis.

Keywords: Indian languages, Bengali, Magahi, Parallel Universal Dependency Treebank, parser

1. Introduction

Sentence parsing is one of the trickiest, yet essential components in the field of Natural Language Processing (NLP). Parsing not only enables better understanding of a sentence structure, but is also useful in the development of various NLP applications like machine translation, and information retrieval. In this paper, we aim to discuss Parallel Universal Dependency (PUD) treebank and parser for two Indian languages, namely, Bengali and Magahi. Bengali, also referred as Bangla, is mostly spoken in the Indian regions of West Bengal, Assam, and Tripura and is the mother tongue of about 97.2 million speakers as per the 2011 Census Report of India.[1] It is one of the 22 scheduled Indian languages and the national language of Bangladesh. Magahi is an Eastern Indo-Aryan language spoken mostly in the Indian states of Bihar and certain areas of Jharkhand. Linguistically, both the languages belong to the Indo-Aryan language family, follow a Subject-Object-Verb (SOV) construction and are head-final languages with a relatively free word order. Like several other Indian languages, they also follow the post-position trait. They are also nominative-accusative languages that allow pro-drop of all arguments, contain complex verb constructions, rich classifiers, differential object marking and has no assigned gender. The verbs show only person agreement with the subject and no agreement with number and gender. However, a distinctive feature of Bengali is that the copula or verb linking the subject and predicate is often found missing in this language.

The objective of UD is to automatically analyze dependency structure of sentences, create multilingual parsers for cross lingual learning, and conduct parsing research for typologically diverse languages under a common framework.[2] The annotation scheme is based on Stanford dependencies (De Marneffe and Manning, 2008), Google universal part of speech, (Petrov et al., 2011) and the Interset Interlingua for morphosyntactic tag sets (Zeman, 2008). Currently, the UD project contains more than 217 treebanks for 122 languages belonging to 24 language families.[3]

It would however be ignorant to state that Indian languages have not progressed at all in the field of NLP (See section-2). The extent and the contribution of their work will be discussed in the later sections of the paper. Nevertheless, discussion on development of PUD treebank and a parser for the above stated languages with English as the source language is what is aimed in this paper.

Section (2), provides an overview of the linguistic resources that have been created for Indian languages. Section (3), discusses the experiment and the data size used to build the parser for the respective languages. Section (4), demonstrates the

[1]`https://censusindia.gov.in/2011Census/Language-2011/Statement-1.pdf`

[2]`https://universaldependencies.org/introduction.html`

[3]`https://universaldependencies.org/`

development of the parser and its outcome. Section (5), illustrates the cross-lingual study of the UD treebank built in this project. The paper concludes with closing remarks and plans for future work.

2. Related Work

In 1991, an initiative was taken up by Technology Development for Indian languages (TDIL), to develop tools for POS tagging, frequency count, spell checkers, and morphological processing for all Indian national (official/scheduled) languages. Thus, a corpus of 3 million words was created for every Indian national language by the end of 1994, including Bengali (Dash, 2004). As per (Kumar et al., 2018), a corpus of 0.17 million sentences is available in Magahi. In 2013, Indian Institute of Information Technology, Hyderabad (IIIT-H) developed monolingual and parallel Pāṇinian Kāraka Dependency (PD) treebanks for Indian languages Hindi, Bengali, Marathi, Kannada and Malayalam.[4] The same was then utilized to annotate Telugu, Urdu, Kashmiri (Bhat, 2017) and a dependency parser for Hindi, Telugu, Bengali, Urdu and Kashmiri was created. Presently, IIIT-H[5] is developing PD treebanks for Indian languages, Bengali, Kannada, Hindi and Malayalam.

As of UD release 2.9, 217 treebanks including the Indian languages, Bhojpuri, Marathi, Hindi, Sanskrit, Tamil, Telugu and Urdu are available(Zeman, 2021).[6] In addition, Magahi UD and Bengali PUD treebanks have been recently reported by (Raj et al., 2021) and (Majumdar, 2021) at *Workshop on Parsing and its Applications for Indian Languages* (in progress) and *Widening NLP workshop 2021* respectively. However, the Bengali UD treebank that was reported at WiNLP has been modified to improve the quality of translation and annotation for the requirements of this paper. Nonetheless, there has been no prior work/resources in Magahi PUD Treebank.

3. Data & Methodology

In order to build the Bengali and Magahi PUD, the English sentences have been taken as the source text from the English PUD (Zeman et al., 2017) which was further translated into the respective target languages, preparing it for the corresponding treebank annotation. In this study both manual and automatic annotation schemas were followed. The sentence alignment is 1-1 but occasionally a sentence-level segment actually consists of two real sentences. The data has been collected from the news domain and Wikipedia. The corpus was then annotated for parts of speech, which was further divided into universal parts of speech (UPOS) and language specific parts of speech (XPOS), and dependency relations. The Bureau of Indian Standards (BIS) tagset[7] has been used for language specific POS tags (Choudhary and Jha, 2014; Ojha and Zeman, 2020). Out of the 37 universal dependency relations, 29 deprel have been used in Bengali and 31 in Magahi (The statistics are given in Table 2). All the 17 UPOS have been used for both Bengali and Magahi (The statistics are given in Table 1). The number of tokens reported for the Bengali and Magahi sentences are 13,110 and 7,575 respectively. Eventually, a total of 50 Bengali sentences were made available for validation to three inter-annotators - native speakers of the language. A kappa score of 0.942613, per dependency, was thus derived. However, we could not do inter-annotators agreement for Magahi.

UPOS Tags	Description	Bengali Statistics	Magahi Statistics
NOUN	Noun	3815	1775
VERB	Verb	1590	780
PUNCT	Punctuation	1720	755
PROPN	Proper noun	805	430
ADJ	Adjective	1275	495
ADP	Adposition	815	1275
DET	Determiner	615	305
PRON	Pronoun	764	214
CCONJ	Coordinating conjunction	385	155
ADV	Adverb	440	150
NUM	Numeral	226	231
PART	Particle	130	110
AUX	Auxiliary	904	783
SCONJ	Subordinating conjunction	270	150
SYM	Symbol	55	33

Table 1: Statistics of used UPOS Tags in the Bengali and Magahi PUD treebank

4. Development of Bengali & Magahi Parser

As mentioned earlier, the Bengali and Magahi treebank was manually annotated using the UD annotation framework. Both, Bengali and Magahi parsers were built on 600 and 200 sentences. The experiment was conducted in two steps.

- **Bengali:** Experiment-1 was run on 200 sentences while Experiment-2 was conducted on

[4]https://www.meity.gov.in/content/language-computing-group-vi

[5]https://kcis.iiit.ac.in/LT/

[6]http://hdl.handle.net/11234/1-4611

[7]http://tdil-dc.in/tdildcMain/articles/134692Draft%20POS%20Tag%20standard.pdf

UD Relations	Description	Bengali Statistics	Magahi Statistics
advmod	Adverbial modifier	530	195
amod	Adjectival modifier of noun	908	324
aux	Auxiliary verb	555	385
case	Case marker	780	1215
cc	Coordinating conjunction	234	102
ccomp	Clausal complement	156	92
compound	Compound	1210	792
conj	Non-first conjunct	276	108
cop	Copula	12	51
det	Determiner	585	175
fixed	Non-first word of fixed expression	180	115
flat	non-first word of flat structure	120	102
goeswith	Non-first part of broken word	-	1
iobj	Indirect object	42	12
mark	Subordinating marker	286	165
nmod	Nominal modifier of noun	995	429
nsubj	Nominal subject	1193	22
nummod	Numeric modifier	186	193
obj	Direct object	179	57
obl	Oblique nominal	860	556
punct	Punctuation	1710	808
root	Root	1000	1000
xcomp	Open clausal complement	230	88

Table 2: Statistics of used UD relations in Bengali and Magahi PUD trebank

600 sentences with the aid of UDPipe open source tool (Straka and Straková, 2017). Cross-validation with an average of 90:10 was used for data splitting where the batch size, learning rate, dropout and embedding size were 50, 0.005, 0.10, 200 respectively, while the other hyper-parameters were randomized for each experiment.

- **Magahi:** Magahi's Experiment-1 was run on 200 sentences using UDPipe similar to Bengali. The data spliting and training features were also the same. Experiment-2 was built on multilingual multi-task model with the aid of UDify open source tool (Kondratyuk and Straka, 2019). We used the same Magahi sentences. In this experiment, the training configurations and features were default including data splitting, batch size, epoch, learning rate, and multilingual BERT layer.

The results are demonstrated in Table 3:

Language	Experiment Details	UPOS	XPOS	UAS	LAS
Bengali	Experiment 1	51.25	62.04	30.23	35.13
Bengali	Experiment 2	78.13	76.09	56.12	47.19
Magahi	Experiment 1	68.08	69.18	34.0	41.74
Magahi	Experiment 2	71.53	66.44	58.05	33.07

Table 3: Results (%) of the Bengali and Magahi Parser

5. Cross-lingual Analysis of Bengali & Magahi PUD

In this section, an extensive linguistic illustration of the language pairs following the annotation schema of the UD v2 guidelines is discussed.

5.1. Nominals

The nominals are divided into three categories in UD - the core arguments, the non-core arguments, and the nominal dependents. These include nsubj (nominal subject), obj (object), iobj (indirect object) under core arguments. The non-core dependents include obl (oblique), vocative, expel (expletive), and dislocated. Lastly, the nominal dependents include nmod (nominal modifier), appos (appositional modifier), and nummod (numeric modifier). In core arguments, nsubj and obj are the most frequently used relations followed by the non-core argument obl. With respect to the nominal dependents, nmod with its subtype nmod:poss is the most frequent followed by the dependency relation nummod.

Figure 1 and Figure 2, showcase the presence of the nominal relations nsubj, obj, iobj, obl. The verb জানিয়েছেন '*janiyechen*' is the root of the sentence. The noun প্রত্যক্ষদর্শী '*protokkhodorshi*' is the nsubj, and the noun পুলিশ '*police*' is the iobj, both of which are dependent on the root. In the lower clause, the noun এপ্রিল '*april*' acts as the obl and the noun ব্যক্তি '*byekti*' acts as the obj, both dependent on the verb করেছিল '*korechilo*', which is further dependent on the root via ccomp relation. In the same way, in Magahi, the noun गबाह *'gabaah'* 'witness' is the nsubj of the root 'told', and the noun पुलिस *'pulis'* 'police' is the iobj. On the other hand, in the lower clause पीड़ित आदमी अप्रील में संदिग्ध आदमी पर हमला कैलकई हल *'piiRit aadamii april meN sandigdh aadamii par hamalaa kailkai hal'* 'the victim had attacked the suspect in April', which is dependent on the root 'told' via ccomp relation, the noun अप्रील *'april'* 'April', has obl relation with the lower verb हमला कैलकई *'hamalaa kailkai'* 'attack'. There are also nsubj and obj in the lower clause, the nominal पीड़ित आदमी *'piiRit aadamii'* 'victim' and संदिग्ध *'sandigdh'* 'suspect' respectively.

5.2. Clauses

In UD, clauses are categorized into five- csubj (clausal subject), ccomp (clausal complement), xcomp (open clausal complement), advcl (adverbial clause modifier), and acl (adnominal clause). The four relations ccomp, xcomp, advcl, and acl are frequently found in both Bengali and Magahi, leaving the csubj. We illustrate xcomp and advcl relations here (see figure 1 and figure 2 where ccomp relation is mentioned.)

The following illustrations, Figure 3, and Figure 4 showcase an example of a clausal construction in Bengali and Magahi respectively. In both the languages, the verb kill মেরে *'mere* in Bengali and मारे *'maare'* in Magahi, which are dependent on the verb root, carry the xcomp relation. The verb চেষ্টা করার *'chesta korar*, 'try do-PRESENT-CONTINUOUS in Bengali and परयास करे *paraaas kare*, 'try do' in Magahi, have advcl relation with the verb kill.

5.3. Predicates

In this section, we will discuss two types of predicate constructions - simple verb construction and compound verb construction. The compound verb construction can further be subdivided into serial verbs and light verb constructions since Indian languages are rich in compound formation. A simple verb construction contains only the verb, which in UD terms is often referred to as the root, and sometimes combines the verb with an auxiliary. A light verb compound construction is formed by combining the main verb (taken as the root) and a corresponding noun/adjective which is dependent on the root. A serial verb compound formation is the amalgamation of the main verb and a corresponding serial verb, which is again dependent on the main verb.

Figure 5 and Figure 6 showcase an example of a simple verb construction in Bengali and Magahi respectively, wherein the verb মনে *'mone'* acts as the root and is combined with the auxiliary হয়ে *'hoye'* in Bengali and होबऽ *'hobe'* acts as the root and is combined with the auxiliary हे *'he'* in Magahi.

The Figure 1 and Figure 3 illustrated, also showcase a light verb compound construction in Bengali, wherein the noun অভিযোগে *'obhijoge'* 'complaints' is dependent on the verb করা *'kora'* 'to-do' and carries the compound:lvc relation in Figure 3. The noun আক্রমণ *akromon* 'attack' is dependent on the verb করেছিল *'korechilo* 'did' and carries the compound:lvc relation in Figure 1. In the same way, the Figure 2 and Figure 4 illustrated, showcase a light verb compound construction in Magahi, wherein the noun आरोप *'aaropa'* 'complaints' is dependent on the verb लगाबल *'lagaabala'* 'place' and carries the compound:lvc relation in Figure 4 and the noun हमला *hamalaa* 'attack' is dependent on the verb कैलकई *'kailkai* 'did' and carries the compound:lvc relation in Figure 2. Compound verb formation is a very common construction found in both Bengali and Magahi.[8]

There is also the presence of another type of predicate construction in UD wherein the adjective or noun acts as the root. In Magahi, it is seen that the noun/adjective is combined with the copula, wherein the corresponding noun/adjective acts as the root of the sentence. However, since Bengali lacks copular construction, the noun/adjective itself acts as the root and the other relations are further dependent on it. Figure 7 showcases such a construction in Bengali, wherein the adjective গুমোট *'gumot'* 'stuffy' acts as the root of the sentence, and Figure-8 illustrates it in Magahi, wherein the adjective उबाऊ *'ubaauu* 'stuffy' is a root of the sentence.

5.4. Coordination

The figures, 9 and 10, showcase examples of coordination constructions. In UD, a conjunct (conj) is a relation between two elements which are connected by a coordinating conjunction (cc). The first conjunct serves as the head and the second conjunct is related to the first through the cc.

The example, Figure 9, showcases a coordination relation in Bengali, wherein the noun স্পনসরশিপ *'sponsorship'* acts as the first conjunct and the noun বিজ্ঞাপন *'biggapon'* acts as the second conjunct and are joined with the coordinating conjunction এবং *'ebong'*. Similarly, Figure 10 showcases a coordination relation in Magahi. The noun परयोजन *'pariyojanaa'* 'sponsorship' is the first conjunct and the noun बिज्ञापन *'bigyaapana'* 'advertising' is the second conjunct, which are conjoined by a coordinating conjunction आउ *'aau'* 'and'.

[8]There could be a different view on which element acts as a root in such a construction (e.g., a noun/adjective is a root and the verb depends on it). We have assumed that the verb is a root and a noun/adjective depends on it. Arguing here in favor of our view will take us in a different direction. Also, there is a space constraint.

Conclusion and Future work

This paper presented an attempt in developing a PUD treebank and a parser for the Indian languages, Bengali and Magahi. Currently, the treebanks consist of 1, 000 sentences. The annotation schema, tags used, and linguistic analysis have also been discussed in the sections above. The built Bengali and Magahi PUD treebank will be publicly released in the UD repository.[9],[10]

In the near future, we plan to encode the morphological information in the same PUD treebank for better usage of the built resource. Additionally, a plan to develop a robust parser on 1,000 parallel annotated sentences using zero-shot and to build an enhanced quality of Machine Translation models and NLP tools will also be aimed. Finally, an attempt will be made in increasing the number of sentences to a minimum of 100 for inter-annotator agreement in both the languages to achieve a better understanding of the quality of annotation.

Acknowledgements

Pritha Majumdar, Deepak Alok and Akanksha Bansal would like to acknowledge Panlingua Language Processing LLP for supporting the creation of these treebanks both academically & financially. Atul Kr. Ojha and John P. McCrae would like to acknowledge the EUs Horizon 2020 Research & Innovation programme through the ELEXIS project under grant agreement No. 731015.

6. Bibliographical References

Bhat, R. A. (2017). Exploiting linguistic knowledge to address representation and sparsity issues in dependency parsing of indian languages.

Choudhary, N. and Jha, G. N. (2014). Creating multilingual parallel corpora in indian languages. In Zygmunt Vetulani et al., editors, *Human Language Technology Challenges for Computer Science and Linguistics*, pages 527–537, Cham. Springer International Publishing.

Dash, N. S. (2004). Language corpora: present indian need. In *Proceedings of the SCALLA 2004 Working Conference*, pages 5–7. Citeseer.

De Marneffe, M.-C. and Manning, C. D. (2008). Stanford typed dependencies manual. Technical report, Technical report, Stanford University.

Kondratyuk, D. and Straka, M. (2019). 75 languages, 1 model: Parsing Universal Dependencies universally. In *Proceedings of the 2019 Conference on Empirical Methods in Natural Language Processing and the 9th International Joint Conference on Natural Language Processing (EMNLP-IJCNLP)*, pages 2779–2795, Hong Kong, China, November. Association for Computational Linguistics.

[9]https://github.com/UniversalDependencies/UD_Bengali-PUD

[10]https://github.com/UniversalDependencies/UD_Magahi-PUD

Kumar, R., Lahiri, B., Alok, D., Ojha, A. K., Jain, M., Basit, A., and Dawer, Y. (2018). Automatic identification of closely-related indian languages: Resources and experiments.

Majumdar, P. (2021). Bengali parallel universal dependency treebank.

Ojha, A. K. and Zeman, D. (2020). Universal Dependency treebanks for low-resource Indian languages: The case of Bhojpuri. In *Proceedings of the WILDRE5– 5th Workshop on Indian Language Data: Resources and Evaluation*, pages 33–38, Marseille, France, May. European Language Resources Association (ELRA).

Petrov, S., Das, D., and McDonald, R. (2011). A universal part-of-speech tagset. *arXiv preprint arXiv:1104.2086*.

Raj, M., Ratan, S., Ritesh, K., Alok, D., and Ojha, A. K. (2021). Developing universal dependencies treebanks for magahi and braj.

Straka, M. and Straková, J. (2017). Tokenizing, POS tagging, lemmatizing and parsing UD 2.0 with UDPipe. In *Proceedings of the CoNLL 2017 Shared Task: Multilingual Parsing from Raw Text to Universal Dependencies*, pages 88–99.

Zeman, D., Popel, M., Straka, M., Hajic, J., Nivre, J., Ginter, F., Luotolahti, J., Pyysalo, S., Petrov, S., Potthast, M., Tyers, F., Badmaeva, E., Gokirmak, M., Nedoluzhko, A., Cinkova, S., Hajic jr., J., Hlavacova, J., Kettnerová, V., Uresova, Z., Kanerva, J., Ojala, S., Missilä, A., Manning, C. D., Schuster, S., Reddy, S., Taji, D., Habash, N., Leung, H., de Marneffe, M.-C., Sanguinetti, M., Simi, M., Kanayama, H., dePaiva, V., Droganova, K., Martínez Alonso, H., Çöltekin, c., Sulubacak, U., Uszkoreit, H., Macketanz, V., Burchardt, A., Harris, K., Marheinecke, K., Rehm, G., Kayadelen, T., Attia, M., Elkahky, A., Yu, Z., Pitler, E., Lertpradit, S., Mandl, M., Kirchner, J., Alcalde, H. F., Strnadová, J., Banerjee, E., Manurung, R., Stella, A., Shimada, A., Kwak, S., Mendonca, G., Lando, T., Nitisaroj, R., and Li, J. (2017). Conll 2017 shared task: Multilingual parsing from raw text to universal dependencies. In *Proceedings of the CoNLL 2017 Shared Task: Multilingual Parsing from Raw Text to Universal Dependencies*, pages 1–19, Vancouver, Canada, August. Association for Computational Linguistics.

Zeman, D. (2008). Reusable tagset conversion using tagset drivers. In *LREC*, volume 2008, pages 28–30.

Zeman, Daniel; et al., . (2021). Universal dependencies 2.9. LINDAT/CLARIAH-CZ digital library at the Institute of Formal and Applied Linguistics (ÚFAL), Faculty of Mathematics and Physics, Charles University.

7. Appendix

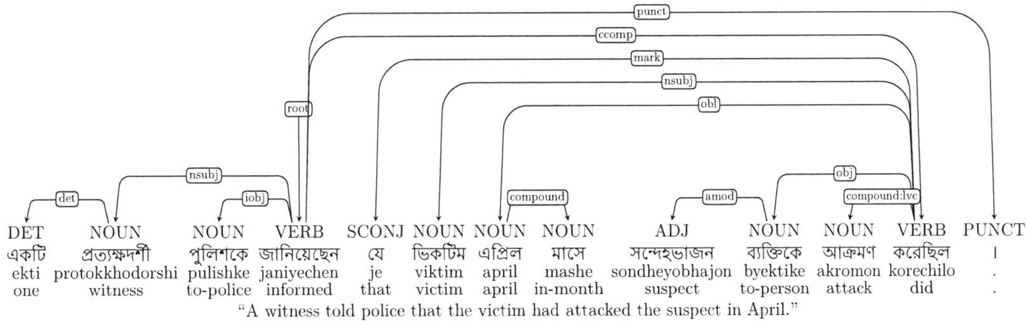

Figure 1: A parallel Bengali construction illustrating the nominal relations

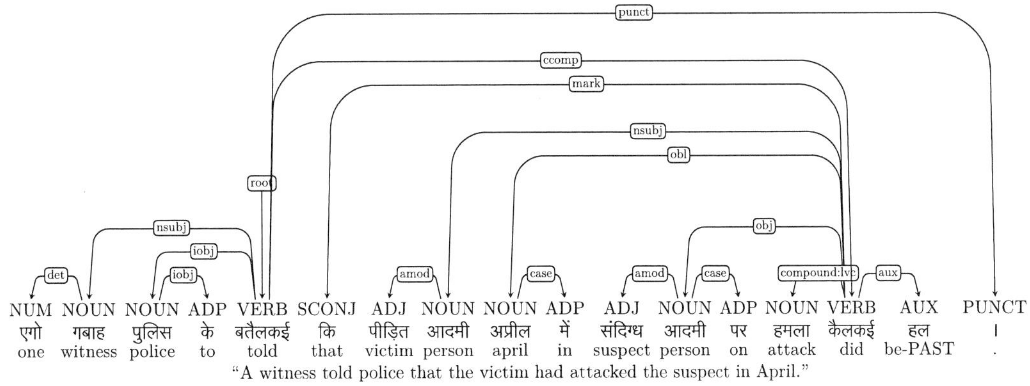

Figure 2: A parallel Magahi construction illustrating the nominal relations

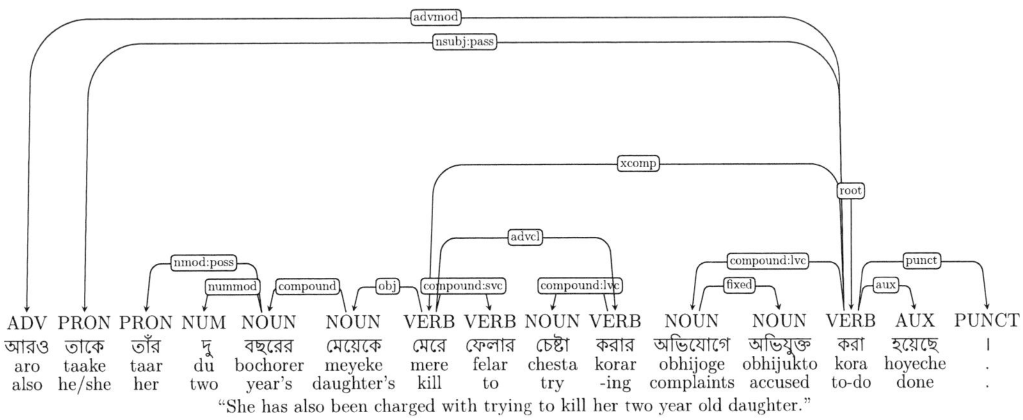

Figure 3: A parallel Bengali construction illustrating the clausal relation

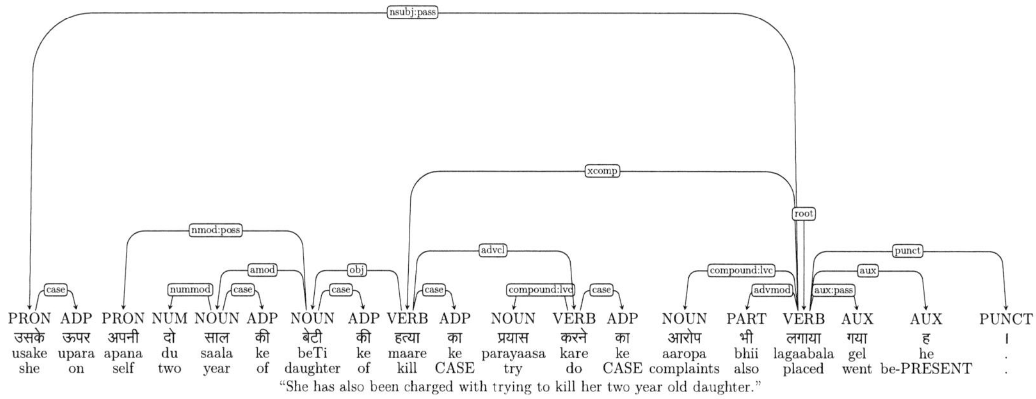

Figure 4: A parallel Magahi construction illustrating the clausal relation

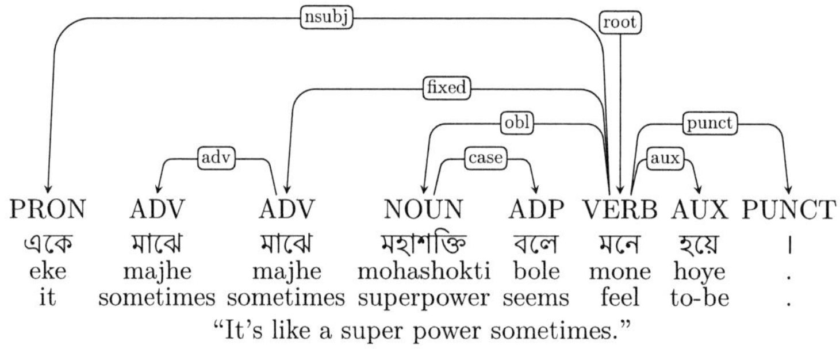

Figure 5: A parallel Bengali construction illustrating the simple verb construction.

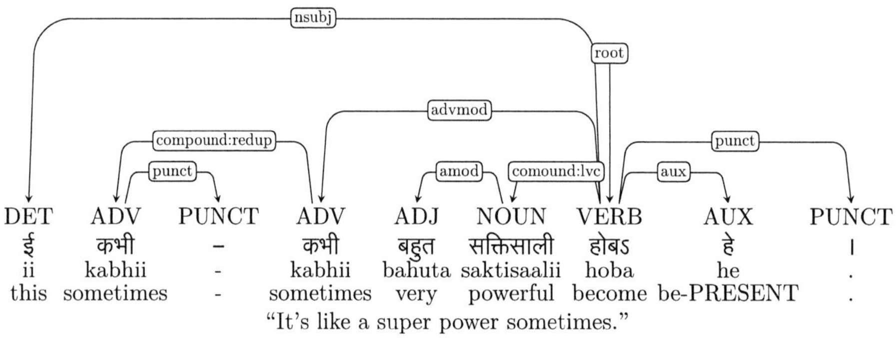

Figure 6: A parallel Magahi construction illustrating a simple verb construction

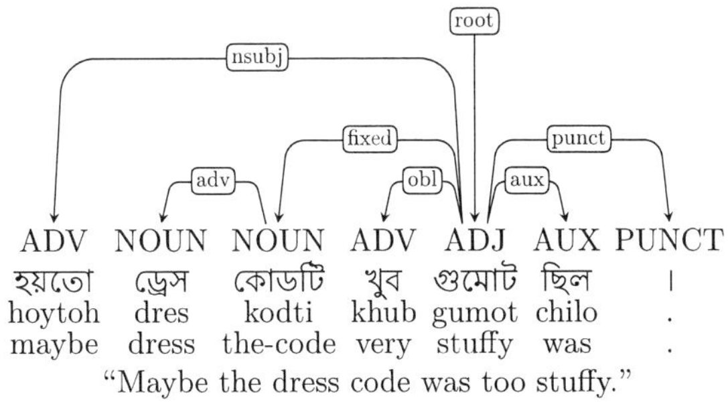

Figure 7: A parallel Bengali construction illustrating the non-verbal predicate construction.

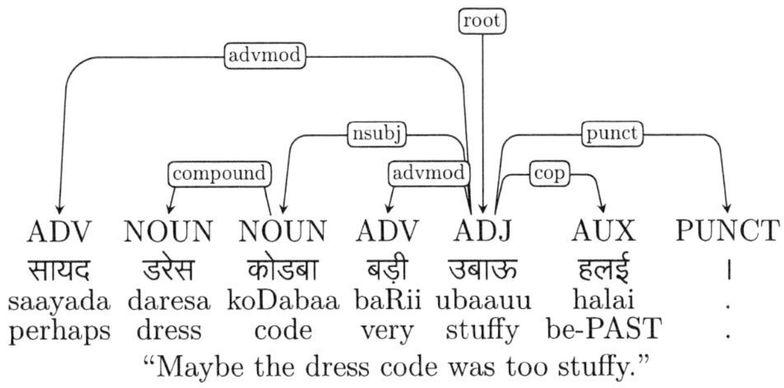

Figure 8: A parallel Magahi construction illustrating a non-verbal predicate

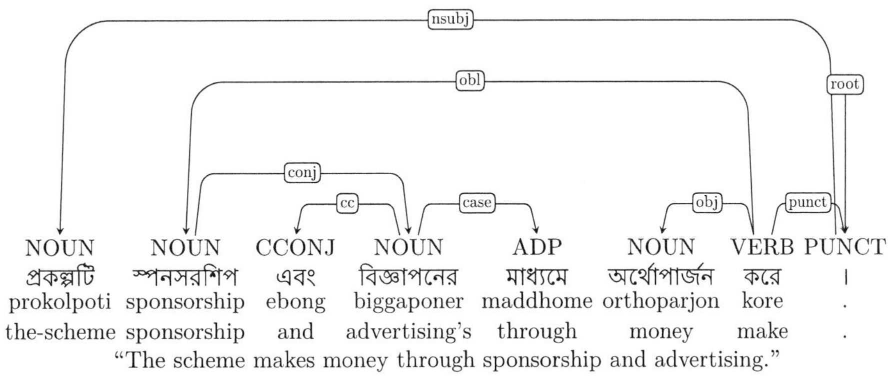

Figure 9: A parallel Bengali construction illustrating the nominal coordinating relation.

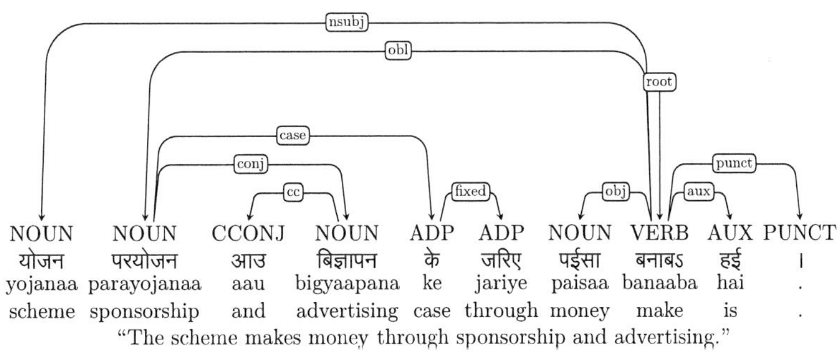

Figure 10: A parallel Magahi construction illustrating the nominal coordinating relation.

Proceedings of the WILDRE-6 Workshop @LREC2020, pages 68–73
Marseille, 20 June 2022

Makadi: A Large-Scale Human-Labeled Dataset for Hindi Semantic Parsing

Shashwat Vaibhav, Nisheeth Srivastava
Department of Computer Science, IIT Kanpur
{shashwatv, nsrivast}@cse.iitk.ac.in

Abstract

Parsing natural language queries into formal database calls is a very well-studied problem. Because of the rich diversity of semantic markers across the world's languages, progress in solving this problem is irreducibly language-dependent. This has created an asymmetry in progress in NLIDB solutions, with most state-of-the-art efforts focused on the resource-rich *English* language, with limited progress seen for low resource languages. In this short paper, we present *Makadi*, a large-scale, complex, cross-lingual, cross-domain semantic parsing and text-to-SQL dataset for semantic parsing in the *Hindi* language. Produced by translating the recently introduced English language *Spider* NLIDB dataset, it consists of 9693 questions and SQL queries on 166 databases with multiple tables which cover numerous domains. It is the first large-scale dataset in the Hindi language for semantic parsing and related language understanding tasks. Our dataset is publicly available at the github repository: https://github.com/neg-loss/Makadi.git.

Keywords: Semantic parsing, Spider dataset, Natural Language Interface to Databases

1. Introduction

Semantic parsing involves mapping natural language sentences to a formal meaning representation, mainly to query an information source. It requires understanding the meaning of natural language sentences and mapping to meaning representations such as logical forms or directly into some programming language like SQL, Python, etc.

Researchers have developed several machine learning models that perform semantic parsing well in test evaluations. Recent advances in semantic parsing have improved the accuracy of neural parsers(Jia and Liang, 2016)(exact match accuracy on ATIS(Price, 1990; Dahl et al., 1994), 83.3), (Dong and Lapata, 2016)(correct answer accuracy percentage on ATIS, 84.6) and (Wang et al., 2020)(exact match accuracy on Spider(Yu et al., 2018), 65.6). These models are fuelled by the training data available to them. Other approaches to NLIDB which do not require large training data based on keywords such as NLP-Reduce(Kaufmann et al., 2007)(69.6% and 67.7% average recall and precision respectively on JOBS(Tang and Mooney, 2001)), and based on parsing such as Athena(Saha et al., 2016)(100% precision and 88.3% recall on MAS[1]) also exist. Since *English* is a resource-rich language, there exist numerous datasets for training such models, for example, Spider(Yu et al., 2018) and WikiSQL(Zhong et al., 2017). We compare our dataset with these two English language NLIDB datasets in Table 1. However, for resource-scarce languages, it becomes very difficult to find such resources, let alone have some model to tackle the problem. In this paper, we present a human-labeled dataset for cross-lingual and cross-domain semantic parsing equivalent to the existing Spider(Yu et al., 2018) dataset in Hindi mixed with the English language. We preferred working with the mixed language because it represents the real-world scenario closely as Hindi speakers generally substituting English terms into their Hindi speech rather than trying to define Hindi equivalents. We combined *Hindi* and *English* words using the *Roman script*, transliterating from Hindi to English using existing libraries (Kunchukuttan, 2020).

Creating such a dataset was challenging for many reasons. First, it wasn't always possible to find *neat Hindi equivalents* of many words from the *English* language or if they were there, they were too complicated to be used since they made look sentences not very appealing. For example, the query *"Return the average price of products that have each category code."* was translated to *"pratyek category code vaale product ka ausat price lautaen."* not translating *category* to *shrenee*. Second, table attributes present in the database were to be renamed mostly to suit the references made in the queries. For example, in most database tables, there was a column named *Name* and we translated it to *naam* such that query like *"Chocolate"* ***naam*** *ke product ka description kya hai?* stay consistent and refer to the existent database attributes. The third and the most ambiguous part was a balance of the languages used in the queries so that it represents real-world scenarios as closely as possible. For example, the query *"Find the phone number of all the customers and staff."* was translated into *"sabhee customer aur staff ke phone number ka pata lagaen."* instead of translating into *"sabhee graahakon aur karmachaariyon ke phone number ka pata lagaen."*. Another possibility related to databases was to even update values available in the database tables. For most of the cases, we chose not to update them as they are just constants and can be referred to in the same way as they were referred to in the queries in the original dataset. To the best of

[1]Microsoft Academic Search Database

our knowledge, there does not exist any such dataset for *Hindi-English mixed* language.

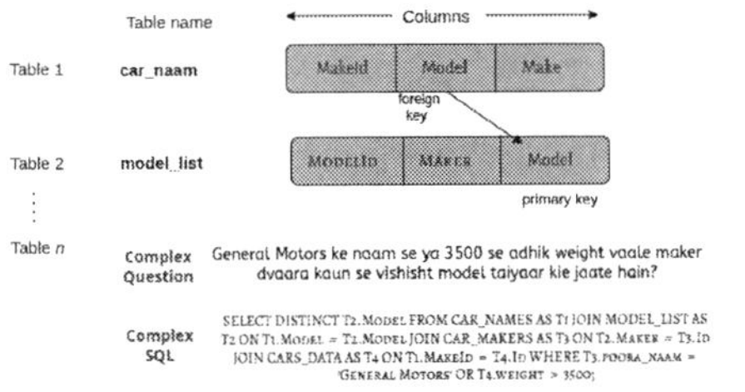

Figure 1: Our corpus contains queries of varying complexity. The above figure shows one such *Natural language query* and the corresponding *SQL* query. A Foreign key constraint is also shown in the above example.

2. Related Work and Existing Datasets

Several semantic parsing datasets with different queries have been created. The natural language used in these datasets is generally *English*. The meaning representations in these datasets can be in any format e.g., logical forms. Historic, monolingual datasets include GeoQuery(Zelle and Mooney, 1996), JOBS(Tang and Mooney, 2001), ATIS(Price, 1990; Dahl et al., 1994). They have been used extensively by (Zelle and Mooney, 1996; Zettlemoyer and Collins, 2005; Wong and Mooney, 2007; Dong and Lapata, 2016; Liang et al., 2011). Other existing text-to-SQL datasets are Restaurants(Popescu et al., 2003; Tang and Mooney, 2001), Scholar(Iyer et al., 2017), Academic(Li and Jagadish, 2014), Yelp, and IMDB(Yaghmazadeh et al., 2017), Advising (Finegan-Dollak et al., 2018) containing 378, 817, 196, 128 and 131 natural language questions respectively. These datasets have been studied for decades in the NLP community(Warren and Pereira, 1982; Popescu et al., 2003; Li et al., 2006; Giordani and Moschitti, 2012; Wang et al., 2017; Xu et al., 2018; Yaghmazadeh et al., 2017).

The very large semantic parsing dataset WikiSQL(Zhong et al., 2017) contained 80,654 natural language queries and 26,521 databases in it. However, each database contained just one table and hence all the queries in it are simple. Spider(Yu et al., 2018) contains 10,181 queries in the English language with over 200 databases covering 138 domains. It contains multiple tables per database with referential constraints allowing to have complex queries in it. The recently published dataset MTOP(Li et al., 2021) consists of 100k annotated utterances in 6 languages(*English, Hindi, Spanish, Thai, French, and German*) across 11 domains for multilingual semantic parsing.

3. Corpus Construction

The original Spider dataset consisting of 200 databases was constructed using mainly three sources. The authors collected 40 databases from DatabaseAnswers[2] having thousands of data models across a wide range of domains. These were populated with dummy data using an online tool[3] and then manually corrected by the authors. Other 70 complex databases from SQL tutorial websites, textbook examples, and database courses were taken, and the remaining 90 databases were created from WikiSQL containing about 500 tables from different domains. The creation of this massive dataset nearly took overwhelming 1100 hours of manual effort. The authors published the dataset which included 1,034 queries in the dev set, 8,659 queries in the train set, and 488 queries in the test set. The authors chose not to make the test set public and is used to evaluate different proposed models and maintain a leaderboard[4]. Along with the queries, it even contained corresponding SQLite databases and SQL scripts to generate those databases. Also, a *table.json* file included with the dataset describes the database table attributes and the foreign key relationship existing among them. We also found that the dataset contained 7 databases with empty tables[5]. It is crucial for models like RAT-SQL(Wang et al., 2020) to have values in the tables as they use value linking. We even found out that one of the databases was missing a table from the SQL script and we took care of it.

Our Approach To start with, we took each statement in the *English language* from the dataset and translated it into an equivalent *Hindi language* statement. The translation process was somewhat controlled in the sense that we did not translate the queries completely(see table 2). We chose to skip translating some very commonly used *English* words and maintained a balanced extent of translation. The motivation behind such balanced translation came from the fact that Hindi speakers in general do not purely use a single language in day-to-day life. Instead, they very frequently use common words from English and sometimes even from local vernaculars. To speed up the translation process, we used *Google translate*[6]. In order to have the references made in the queries relevant, we even updated the table attributes like column names and table names suitably keeping the changes minimal. Although we had the option of translating values from the tables but we strongly avoided that because they are constants and can be referred to in a fashion similar to the original dataset. However, some of the values were changed to make the queries look more natural. For example, in the query *"sabhee mahila sankaay sadasyon ke lie pahala naam, antim naam*

[2]http://www.databaseanswers.org/

[3]http://filldb.info/

[4]https://yale-lily.github.io/spider

[5]Academic, Music, Scholar, Yelp, Geo, Restaurants, IMDB

[6]https://translate.google.com/

Dataset	# Q	# SQL	# DB	# Domain	# Table/DB	ORDER BY	GROUP BY	HAVING
WikiSQL	80,654	77,840	26,521	-	1	0	0	0
Spider	10,181	5,963	200	138	5.1	1335	1491	388
Makadi	9,693	5,294	166	133	5.27	1150	1261	313

Table 1: Statistics about different text-to-SQL datasets. **Makadi** is the *only* text-to-SQL dataset in code-mixed *English* and *romanized Hindi* language.

Original Query	Google Translation	Balanced Translation
What are the names of the pilots in alphabetical order?	paayalaton ke naam varnaanukram mein kya hain?	pilots ke naam varnaanukram mein kya hain?
Which accelerator name contains substring "Opera"??	kis tvarak naam mein "opera", sabastring shaamil hai?	kis accelerator naam mein "Opera" substring shaamil hai?
What is the model of the car with the smallest amount of horsepower?	sabase kam ashvashakti vaalee kaar ka modal kya hai?	sabase kam horsepower vaalee car ka model kya hai?

Table 2: This is how we did the balanced annotation. We avoided translating queries completely.

aur phone number dikhaen", the word *mahila* is value in one of the tables of *Activity* database. Keeping the consistency with the updated queries, we updated corresponding SQL queries. Since our dataset is derived from the Spider dataset, it also inherits all the qualities automatically. For example, our dataset covers a vast range of SQL patterns with the SQL components `SELECT` with multiple columns and aggregations, `WHERE, GROUP BY, HAVING, LIMIT, JOIN, INTERSECT, EXCEPT, UNION, AND, EXISTS, OR, NOT IN, LIKE` along with several nested queries. However, we faced another set of challenges while annotating the original dataset. We considered the following points.

A) Language balance. While creating the dataset, we felt that making a complete translation won't be the best thing to do. Because, in general, *Hindi* speakers often use *English* and this has become so normal that everybody does that. So to make our dataset more general and near-real world, we decided to keep a few English words. But now the question was about to what extent the translations were to be made. The commonality of a word in a language differs from person to person, as one person might be using some particular word than some other person. So, it was difficult on deciding which word to consider common and which word to not. To assure that the language style is consistent enough, two *Hindi speakers* did the validation and suggested improvements.

B) Query reference. While doing the translations, it was an absolute possibility to produce a translation in such a way that the query does not refer to the tables and columns in it at all and at the same time keep the query intent. We focused on avoiding such kinds of translations as it is natural to have references to the database in the query presented. RAT-SQL (Wang et al., 2020; Guo et al., 2019) have used the idea of *schema linking* and *value linking* extensively and have shown improvement. Another work (Bogin et al., 2019) too emphasize schema encoding and schema linking to produce the results.

C) Missing SQL script. We found out that in the original dataset, 7 SQL scripts were missing from the dataset. We created them ourselves. For this, we used `sqlite_web`[7] to read the corresponding SQLite databases and write the script. We also found out that several databases just had empty tables in the dataset.

4. Dataset Statistics and Comparison

We have summarized the statistics about our corpus already in table1. To the best of our knowledge, no such dataset is known to exist. In our dataset, we provide a dev set and a train set consisting of respectively 1,034 and 8,659 queries along with their SQL equivalents. We also ship 166 SQLite databases along with SQL scripts to generate them. We could not provide the test set and corresponding SQL queries as we did not have access to them as of writing. Since there does not exist any dataset like ours, providing a detailed comparison is a difficult task. Our dataset poses a little varied challenge to the models from what other text-to-SQL datasets present. It tests the generalization ability of the models to new and varied domains under cross-language settings.

5. Task Definition

With our dataset, we define a text-to-SQL task that differs from earlier text-to-SQL or more generally semantic parsing datasets which are monolingual in nature. Our dataset contains *English* transliterated natural language queries in the *Hindi* language and SQL queries distributed over vast domains. Thus, we evaluated a state-of-the-art text-to-SQL model using Hindi word embeddings on our dataset. Since our dataset contains

[7]https://github.com/coleifer/sqlite-web

	Query Type				
Component	Easy	Medium	Hard	Extra Hard	Overall
`SELECT`	62.22(90.32)	44.59(80.44)	64.36(93.10)	40.36(80.12)	51.47(84.89)
`WHERE`	33.63(84.01)	30.60(72.58)	18.18(64.89)	15.02(46.15)	26.09(68.67)
`GROUP BY`	48.64(76.92)	44.79(71.96)	36.36(88.31)	38.09(71.89)	41.87(74.67)
`ORDER BY`	49.99(73.46)	28.77(74.66)	55.55(83.33)	73.07(77.70)	52.77(77.58)
`KEYWORDS`	78.80(89.90)	73.49(91.79)	64.07(84.39)	61.16(75.30)	70.20(86.84)
Query Count	248	446	174	166	1034

Table 3: F1 scores for different levels of the SQL queries on our dataset. Values shown in brackets correspond to F1 scores of *GloVe* version of RAT-SQL(Wang et al., 2020) on the dev set of the Spider dataset.

mixed code i.e. *English* and *romanized Hindi*, we expected reduced performance on this dataset than English datasets. The size of the performance gap is expected to be informative about the opportunity cost of attempting to tailor semantic parsing tasks to multilingual datasets such as ours. As is conventional in such analyses, we do not include queries that require any form of common sense or knowledge from the outside world.

6. Evaluation Metrics

To measure the performance of different models, we consider Component matching and Exact matching as described in Spider Dataset.

Component Matching In a SQL query, there is a possibility of having several components for which order doesn't matter. To avoid ordering of components, we can first parse the gold SQL and decoded SQL into several sub-components and see if the same components exist in both sets.

Exact Matching We use the concept of component matching described above to find if the gold SQL and predicted SQL are exactly the same or not. This way equivalent gold SQL and predicted SQL will be treated the same even if some components in predicted SQL are in a different order from those in gold SQL.

Hardness Criteria As in the original dataset, our dataset too contained SQL queries of varying hardness. The hardness criteria depend upon a number of SQL components included in it. For example, queries consisting of just one `SELECT` component would be considered easier than the one with multiple `SELECT` components. There are four categories related to hardness: easy, medium, hard and extra hard.

7. Result and Analysis

To test the usability of our corpus, we evaluated our corpus on the model given by (Wang et al., 2020). We made minor modifications to it. For example, we used *Hindi* word embeddings from *FastText*[8] which also consisted of a few *English* words. We did the transliteration of the Hindi words and then used them. Since the model was not designed for a dataset like ours, unsurprisingly, it gave Exact match accuracy of 35.48% and 9.03% on easy and extra hard level queries respectively when trained for 40,000 steps. On medium and hard queries, it gave 21.97% and 14.36% exact match accuracy respectively, and overall it was found to be 21.85%. We present F1 scores of component matching in Table 3. The results described above are based on how the model performed on the dev set and not on the test set as we did not have access to the test set.

There is a clear performance gap in model performance going from English to Hindi. RAT-SQL manages to identify individual SQL clauses in natural language Hindi sentences in Makadi, leading to component matching performance of between 0.26-0.70, compared with 0.68-0.86 for similar tasks in English. However, exact match accuracy shows a much larger performance deficit, with overall accuracy at 21.85% in contrast with 59.67% ($\pm$ 2% depending on a random seed) seen in English semantic parsing.

We consider some possible explanations for this gap below. First, RAT-SQL(Wang et al., 2020) uses GloVe[9] and BERT pre-trained word embeddings for English semantic parsing, which offer comprehensive coverage for all English language words. Since a large number of English words were missing from the FastText Hindi embeddings used in our test, it is obvious to have poor performance for any model. Thus, an obvious direction of future work is to produce word embeddings for *English* and *(romanized) Hindi* words in a single vector space. Second, sometimes there exist several different transliterations for a word and in that case, which produces ambiguity in naive approaches like the one we have currently used. More sophisticated approaches could use approximate string matching techniques to map these possibilities to a single word embedding for that word. Thus, finding good semantic parsing models for mixed language datasets like Makadi offers several clear directions for improvement.

[8]https://fasttext.cc/

[9]https://nlp.stanford.edu/projects/glove/

8. Conclusion

In this paper, we present **Makadi** covering a variety of domains, containing complex queries in code-mixed *English* and *Hindi* language for semantic parsing and Text-to-SQL task. It is unique in the sense that it is the first such large corpus introduced in mixed language and it also happens to be the first such resource in the Hindi language. We expect that it would prove beneficial to the researchers in NLP and DB community.

9. Bibliographical References

Bogin, B., Berant, J., and Gardner, M. (2019). Representing schema structure with graph neural networks for text-to-SQL parsing. In *Proceedings of the 57th Annual Meeting of the Association for Computational Linguistics*, pages 4560–4565, Florence, Italy, July. Association for Computational Linguistics.

Dahl, D. A., Bates, M., Brown, M., Fisher, W., Hunicke-Smith, K., Pallett, D., Pao, C., Rudnicky, A., and Shriberg, E. (1994). Expanding the scope of the ATIS task: The ATIS-3 corpus. In *Human Language Technology: Proceedings of a Workshop held at Plainsboro, New Jersey, March 8-11, 1994.*

Dong, L. and Lapata, M. (2016). Language to logical form with neural attention. In *Proceedings of the 54th Annual Meeting of the Association for Computational Linguistics (Volume 1: Long Papers)*, pages 33–43, Berlin, Germany, August. Association for Computational Linguistics.

Finegan-Dollak, C., Kummerfeld, J. K., Zhang, L., Ramanathan, K., Sadasivam, S., Zhang, R., and Radev, D. (2018). Improving text-to-sql evaluation methodology. In *Proceedings of the 56th Annual Meeting of the Association for Computational Linguistics (Volume 1: Long Papers)*, pages 351–360. Association for Computational Linguistics.

Giordani, A. and Moschitti, A. (2012). Translating questions to SQL queries with generative parsers discriminatively reranked. In *Proceedings of COLING 2012: Posters*, pages 401–410, Mumbai, India, December. The COLING 2012 Organizing Committee.

Guo, J., Zhan, Z., Gao, Y., Xiao, Y., Lou, J.-G., Liu, T., and Zhang, D. (2019). Towards complex text-to-SQL in cross-domain database with intermediate representation. In *Proceedings of the 57th Annual Meeting of the Association for Computational Linguistics*, pages 4524–4535, Florence, Italy, July. Association for Computational Linguistics.

Iyer, S., Konstas, I., Cheung, A., Krishnamurthy, J., and Zettlemoyer, L. (2017). Learning a neural semantic parser from user feedback. *CoRR*, abs/1704.08760.

Jia, R. and Liang, P. (2016). Data recombination for neural semantic parsing. In *Proceedings of the 54th Annual Meeting of the Association for Computational Linguistics (Volume 1: Long Papers)*, pages 12–22, Berlin, Germany, August. Association for Computational Linguistics.

Kaufmann, E., Bernstein, A., and Fischer, L. (2007). Nlp-reduce: A "naıve" but domain-independent natural language interface for querying ontologies. *4th European Semantic Web Conference (ESWC 2007)*, 01.

Kunchukuttan, A. (2020). The IndicNLP Library. `https://github.com/anoopkunchukuttan/indic_nlp_library/blob/master/docs/indicnlp.pdf`.

Li, F. and Jagadish, H. V. (2014). Constructing an interactive natural language interface for relational databases. *Proc. VLDB Endow.*, 8(1):73–84, sep.

Li, Y., Yang, H., and Jagadish, H. V. (2006). Constructing a generic natural language interface for an xml database. In Yannis Ioannidis, et al., editors, *Advances in Database Technology - EDBT 2006*, pages 737–754, Berlin, Heidelberg. Springer Berlin Heidelberg.

Li, H., Arora, A., Chen, S., Gupta, A., Gupta, S., and Mehdad, Y. (2021). Mtop: A comprehensive multilingual task-oriented semantic parsing benchmark. *ArXiv*, abs/2008.09335.

Liang, P., Jordan, M. I., and Klein, D. (2011). Learning dependency-based compositional semantics.

Popescu, A.-M., Etzioni, O., and Kautz, H. A. (2003). Towards a theory of natural language interfaces to databases. In *IUI*.

Price, P. J. (1990). Evaluation of spoken language systems: the ATIS domain. In *Speech and Natural Language: Proceedings of a Workshop Held at Hidden Valley, Pennsylvania, June 24-27,1990.*

Saha, D., Floratou, A., Sankaranarayanan, K., Minhas, U. F., Mittal, A., and Özcan, F. (2016). Athena: An ontology-driven system for natural language querying over relational data stores. *Proceedings of the VLDB Endowment*, 9:1209–1220, 08.

Tang, L. R. and Mooney, R. J. (2001). Using multiple clause constructors in inductive logic programming for semantic parsing.

Wang, C., Cheung, A., and Bodik, R. (2017). Synthesizing highly expressive sql queries from input-output examples. In *Proceedings of the 38th ACM SIGPLAN Conference on Programming Language Design and Implementation*, PLDI 2017, page 452–466, New York, NY, USA. Association for Computing Machinery.

Wang, B., Shin, R., Liu, X., Polozov, O., and Richardson, M. (2020). RAT-SQL: Relation-aware schema encoding and linking for text-to-SQL parsers. In *Proceedings of the 58th Annual Meeting of the Association for Computational Linguistics*, pages 7567–7578, Online, July. Association for Computational Linguistics.

Warren, D. H. and Pereira, F. C. (1982). An efficient easily adaptable system for interpreting natural language queries. *American Journal of Computational Linguistics*, 8(3-4):110–122.

Wong, Y. W. and Mooney, R. (2007). Learning synchronous grammars for semantic parsing with lambda calculus. In *Proceedings of the 45th Annual Meeting of the Association of Computational Linguistics*, pages 960–967, Prague, Czech Republic, June. Association for Computational Linguistics.

Xu, X., Liu, C., and Song, D. (2018). SQLNet: Generating structured queries from natural language without reinforcement learning.

Yaghmazadeh, N., Wang, Y., Dillig, I., and Dillig, T. (2017). Sqlizer: Query synthesis from natural language. *Proc. ACM Program. Lang.*, 1(OOPSLA), oct.

Yu, T., Zhang, R., Yang, K., Yasunaga, M., Wang, D., Li, Z., Ma, J., Li, I., Yao, Q., Roman, S., Zhang, Z., and Radev, D. (2018). Spider: A large-scale human-labeled dataset for complex and cross-domain semantic parsing and text-to-sql task. In *EMNLP*.

Zelle, J. M. and Mooney, R. J. (1996). Learning to parse database queries using inductive logic programming. In *Proceedings of the Thirteenth National Conference on Artificial Intelligence - Volume 2*, AAAI'96, pages 1050–1055. AAAI Press.

Zettlemoyer, L. S. and Collins, M. (2005). Learning to map sentences to logical form: Structured classification with probabilistic categorial grammars. In *Proceedings of the Twenty-First Conference on Uncertainty in Artificial Intelligence*, UAI'05, page 658–666, Arlington, Virginia, USA. AUAI Press.

Zhong, V., Xiong, C., and Socher, R. (2017). Seq2sql: Generating structured queries from natural language using reinforcement learning. *CoRR*, abs/1709.00103.

Proceedings of the WILDRE-6 Workshop @LREC2020, pages 74–79
Marseille, 20 June 2022

Automatic Identification of Explicit Connectives in Malayalam

Kumari Sheeja S, Sobha Lalitha Devi
AU-KBC Research Centre, MIT Campus of Anna University, Chennai, India
{sheeja,sobha}@au-kbc.org

Abstract

This work presents an automatic identification of explicit connectives and its arguments using supervised method, Conditional Random Fields (CRFs). In this work, we focus on the identification of connectives and their arguments in the corpus. We consider explicit connectives and its arguments for the present study. The corpus we have considered has 4,000 sentences from Malayalam documents and manually annotated the corpus for POS, chunk, clause, discourse connectives and its arguments. The corpus thus annotated is used for building the base engine. The percentage of the performance of the system is evaluated based on the precision, recall and F-score and obtained encouraging results. We have analysed the errors generated by the system and used the features obtained from the anlaysis to improve the performance of the system.

Keywords: discourse, machine learning, discourse relations, conditional random fields, malayalam, NLP

1. Introduction

Discourse analysis is concerned with analysing how phrase, clause and sentence level units of text are related to each other within the larger unit of text. Discourse structure in the documents are important in discourse analysis because it makes the text coherent and meaningful. The pre-processing module also contains the Part of Speech (POS), Chunking and NER which are the essential tool for information retrieval and question answering system. Connectives can be inter or intra sentential. Inter sentential connective occupies the initial position of the sentence which is considered as the one of the argument of the connective and the other argument in the previous sentence. The intra sentential connective appears within the sentence and the two arguments are the main and subordinate clause of the sentence. The clause which follows the connective is the second argument and the other clause is the first argument. The process of discourse annotation involves tokenization and tagging of POS, Chunk and NER using various tag sets.We also annotated the corpus in terms of more basic characterization of discourse structure in terms of identifying discourse connectives in the text and annotating their arguments with semantics. Finally we developed a system for the identification of connectives and their arguments using Machine Learning Technique CRF.

2. Related Work

The annotation study for discourse relations in Arabic (Al-Saif and Markert, 2010) used Machine learning algorithms for automatically identifying explicit discourse connectives and its relations in Arabic language. The sense annotation and sense ambiguities of discourse connectives (Miltsakaki et al., 2005) used syntactic features and simple MaxEnt model and identified several features helped in disambiguation of the connectives since, when and while. (Elwell and Baldridge, 2008) improved the system performance using models for specific connectives and the types of connectives and interpolating them with a general model by using maximum entropy rankers. The work on tagging German discourse connectives using English training data and a German– English parallel corpus (Versley, 2010) and an approach to transfer a tagger for English discourse connectives by annotation projection using a freely accessible list of connectives. This system obtained the F-score of 68.7% for the identification of discourse relations. (Webber et al., 2016) Showed the further procedure of more frequent annotation of more than one discourse relation between the same pair of spans. PDTB annotation also mentioned about another possible source of multiple discourse relations holding concurrently in large corpus. A lexicon of English discourse connectives called DiMLex-Eng (Das et al., 2018) compiled from a lexicon of German discourse connectives DiMLex which focused on modifications to the sense classification of discourse relation in Hindi and comparison based on some initial annotations. (Sobha et al., 2014) used the health domain corpus for the purpose of analysing the discourse connectives and its arguments for languages Hindi, Tamil and Malayalam. They have also presented an automatic discourse relation identifier for the languages Hindi, Tamil and Malayalam (Sobha et al., 2017).

(Faiz and Mercer, 2013) considered the problem of identifying explicit discourse connectives in text using applied machine learning. They used syntactic features to build maximum entropy classifiers for better performance. (Patterson and Kehler, 2013) developed a system for predicting the presence of discourse connectives using classification model. It focused on contrast relation which is the type with lowest model accuracy. An unsupervised approach (Marcu & Echihabi, 2002) to recognize discourse relations that hold between arbitrary spans of texts and show that discourse relation classifiers that use very simple features achieve unexpectedly high levels of performance when trained on extremely large datasets. (Rysova, 2018) introduced the constraints and preferences in the use of discourse connectives in the written Czech texts. An automated system for the identification of arguments of discourse connectives (Wellner & Pustejovsky, 2007) used head based representation for identification of arguments and used re-ranking model for modelling the arguments. Chinese discourse structure (Li et al., 2013) used the advantages of the tree structure from RST and connective from PDTB. Chinese Discourse Tree Bank is developed from 500 Xinhua Newswire documents and employed top-down strategy. Turkish Corpus (Zeyerk and Webber, 2008) based on the principles of PDTB and determined the set of explicit discourse connectives and the syntactic classes. Coordinating and subordinating are not classes in Turkish and most of the existing grammars of Turkish describe clausal adjuncts and adverbs in semantic rather than syntactic terms.

This work proposes an identification of connectives and arguments in the corpus using the machine learning technique CRFs. Malayalam is a morphologically rich Dravidian language spoken in India. It is a highly inflectional and agglutinative language. It has very different writing style where two or three words are joined together. Features used are rich linguistic features such as suffixes of words, POS, Chunk, Clauses, Connectives and its arguments. The focus of the study is to identify the connectives and its arguments in our corpus. Here Section 3 describes the corpus collection and annotation process. Section 4 describes the method used to develop the system. Feature selection is described in Section 5. The results are discussed in Section 6 and the conclusion is presented in section 7.

3. Corpus Collection and Annotation

A corpus from tourism website consists of 4000 sentences and 47,897 tokens. We have developed the system using machine learning technique CRFs. The training corpus consist of 39,046 tokens and and the testing corpus consists of 8851 tokens. We developed the corpus annotated with discourse connective along with binary arguments by following the guidelines of PDTB (Prasad et al., 2008), a large-scale resource of annotated discourse relations and their arguments. The first argument is tagged as<ARG1> and </ARG1>,the second argument as <ARG2> and </ARG2> and the connective as <CON> and </CON>. The tag sets used for connective and argument identification is described in Table 1.

Sl. No.	Main Tags	Labels
1	Connective begin	<CON>
2	Connective end	</CON>
3	Argument1 begin	<ARG1>
4	Argument1 end	</ARG1>
5	Argument2 begin	<ARG2>
6	Argument2 end	</ARG2>

Table 1: Tag sets-connectives and arguments

In our corpus, the connectives that do not occur as free words were considered to be part of arg1 and the other relation will be arg2. As Malayalam is free word order and inflectional, it consists of many connectives are morphemes and these type of connectives occur intra-sentential. The discourse relation in our corpus can be syntactic (a suffix) or lexical. Discourse relations can be within a clause, inter-clausal or inter-sentential. Examples of annotation of connectives and its arguments are given in example 1 and example 2.

Example 1:

[shareera vedhana kurakkaan idakkide vedhana

body pain decrease frequently pain

samharikal upayogich**aal<con><cont-cond>]** </arg1>

killer use+**if**

[athu arogyathe dosham cheyyum]/</arg2>

that health harm do

(**If** pain killers are used frequently for body pain, it will be harmful to our health)

In Example 1, the first argument and the second argument are marked as <arg1> and <arg2>.The connective is "**aal**" and it is a subordinate connective and if we take the first argument independently, "shareera vedhana kurakkaan idakkide vedhana samharikal upayogich**aal<con>**" (If pain killers are used frequently for body pain), it will be meaningless. So the use of connectives for relating the arguments makes the text more coherent in the corpus.

Example 2:

[aavaSyaththinu uRakkam kiTTAthe varum**pOL]**</arg1>

enough sleep not+ getting

[SarIraththinu kshINam anubhavappeTunnu]</arg2>

Body tiredness experiencing

(When we do not sleep properly, it leads to body tiredness.)

In Example 2, the verb "varum" (will+come) is combined with the connective **'mpoL' (when),** occur intra-sentential and connects the main clause with the adverbial clause. This representation of the connectives and arguments bring coherence in corpus.

The causal relation is characterized by the cause, the effect and a causal marker. The marker indicates the presence of a causal relation. The cause is the event that has an effect and it acts as a reason for another event to happen. At the discourse level, the causal discourse connective connects two discourse units, arg1 and arg2. The clause that follows the connective is arg2 and the other clause is arg1. The arg2 acts as the reason for the event occurred in arg1.

Example 3:

[Ramuvinu nalla Ormashakthiyundu,] /arg1 **athu kond <con>**

Ramu good memory power so

[avanu pareekshayil mikachcha pragadanam nadaththaan kazhiyum]/arg2

He examination well can+perform

(Ramu has good memory power, **so <con>** he can perform well in the examination.)

The connective "so" in the Example 3 shows "result" relation between two units, where the event in second discourse unit is the result of event in first discourse unit. Here, "Ramuvinu nalla Ormashakthiyundu" (He has good memory power) is the cause and "avanu pareekshayil mikachcha pragadanam nadaththaan kazhiyum"(he can perform well in the examination) is the effect of the cause.

4. Method

The method adopted here uses the machine learning technique CRFs. CRFs uses syntactic and semantic features. These features are obtained by analysing the data. The syntactic features include the suffixes for the words, part of speech, chunk and the clause boundaries and the semantic features include the connective markers and arguments of the connectives.

4.1 Syntactic Pre-Processing

Pre-processing of the text is required as syntactic and semantic information are required for any high level analysis. The pre-processing modules impart the above two information to the text so that the text will have the necessary information required for high end analysis. Syntactic pre-processing is the next step in text analysis after the preliminary processing of sentence splitting and tokenizing. We used the following syntactic pre-preprocessing techniques for developing the connectives and its argument identification of the corpus.

POS Tagger: Part of Speech tagger disambiguates the multiple parse given by the morphological analyser, using the context in which a word occurs. It is the process of tagging the word in a text tagged with its corresponding part of speech such as noun, verb, adjective, adverb, etc. The Part of speech tagger is developed using the machine learning technique Conditional Random fields (CRF++). The features used for machine learning is a set of linguistic suffix features along with statistical suffixes and uses a window of 3 words. The tag set used for developing the POS tagger BIS tag set. These tag sets indicate syntactic classification like noun or verb, and sometimes include additional information, with case markers (number, gender etc.) and tense markers.

Noun Chunk: Chunking is the task of grouping grammatically related words into chunks such as noun phrase, verb phrase, adjectival phrase etc. The system is developed using the feature POS tag, word and window of 5 words.

Clause boundary: Clause is the smallest grammatical unit that has a subject and predicate and expresses a proposition. In Malayalam the subordinate clauses are formed using non-finite verbs. Non-finite verbs are verbs which cannot perform action as the root of an independent clause. The subject of a clause can be explicit or implicit as this language has the subject drop phenomena. In this system we identify the following clauses: Main clause (MC), Relative participle clause (RPC), Conditional clause (CONC), Infinitive clause (INFC), Non-finite clause (NFC), Complementizer clause (COMC). The system is a hybrid system using ML(CRFs) and Linguistic rules combined. The CRFs are trained using annotated corpus and uses linguistic features such as suffix, POS and chunk for learning and mark the beginning and end of a clause. The clause boundary identification depends on word, morphological information and chunk. As begin and end boundaries of the clause matches with the chunk boundaries, chunk boundaries are an important feature of clause boundary identification.

4.2 Semantic Pre-Processing

Once the syntactic pre-processing of the text is over, the system will attempt to produce the logical form of the sentence. The semantic pre-processing is required to ascertain the meaning of the sentence. We used the following semantic pre-preprocessing techniques for developing the system for the identification of explicit connectives and its arguments.

4.2.1 Connective identifier

Connectives are grammatical features such as "but", "whereas", which connect two discourse units semantically. The discourse units are called arguments of the connectives. Thus connectives connect two arguments to bring in coherence to the discourse. The discourse unit or the arguments can be intra or inter sentential. If it is intra sentential, it connects the clauses with in a sentence and if it is inter sentential then it connects two sentences.

4.2.2 Discourse argument

The assignment of arguments is syntactic in this work. The arguments can be in the same sentence as the connective or can be outside in the immediately preceding sentence. It is also observed that the argument can be a non-adjacent sentence. But the text span follows the minimality-principle. The position of argument start is on the start of the sentence and this may vary depending on the connectivity with the previous sentence. We used the ML technique CRFs for identifying the beginning and end of each argument.

Example 4 :

[naTuvEdanakku pala kAraNangngaL uNT.] </arg1>

Backpain many reasons are+ there

athinAl<con>

therefore

[yathArththa kAraNam kaNTeththi

Real reason to+be+finding+out

chikilsikkukayANu vENTath.]</arg2>

to+do+treatment

(There are many reasons for back pain. **So** treatment should be taken based on the real reason.)

In Example 4, the connective **"athinaal" (therefore),** occurs inter-sentential by connecting two sentences. Connectives occur at the initial position in the second argument. We see that the connectives are explicitly realizing relations between two arguments arg1 and arg2.

5. Feature selection

Feature selection plays an important role in machine Learning and the learning depends on the features and hence the system's performance. A set of linguistic features are used for identification of connectives and its arguments. The features are discussed below.

5.1 Features for Connective Classification

For connective identification, we used lexical and syntactic features such as word, POS, chunk, clause and their combinations. The connectives which link groups of words together are mostly conjunction and hence POS features for the identification of connectives is important. Chunk feature segments a sentence into sequence of syntactic constituents and hence it helps to identify the boundary of the connectives and arguments. As connective links clauses or sentences, clause beginning and end of the corpus is used as feature for connective identification.

A baseline system is developed for the identification of connectives using word as feature. Features such as word, POS, chunk, combination of word, POS and chunk and clause are used for developing an extended system. The connective identification for baseline system is performed with minimal features. While developing the baseline system, we considered the first word as one of the features and obtained the f-score as 76.04%. Using word and POS features, we obtained the f-score as 83.47%. This improves the f-score by 7.43%. The inclusion of the chunk feature improves the result by 3.87%. Addition of Clause boundary improves the result by 5.74% and obtained the f-score as 93.08% descibed in Table 2.

Corpus	Word	Word+ POS	Word +POS +Chunk	Word+POS+ Chunk +Clause Boundary
Connectives	76.04	83.47	87.34	93.08

Table 2 : Feature-wise f-measure of connectives

5.2 Features for Argument Identification

The arguments of the connective are also clauses, clause tagging also helps in the identification of the argument boundaries arg1 and arg2. Connectives are used as the key feature in identification of argument boundary. The start and end position of the sentence with respect to the connective are also used as the feature for the identification of arguments. In inter sentential relation, arg1 start and end will be the start and end of the previous sentence of the connective word. The start of arg2 will be after the connective and end of arg2 will be the end of the same sentence. In intra sentential relation, arg2 mostly starts immediately after a connective and ends at the end of the sentence. The arg1 start will be the beginning of the sentence and ends at the clause boundary end in case of intra sentential relation.

Example 5:

[Moonnaar pragrithi souandharyaththinu peru kettathaN] /arg1. **Athinaal<con>**

Munnar scenic beauty known for so [ithu Sthalam sandharshikkan aaLukaLe aakarshikkunnu.]/arg2

it place to visit people attract

(Munnar is known for its scenic beauty. **So** it attracts people to visit the place.)

In the example 5, the connective is inter-sentential, then the end of the preceding sentence is arg1 end, beginning of the preceding sentence is arg1 begin and next token of the connective is arg2 begin, last token of the sentence with connective is arg2 end.

6. Results

In this work, we have used supervised machine-learning approach Conditional Random field for automatically identifying discourse connectives and its arguments of the corpus. This section describes the evaluation and performance of each module using precision, recall and F-score. The evaluation and performance of the system is described using precision, recall, and F-score. For connective identification, we obtained the precision of 92.35%, recall of 93.83% and f-score of 93.08%. The precision of arg1 begin, arg1 end, arg2 begin and arg2 end are 77.81%, 80.14%, 85.53% and 79.28% respectively.

Label	Precision (%)	Recall (%)	F-score (%)
<con>	92.35	93.83	93.08
<arg1>	77.81	79.01	78.39
</arg1>	80.14	83.02	81.54
<arg2>	85.53	87.22	86.35
</arg2>	79.28	80.09	79.69

Table 3: Results of connective and argument identification of corpus

The recall of arg1 begin, arg1 end, arg2 begin and arg2 end are 79.01%, 83.02%, 87.2% and 80.09%. We obtained the f-score of arg1 begin, arg1 end, arg2 begin and arg2 end are 78.39%, 81.54%, 86.35% and 79.67%. This is described in Table3.

The errors generated by the system while classifying the connectives are analysed and the type of errors generated is discussed in the section 6.1.

6.1 Error Analysis

- Some connectives cannot be identified by the system due to some conjunctions identified in POSs which are not connectives and it is not considered as connectives during system identification which affects the performance measures of our system.
- Variation of connective position: Other reasons for occurring errors in the corpus are variation of the position, distribution and sharing of connectives, effect of errors from the previous steps. The connectives such as "allengil"(if+not), "undenkil"(if+so) etc. occur inter or intra sentential depends on the formation of sentence and agglutinative level of the sentence.
- Agglutinative Connective: If corpus contains agglutinative words, system couldn't identify some of the agglutinated connective words which causes error in connective classification. Connectives such as "vannengil" (if+comes), "poyaal" (if+go), "vannappol" (when+did+come) etc. are morpheme connectives where the verbs are found agglutinated with the connectives "engil", "-aal", "-mbol", " appoL" (if+so, if, when etc.). Here both lexical and morphemes can become the connectives.

Example 6:

[naam vedhana samharikaL

We pain killers

amithamaaupayogichaal] /arg1

if+ over+use

[athu aarogyathe dosham cheyyum]/arg2

that health harm will+do

(If we use more pain killers, it will be harmful to our body)

In Example 6, "amithamaaupayogichaal" (if+over+use) is an agglutinated connective word, and the system fails to identify this type of connective during connective classification.

- Multiple sentences with different connective: Sometimes argument may contain multiple sentences bound with different connectives and it is difficult for the system to identify the position of connectives and results in errors. If multiple connectives (intra and inter sentential) occur in the two consecutive sentences, the system correctly tagged the intra-sentential connective and arguments. At the same time, if the inter sentential connective occurs in the next sentence, the system failed to identify the beginning and end of the first argument of inter sentential connective.
- Most of the errors occur in argument identification is variation of the position of arguments, distribution and sharing of arguments and also the effect of errors from the previous steps.
- When the arguments of the connective appear in different sentences, system couldn't identify the argument boundary of the relation.
- The correlative conjunction such as mAthramalla - pakshe(not only –but also), the system generate errors due to the identification of the pair of conjunctions as a single relation. In this situation, the error occurred in the identification of argument boundaries.

Example 7 :

[bhakshaNakramIkaraNam nAm SIlamAkkiyAl
Dieting we practise

athu SarIravaNNam
that body weight

kuRaykkunnathu **mAthramalla**]/arg1.
Reduce not only

[**pakshe** bhAviyil ArOgyaththOTe
But future health

jIvikkukanum vazhiyorukkunnu.]/arg2
also living will+be+ leading

(Dieting in our daily life **not only** reduces our body weight **but also** helps to lead a healthy life in future)

In example 7, **"maathramalla-pakshe" (not only-but also)** is the correlative connective. But the connective **"pakshe" (but)** is dropped in certain cases.

7. Conclusion

In this work, we have used the syntactic features for identifying the connectives and their arguments in our corpus and consider explicit connectives in our corpus to identify the discourse arguments. In identifying connectives and discourse arguments, we use supervised method, Conditional Random Fields (CRFs). We have developed an annotated corpus of POS, chunk, NER, discourse connectives and its arguments of the corpus. We focussed on the identification of explicit connectives and their arguments in the corpus. We have analysed the errors to improve the performance of the system. In future, we can work with other datasets with better features to improve the performance of the system. We can also work with implicit connectives and arguments of our language based on the semantics and the context of the text by providing a word or phrase to express the relation.

8. Bibliographical References

Al-Saif, A. & Markert, K. (2010). The leeds arabic discourse treebank: Annotating discourse connectives for arabic. *In Proceedings of the 7th International Conference on Language Resources and Evaluation (LREC-2010),* ed. Calzolari, N, Choukri, K, Maegaard, B, Mariani, J, Odijk, J, Piperidis, S, Rosner, M & Tapias, D, Valletta, Malta, pp. 2046-2053.

Miltsakaki, E., Dinesh, N., Prasad,R., Joshi, A. & Webber, B. (2005). Experiments on sense annotations and sense disambiguation of discourse connectives. *In Proceedings of the Fourth Workshop on Treebanks and Linguistic Theories*,Spain,Barcelona.

Elwell, R. & Baldridge, J. (2008). Discourse connective argument identification with connective specific rankers. *In Proceedings of the IEEE International Conference on Semantic Computing*, ed. Kawada, S, Santa Monica, CA, USA, pp. 198-205.

Versley, Y. (2010). Discovery of ambiguous and unambiguous discourse connectives via annotation projection. *In Proceedings of Workshop on Annotation and Exploitation of Parallel Corpora (AEPC)*, University of Tartu, Estonia, vol.10, pp. 83-92.

Webber, B., Prasad, R., Lee, A. & Joshi, A. (2016). A discourse-annotated corpus of conjoined VPs. *In Proceedings 10th Linguistic Annotation Workshop, Association for Computational Linguistics,* Berlin, Germany, pp. 22–31.

Das, D., Scheffler, T. Bourgonje, P. & Stede, M. (2018). Constructing a lexicon of English discourse connectives. *In Proceedings of SIGDIAL 2018 Conference, Association for Computational Linguistics,* Melbourne, Australia,pp. 360–365.

Sobha, L., Lakshmi, S. & Gopalan, S. (2014). Discourse tagging for Indian Languages. *In Proceedings of CICLing 2014, Springer,* Berlin, Heidelberg, vol 8403, pp. 469-480.

Sobha, L., Sindhuja, G. &.Lakshmi, S. (2017). Cross linguistic variations in discourse relations among indian languages. *In Proceedings of the 14th International*

Conference on Natural Language Processing, NLP Association of India, Kolkata, India, pp. 402-407.

Faiz, S. I., & Mercer, R. E, (2013). Identifying explicit discourse connectives in text. *Advances in Artificial Intelligence, Springer*, Berlin, Heidelber, vol 7884. pp.64-76.

Patterson, G. & Kehler, A.(2013). Predicting the presence of discourse connectives. *In Preceedings of conference on Emperical Methods in Natural Language Processing*, Association for Computational Linguistics,Seattle, Washington, USA, pp. 914–923..

Marcu, D. & Echihabi, A. (2002). An unsupervised approach to recognizing discourse relations. *In Proceedings of the 40th Annual Meeting of the Association for Computational Linguistics*, Philadelphia, Pennsylvania, USA, pp. 368-375.

Rysova, M. & Rysova, K. (2018). Primary and secondary discourse connectives: Constraints and preferences. *Journal of Pragmatics,* vol. 130, pp.16-32.

Wellner, B. & Pustejovsky, J. (2007). Automatically identifying the arguments of discourse connectives. *In Proceedings of the Joint Conference on Empirical Methods in Natural Language Processing and Computational Natural Language Learning*, Association of Computational linguistics, Prague, pp. 92–101.

Li, Y., Feng, W., & Zhou, G. (2013). Elementary discourse unit in chinese discourse structure analysis. Chinese lexical semantics, Lecture Notes in Computer Science, vol. 7717, pp. 186-198.

Prasad, R., Dinesh, N., Lee, A., Miltsakaki, E., Robaldo, L., Joshi, A. & Webber,B. (2008). The penn discourse treebank2.0. *In Proceedings of the Sixth International Conference on Language Resources and Evaluation*.

Zeyerk, D. & Webber, B. (2008). A discourse resource for turkish: annotating discourse connectives in the METU corpus. *In Proceedings of the 6th Workshop on Asian Language Resources*, Hyderabad, India, pp. 65-72.

Proceedings of the WILDRE-6 Workshop @LREC2020, pages 80–83
Marseille, 20 June 2022

Web-based System for Derivational Process of Kṛdanta based on Pāṇinian Grammatical Tradition

Sumit Sharma, Subhash Chandra
Ph.D. Research Scholar, Assistant Professor
Department of Sanskrit, University of Delhi
New Delhi-110007, India
Sumitpunjab96@gmail.com, schandra@sanskrit.du.ac.in

Abstract

Each text of the Sanskrit literature is wadded with the uses of Sanskrit kṛdanta (participles). The knowledge and formation process of Sanskrit kṛdanta play a key role in understanding the meaning of a particular kṛdanta word in Sanskrit. Without proper analysis of the kṛdanta, the Sanskrit text cannot be understood. Currently, the model of Sanskrit learning is traditional classroom teaching which is accessible to the students but not to general Sanskrit learners. The acute growth of Information Technology (IT) is changed the educational pedagogy and web-based learning systems evolved to enhance the teaching-learning process. Though many online tools are being developed by researchers for Sanskrit these are still scarce and untasted. Globe genuinely demands the high-impacted tools for Sanskrit. Undoubtedly, Sanskrit kṛdanta is part of the syllabus of all universities offering Sanskrit courses. Approximately 100 plus kṛt suffixes are added with verb roots to generate kṛdanta forms and due to complexity, learning these forms is a challenging task. Therefore, the objective of the paper is to present an online system for teaching the derivational process of kṛdantas based on Pāṇinian rules and generate a complete derivational process of the kṛdantas for teaching and learning. It will also provide a platform for e-learning for the derivational process of Sanskrit kṛdantas.

Keywords : Computation and Digital Access of Sanskrit Grammar, kṛdanta, Pāṇinian Grammatical Tradition, Sanskrit Grammar, Derivational Process.

1. Background and Introduction

Sanskrit grammar is exigent to develop an elementary understanding of the ancient Indian philosophy, religious views, social issues, community laws, etc. as they are indicted in the Sanskrit language. Disparate grammars based on Sanskrit have been authored, but *Pāṇinīan* grammar *Aṣṭādhyāyī* (AD) is considered to be cardinal. It is a model of exhaustive grammar for any natural language yet small enough to memorize (Kulkarni, Sanskrit and Computational Linguistics, 2007). As the name of the AD suggests itself, there are eight chapters in AD (Pandey, 2017). Each chapter of AD is further divided into four sub-chapters, so there are a total of 32 (8*4) sub-chapters in AD. It consists of about 4000 aphoristic rules, which are called *sūtras*. Written in less than 4000 *sūtras*, this grammar structure is similar to that of a modern computer programming language. AD contains special sections on the phonological changes, morphological generator (Kulkarni & Shukl, Sanskrit morphological analyzer: Some issues, 2009), syntax, and semantics. The rule of *kṛt* suffixes is discussed in chapter third and other operational rules related to the derivational process of *kṛt* are discussed in the fourth and fifth chapters.

Around 1,190 *sūtras* are dealing with secondary nouns derived by *taddhita* suffixes and 631 *sūtras* are dealing with secondary nouns derived by *kṛt* suffixes. In this way, 1,821 i.e almost half of AD's *sūtras* discuss the derivational process of secondary nouns derived by *taddhita* and *kṛt* suffixes. The sixth, seventh and eighth chapters refer to the phonological changes that occur in the word's phonemes. These changes are either due to the addition of suffixes to the root word/verb or due to the sandhi. From the fourth sub-chapter of the sixth chapter to the end of the seventh chapter, there is a specific subject called *aṃgādhikāra*, which describes the changes that occur in the root words due to the suffix or in the suffix due to the root word. These changes are also seen as phonological changes. *Kātyāyanamuni* wrote 4300 *vārtikas* and *maharṣi Patañjali* wrote *Mahābhāṣya* on these *sūtras* of AD. Together they are called the *Trimuni* of Sanskrit Grammar. Albeit, based on their compositions, an infinite number of scholars wrote multiple scriptures and commentaries, yet, it is very challenging to understand Sanskrit grammar in the sequence of AD. This technical complexity diminished the understanding capabilities of the learners. Therefore, an emergent need for procedural texts, in which the different *sūtras* of AD were classified into different topics based on the subjects like Sandhi, *samāsa,* karaka, etc. to enhance understanding, and grasping of the concepts and kept in order with the point of view of their potential use. Keeping this in mind, a grammarian named *Bhaṭṭojidīkṣita* composed a procedural text called *Vaiyākaraṇasiddhāntakaumudī*. His disciple *Varadarāja* wrote the texts named *Madhyasiddhāntakaumudī* and *Laghusiddhāntakaumudī* in the concise form of the aforementioned text. Presently, the teaching-learning method (Chandra, Kumar, Sakshi, & Kumar, 2017) of Sanskrit grammar is of two types - ancient and modern. Where in ancient grammar, the *Kashika, Mahabhashya*, etc. are read and taught in the AD sequence, whereas, in the modern grammar, various subjects are taught through procedural texts like *vaiyākaraṇasiddhāntakaumudī, laghusiddhāntakaumudī, madhyasiddhāntakaumudī*, etc.

2. Scope and Objective of the Paper

AD is opined and envisaged as the idol grammar written in any language by scholars of Sanskrit and linguistics in India and abroad. *kṛdanta* words use and derivational process are precisely taught as a component subject at undergraduate and postgraduate levels in all major universities worldwide having Sanskrit or Indic languages departments and Sanskrit Universities. According to the sutra, *'kṛdatiṅ'* except the 18 tiṅ suffixes all those suffixes prescribed from the main verb is called kṛt, i.e., all those nominal words derived from the verbs are *kṛdanta* (Singh & Jha, Primary Derivational process in Sanskrit: A Computational Approach to Analysis of *Kridanta,* 2011). Hereby, without any verb phrase in Sanskrit sentence behavior becomes possible only with *kṛdanta* words like- *snānīyam cūrṇam*, etc. according to AD, there are hundreds of kṛt suffixes which represent different situations and conditions. But it is also not necessary that all the *kṛdanta* words should be used as verbs. Most are used as nominal words even some *kṛt* suffixes denote the meaning of helping verbs, and prepositions too. So, it is clear that *kṛdanta* words are superabundantly used in Sanskrit texts. Without the knowledge of *kṛt* suffixes, Sanskrit texts cannot be understood. Consequently, identifying and analyzing these *kṛdanta* words is exacting.

In today's era of globalization of information technology, where the entire world is connected by a click of a button, world news is generated, accessible, and received through web organizations. There has also been a change in the medium of exchange of knowledge traditions. Online tools and content have taken the place of traditional access to the content. There is a lot of deficiency in the Sanskrit language. Many institutions are working to bring Sanskrit on the platform yet, to date, any online derivational process system for secondary nouns is not available where a person can find a complete derivational process of the given secondary noun as an output.

The purpose of this paper is to develop an online system for the analysis and derivational process according to AD by digitizing the *sūtras* related to *kṛdanta.* Through which anyone can easily solve their doubts and queries online related to the *kṛdanta* words according to *Pāṇinīan* grammar. As of now, the system accepts input in Devanagari and generates output in Devanagari.

Figure 1: User Interface

3. Data Collection and Digitization

The morphological analyzer and generator System is a web-based system for kṛdanta words, Sūtras of AD and vārtikas of Kātyāyana are stored in a text file/database with its reference, meaning, type, and explanation in UTF-8 format in Devanagari script. The sūtras and vārtikas are digitized, proofread, and stored in text files. Around 600 Sūtras of AD-related to kṛdanta are digitalized. The entire programming of the developed system is based on the pāṇinīya grammatical tradition (Pandeya & Pandeya, 1938).

3.1 Databases and Rules

The system uses various rules and databases to execute the result. Major rule files are listed below:

1. **Kṛt Recognition Rules**: It contains two major rules one is verb roots database and the other is recognition rules. The sample is shown in Tables 1 and 2.

MainRootVerb	kṛtDhatu
भू	भू
भू	भव
भू	भाव
ष्वद्	स्वद
ष्वद्	स्वाद
षूद्	सूद्

Table 1: verb roots database

SR	Start	Mid	End	Suffix
1		ि	तव्य	तव्यत्
2			तव्य	तव्यत्
3		ि	तव्य	तव्य
4			तव्य	तव्य
5			णीय	अनीयर्
6			नीय	अनीयर्
7			एलिम	केलिमर्

Table 2: recognition rules

2. **Kṛt Siddhi Generation Rules:** It contains two major rules one *kṛt* siddhi generation rules and the other AD rules. The sample is shown in Tables 3 and 4.

RecCode	Rule
तव्य_2_RB	Rule_01254#VF+तव्य Rule_153#VF+तव्य Rule_151#VF+तव्य Rule_157#VF+तव्य Rule_2541#VF+ितव्य Rule_0#
तव्यत्_1_RB	Rule_1308#VF+तव्यत् Rule_1254#VF+तव्यत् Rule_153#VF+तव्यत् Rule_151#VF+तव्यत् Rule_157#VF+ तव्य Rule_2541#VF+ितव्य Rule_0#
यत्_1_EB	Rule_1254#VF+यत् Rule_153#VF+यत् Rule_151#VF+यत् Rule_157#VF+यत् Rule_3441#MF+य Rule_2541#MF+ेय Rule_0#

Table 3: kṛt siddhi generation rules

AD-SR	RULE	MEAN	TYPE	WORK
3.1.93	कृदतिङ्		सञ्ज्ञा	
3.1.94	वाऽसरूपोऽस्त्रियाम्		परिभाषा	
3.1.95	कृत्याः		अधिकार	
3.1.96	तव्यत्तव्यानीयरः		विधि	
3.1.97	अचो यत्		विधि	
3.1.98	पोरदुपधात्		विधि	
3.1.99	शकिसहोश्च		विधि	

3.2 Computational Platform and Techniques

The online derivational process system for words ending with *kṛt* suffixes is a cohesive mechanism as it works with the help of many small self-built digital components. To develop the system, computational rules were developed for analysis and derivational processes based on the *sūtras* of AD. The major components are User Interface, Preprocessor, Analyzer, Output Generator, and Table Generator. The computational environment for developing this morphological mechanism was created through building various databases and modules.\

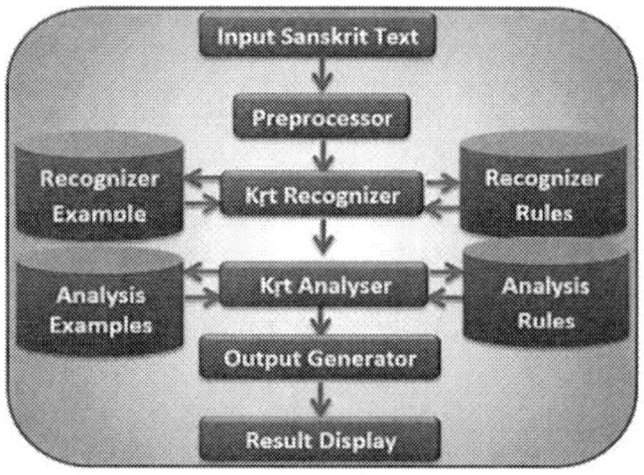

Figure 2: Flow Chart of the System

Databases and Text files are used for storing the data and rules. Any web-based system has two major parts: Front-End and Back-End. The front-end is developed using HTML, CSS, and JS codes embedded in HTML codes for page decoration and beautification of the User Interface. The back-end contains a lot of programming languages, databases, and servers. For this, the Python programming language, Text files, and Flask as a server have been used.

3.3 Methodology

The elevated system is an input-output generating system. It works with a reverse *Pāṇinian* approach. The methodology accepted to create a database is clearly in line with the well-defined and structured process of AD stated by *Pāṇini*. It takes input from the user and generates the corresponding output. The user can give input in Hindi (Devanagari). Once the input is given, a lot of self-built functions work simultaneously to give the output. The preprocessor initially runs the query at the back end syncing it with the digital analyzer. Then the following query is searched one by one from different databases and the corresponding result is generated. The generated result is formatted according to the users' query input and then displayed on the client's end. The methodology can be understood in Figure 1.

4. Major Features of the Developed System

The developed system has a very user-friendly and easy approach. This web-based matured system consists of a variety of features, it accepts the input query in Devanagari UTF-8 format. It further has the scope for creating multi-script input systems such as Ròman, Gurumukhi, etc. Since the system is available online, it is widely accessible. *Kṛdanta* analyzer is a key feature of this system. We get the analysis of the given word as the main verb + suffixes added in the word. The main verb and suffix are also hyperlinked with their specifications like the verb's meaning, *gaṇa,* etc. The complete derivational process according to AD is the major highlight of this system. The whole process is quick and error-free. The system works on Rule and example base, which is similar to *Pāṇini's utsarga* and *apavāda* method. All digitize *sūtras/ vārtikas* are hyperlinked with their meaning and explanation in Hindi. The entire system will be available for public access over the web. Users can get a derivational process by using it from anywhere at any time.

5. Proposed Result and Future Direction

Kṛdanta analyzer and generator is a very useful system in teaching-learning pedagogies (Chandra, Kumar, Sakshi, & Kumar, 2017) for students, teachers, or researchers for immediate analysis or derivational process. In Sanskrit grammar derivational process has a key role in determining the meaning of any word because different suffixes conjoined with verbs denote exclusive meanings. So, learners can enhance their Sanskrit learning skills by assimilating the information, which can be easily obtained on this system. As this system is developed for E-learning, so it will be available 24*7 and with help of this system, more and more interested persons can receive education according to their desire and convenience. Users can get the *sūtras* used in the derivational process along with their AD number, Hindi meaning, type, and as well as explanation. Therefore, any teacher can easily teach this aspect by this system in online or offline mode. Currently, this system is under development. The prototype of the system has been developed. In the future, it is planned to make a morphological analyzer and generator for all major parts of *pāṇinīya* grammar such as *ṇijanta, yaṅanta, subanta* (Chandra, Sanskrit Subanta Recognizer and Analyzer, 2006), *sanādyanta, samāsa, sandhi, taddhita,* etc. Later on, the separate morphological analyzers can be combined into a single system of sentence analysis with karaka elucidation. This system is developed only for Hindi medium and Devnagari script. Developing this system further can be outbid for input/output in other languages and scripts like Sanskrit, English, Punjabi, Bangla, Tamil, Telugu, Roman, Gurumukhi, etc. It is hoped that this web-equipped system will play an important role in the Digital India scheme and new education policy run by the Government of India in the field of education. Also, in the field of e-learning, it will prove to be very useful for teachers and learners. It can be hortative for Computational Linguists.

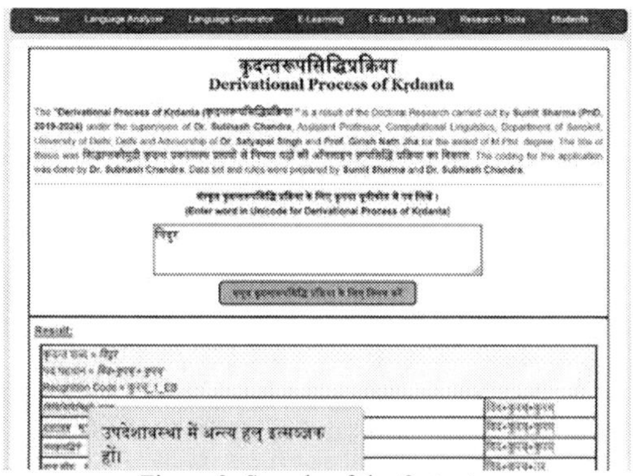

Figure 3: Sample of the Output

6. Bibliographical References

Singh, S. K. (2008). Kridanta recognition and processing for Sanskrit. . *M.Phil. Dissertation*. New Delhi, India: School for Sanskrit and Indic Studies, Jawaharlal Nehru University.

Briggs, R. (1985). Knowledge Representation in Sanskrit and Artificial Intelligence. *AI Magazine, 6(1)*.

Chakraborty, S. (2021). The Role of Specific Grammar for Interpretation in Sanskrit. *Journal of Research in Humanities and Social Science, 9(2)*, 107-187.

Chandra, S. (2006). Sanskrit Subanta Recognizer and Analyzer. *M.Phil. Dissertation*. New Delhi, India: School of Sanskrit and Indic Studies, Jawaharlal Nehru University.

Chandra, S., Kumar, V., Sakshi, & Kumar, B. (2017). Innovative Teaching and Learning of Sanskrit Grammar through SWAGATAM (स्वगतम्). *Language in India, 17*(1), 378-391.

Chaudhary, A. (2018). *Vaiyākaraṇasiddhāntakaumudī.* Jaipur: Jagdish Sanskrit Pustakalya.

Govindacharya. (2011). *vaiyākaraṇasiddhāntakaumudī śrīdharamukhollāsinī hindī vyākhyā samanvitā .* Banaras: Chaukhamba Subharati Prakashan.

Jha, G. N., Aggarwal, M., Chandra, S., Mishra, S. K., Mani, D., Mishra, D., . . . Singh, S. K. (2007). Inflectional Morphology Analyzer for Sanskrit. *First International Symposium on Sanskrit Computational Linguistics*, (pp. 47-66). Paris, France.

Kulkarni, A. (2007). Sanskrit and Computational Linguistics. *First International Sanskrit Computational Symposium*, (pp. 1-11). Paris.

Kulkarni, A., & Shukl, D. (2009). Sanskrit morphological

Proceedings of the WILDRE-6 Workshop @LREC2020, pages 84–89
Marseille, 20 June 2022

Universal Dependency Treebank for Odia Language

Shantipriya Parida[1], Kalyanamalini Sahoo[2], Atul Kr. Ojha[3], Saraswati Sahoo[4], Satya Ranjan Dash[5] and Bijayalaxmi Dash[6]
[1]Silo AI, Helsinki, Finland
[2]University of Lille, France
[3]Insight Centre for Data Analytics, DSI, NUI, Galway, Ireland
[4]Institute of Mathematics and Applications, India
[5]KIIT University, Bhubaneswar, India
[6]Ravenshaw University, Cuttack, India
shantipriya.parida@silo.ai, kalyanamalini.shabadi@univ-lille.fr, atulkumar.ojha@insight-centre.org, sahoosaraswati455@gmail.com, sdashfca@kiit.ac.in, rudrabijayalaxmi@gmail.com

Abstract

This paper presents the first publicly available treebank of Odia, a morphologically rich low resource Indian language. The treebank contains approx. 1082 tokens (100 sentences) in Odia selected from "Samantar", the largest available parallel corpora collection for Indic languages. All the selected sentences are manually annotated following the "Universal Dependency (UD)" guidelines. The morphological analysis of the Odia treebank was performed using machine learning techniques. The Odia annotated treebank will enrich the Odia language resource and will help in building language technology tools for cross-lingual learning and typological research. We also build a preliminary Odia parser using a machine learning approach. The accuracy of the parser is 86.6% Tokenization, 64.1% UPOS, 63.78% XPOS, 42.04% UAS and 21.34% LAS. Finally, the paper briefly discusses the linguistic analysis of the Odia UD treebank.

Keywords: Universal Dependency, Odia UD Treebank, UPOS tags

1. Introduction

Odia (earlier known as Oriya) is an Indian language belonging to the Indo-Aryan branch of the Indo-European language family. It is the predominant language of the Indian state of Odisha. Odia is written in Odia script, which is a Brahmic script. There are 37 million Odia speakers in India.[1] Odia is one of the many official languages of India and is designated as a Classical language.

Odia is an agglutinative language (Sahoo, 2001), and hence, a morphologically rich language. Odia's verb morphology is rich with a three-tier tense system, person, number, and honorific markers. The prototypical word order is subject-object-verb (SOV) (Parida et al., 2020a; Parida et al., 2020b). Odia nominal morphology differentiates between plural and singular numbers; case marking on nouns; first, second, and third-person pronouns. But it does not have grammatical gender marking, which reduces the complexities of learning the language. Odia language allows Noun-verb, Adjective-verb, and Verb-verb compounding but does not allow elision. It has 28 consonants, 6 vowels, 9 diphthongs, and 4 semivowel phonemes. Most vowels can be short or long, and care must be taken to remember that the length of the vowel changes the word meaning completely. Odia's vocabulary is influenced by Sanskrit and also a little influence from Arabic, Persian, and Austronesian languages as the Kalinga empire (Odisha's ancient name) was connected to different other kingdoms.[2]

Odia language lacks online content and resources for natural language processing (NLP) research.

Unlike Treebanks of widely accepted languages such as English, Mandarin, Hindi, and Spanish for Natural Language Processing applications, applications based on low resource language like Odia is stagnated due to low resources. This paper is one step toward providing resources for such a low resource language. To start with we have worked on making a treebank in the Odia language. This project will surely help the Odia community and NLP researchers in providing resources for NLP applications.

2. Odia Language Grammar

Odia is an SOV language. Usually, a simple sentence begins with a subject and ends with a finite verb. The major word classes found in Odia are nouns, pronouns, verbs, adjectives, and postpositions. Certain minor categories like classifiers, complementizers, and conjunctions are also found. The objects occur between the subject and the verb, the Indirect Object precedes the Direct Object. The modifier precedes the item it modifies: the adjective precedes the substantive it qualifies, and the adverb precedes the verb. Although scrambling is allowed, usually, the word-order sticks to the V-final constructions except for poetic inversion (Sahoo, 2001).

Declension Odia has two numbers: singular and plural; and three persons: 1st person, 2nd person, and 3rd person. The subject NP agrees with the verb in person, number, and honorific. Honorificity goes along with person and number and it is marked in various word classes like nouns, pronouns, verbs, and, interestingly enough, with some of the post-positions that function as genitive, locative, and ablative markers. Generally, the person-number suffixes also go together.

There are eight cases in Odia: nominative, accusative, in-

[1]https://censusindia.gov.in/2011Census/Language_MTs.html

[2]https://www.nriol.com/indian-languages/oriya-page.asp

strumental, dative, ablative, genitive, locative, and vocative. Except for the nominative case, all the other cases are marked morphologically.
Phonologically, there is no distinction in the form of a word in masculine, feminine, or neuter gender in Odia. E.g. *pua* 'son' (masc), *jhia* 'daughter' (fem), *phaLa* 'fruit' (neuter). But there are certain cases, where one finds such differences between the masculine and the feminine form of the words phonologically. E.g. *chhaatra* 'male student', *chhaatri* 'female student'.

Pronouns Odia pronouns are shown in Figure 1.

(Sahoo, 2001)

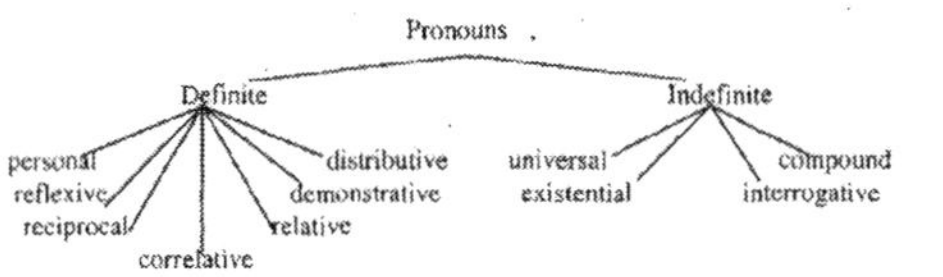

Figure 1: Odia Pronouns

- Personal: *mun* 'I', *tu* 'you', *tume* 'you', *aapaNa* 'you', *se* 'she' / 'he'
- Reflexive: *se nije* 'he himself / she herself'
- Reciprocal: *paraspara* 'each other'
- Correlative: *jie* 'who (ever)' —*se* 'he' / 'she'
- Relative: *je* 'whoever', *jaahaaku* 'whomsoever'
- Demonstrative: *eha / ehi* 'this', *eguDika / eguDaaka* 'these', sehi 'that' and seguDika / seguDaaka 'those'
- Distributive: *pratyeka* 'each' / 'every'
- Universal: *samaste* 'all'
- Existential: *jaNe* 'one person', *goTe* 'a'/ 'one'
- Interrogative: *kie* 'who', *kaahaaku* 'whom','
- Compound: *kehi jaNe / kie jaNe* 'somebody'

Case morphemes Odia case morphemes are shown in Table 1.

Case	Singular	Plural/[+Hon] sg
Nominative (NOM)	-	-e
Accusative (ACC)	*ku*	*nku, maananku*
Instrumental (INST)	*re, dwaaraa, dei*	*re, dwaaraa, dei*
Dative (DAT)	*ku*	*nku, maananku*
Ablative (ABL)	*ru, Thaaru*	*MaanankaThaaru*
Genitive (GEN)	*ra*	*nkara, maanankara*
Locative (LOC)	*re, Thaare*	*MaanankaThaare*
Vocative (VOC)	*he, bho*	

Table 1: The Case morphemes in Odia

Postpositional words The following postpositional words are used to express different case relations.

- *aagare* 'before'
- *pare* 'after'
- *kari* 'by'
- *nimitte* 'for
- *parjyante* 'up to'
- *paain* 'for'
- *prati* 'to', 'against'
- *baahaara* 'out', 'outside'
- *byatita* 'without'
- *binaa* 'without'
- *boli* 'because of', 'literally speaking', e.g. *goli boli goTe pilaa thilaa* 'there was a child called Goli'
- *bhitare* 'in', 'inside'
- *majhire* 'inside', 'in the midst of'
- *laagi* 'for' e.g. *raatidina laagi* 'for day and night'
- *sahite* 'with'

Conjunctions Conjunction markers include *o / eban / aau* 'and', *kimbaa / abaalathabaa* 'or', *madhya* 'also', *tathaapi* 'still', *kintu* 'but' etc.

Classifiers A classifier is a noun-related element but has no independent nominal reading. Having insufficient referential or predicative content, it is not fully lexical. *-Taa* 'one$_{[+def]}$', *Topaa* 'drop', *muThaa* 'fist', *gochhaa* 'bundle', *jaNa* 'one$_{[+Human]}$', *paTa* 'slice', *asaraa* 'shower', *menchaa*, etc. are usually are identified as classifiers.

Complex verbs Complex verb constructions like the combination of a verbal with a nominal (N-V sequences), and the combination of a verbal with a verbal (V-v sequences) are found in Odia.

Serial verbs Odia is a verb serializing language. A series of verbs along with their complements and adjuncts (if any) can occur in a single clause having a common subject. Very often, the series of verbs have a common object too.

Verbal Nouns Many verbal nouns are found in Odia, such as *chaasa* 'ploughing', *chaaDa* 'release', *maajaNaa* 'bath', *rahaNi* 'stay' *bikaa* 'selling', *baahuDaa* 'return'. Some verbal nouns have been borrowed from Sanskrit, e.g. *anubhaba* 'feeling', *bidroha* 'revolution', *prabesha* 'entrance', *sthiti* 'existence', etc. which are used along with a light verb in Odia.

Copular sentences Copular constructions are usually sentences with a subject and a predicate. The predicate may be either a noun (nominal predicate) or an adjective (adjectival predicate).

Adverbs Like English, Odia also has Time, Place, and Manner adverbials.

Finite Verbal Forms Agreement features contribute to the finiteness of a verbal form in Odia. All the finite verbal forms have an agreement in concord with the subject NP. The agreement features of the verbal form are marked for the person, number, and honorific of the subject NP.

The Infinitive In Odia, the infinitival form is realized by the verbal ending – *ibaaku* 'to do'.

The Conditional affix *-ile* (or *–le*) The morpheme *-ile* (or *–le*) functions as a conditional marker. It is suffixed to the bare verbal root. It is nonfinite as it does not carry any Agr feature and thus can co-occur in a verbal form irrespective of person, number, or gender of the subject.

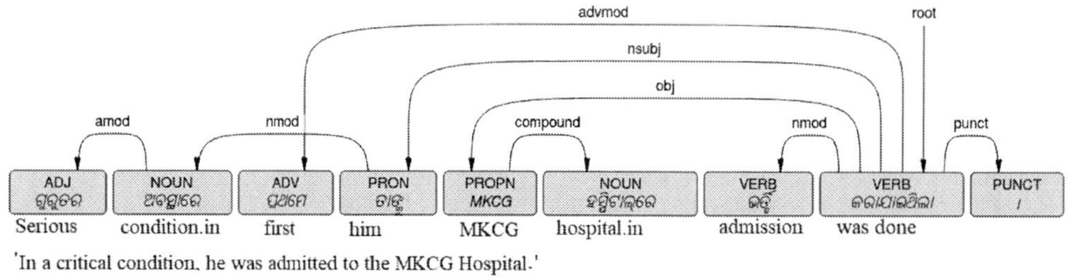

Figure 2: Passivization with Adverbial modifier construction in UD Odia

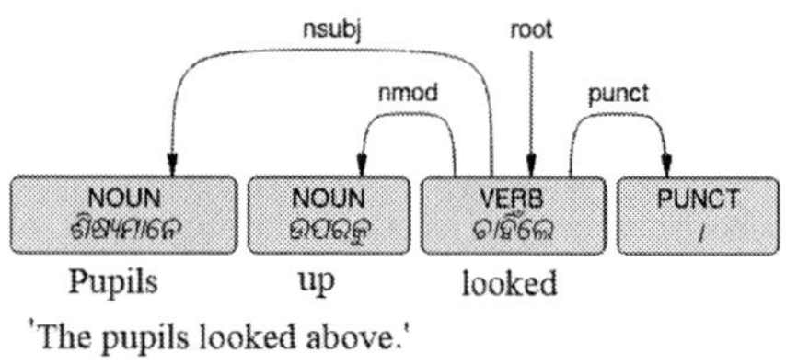

Figure 3: Finite intransitive verb construction in UD Odia

3. Related Work

Under the leadership of IIIT-Hyderabad, a consortium was formed in 2013 to start a project sponsored by TDIL (Government of India), called Development of Dependency Treebank for Indian Languages.[3] This project aimed to restore annotation work in monolingual treebanks for various languages such as Hindi, Marathi, Bengali, Kannada, and Malayalam. To achieve this model, the Pāṇinian Kāraka Dependency scheme was followed (Begum et al., 2008; Husain et al., 2010; Bhat, 2017; Ojha and Zeman, 2020). The same annotation scheme was used to annotate data in Telugu, Urdu, and Kashmiri.

NLP research of Odia has led to development of a statistical POS tagger (Ojha et al., 2015), neural network based POS tagger (Das and Patnaik, 2014), POS tagging using Support Vector Machine (SVM) (Das et al., 2015), a shallow parsing tool [4], and English-Odia machine translation system (Parida et al., 2020a).

Within the Universal Dependencies framework, as of UD release 2.8, treebanks and parsers are available for Bhojpuri, Hindi, Marathi, Sanskrit, Tamil, Telugu and Urdu (Zeman and et al., 2021). Nevertheless, there is no prior work on Odia dependency treebanking and parser.

4. Data and Methodology

To collect Odia text, we used *Samanantar*, the largest parallel corpora collection for 11 Indian languages (Ramesh et al., 2021). The parallel corpora collection includes English-Odia parallel text that covers many domains. We selected the Odia sentences of word length between 5 to 15 words per sentence. For annotation, all selected sentences are converted into CoNLL-U format consisting of 10 fields (Buchholz and Marsi, 2006). The fields are "ID", "Word", "Lemma", "UPOS", "XPOS", "FEATS", "HEAD", "DEPREL", "DEPS", and "MISC". The "UPOS" tags are based on the universal POS tags [5] following the UD guidelines, version 2. For "XPOS", we annotated according to Bureau of Indian Standards (BIS) Part of Speech (POS) tagset [6] guideline released by the department of information technology ministry of communications & information technology, the government of India. The guideline includes a POS tagset for the Odia language. The dependency relations were marked on Universal dependency tags which is an updated version of Stanford Dependencies (de Marneffe et al., 2014). Out 17 UPOS tags, we use 15 UPOS tag in this dataset, while out of 37 dependency tags, we use only 24 tags (see the Table 2 & 3). The annotation task was performed by 6 native Odia speakers including 2 linguists.

UPOS Tags	UPOS description	Statistics
NOUN	Noun	570
VERB	Verb	234
PUNCT	Punctuation	192
PROPN	Proper noun	170
ADJ	Adjective	102
ADP	Adposition	82
DET	Determiner	75
PRON	Pronoun	55
CCONJ	Coordinating conjunction	48
ADV	Adverb	45
NUM	Numeral	26
PART	Particle	23
AUX	Auxiliary	13
SCONJ	Subordinating conjunction	7
SYM	Symbol	1

Table 2: Statistics of used UPOS Tags in the Odia treebank

[3] http://meity.gov.in/content/language-computing-group-vi

[4] http://calts.uohyd.ac.in/calts/sptil-parser.html

[5] https://universaldependencies.org/u/pos/

[6] http://tdil-dc.in/tdildcMain/articles/134692Draft%20POS%20Tag%20standard.pdf

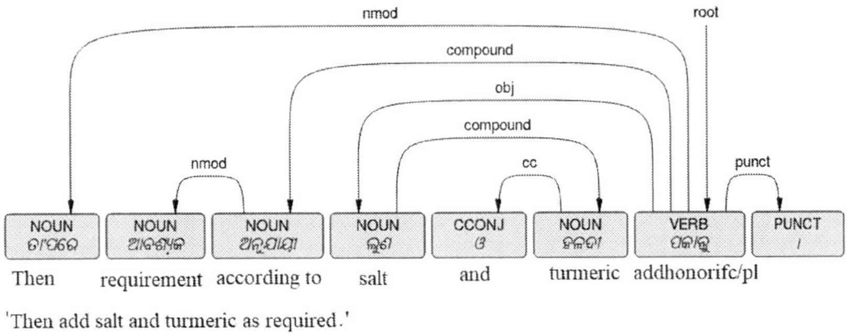

Figure 4: Finite verb in imperative sentence in UD Odia

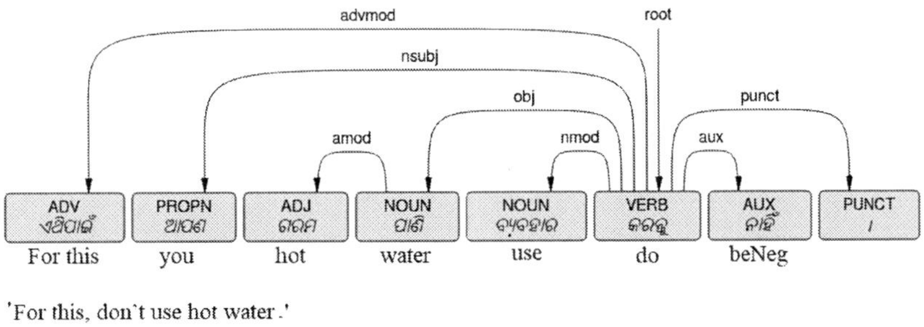

Figure 5: Main verb construction in UD Odia

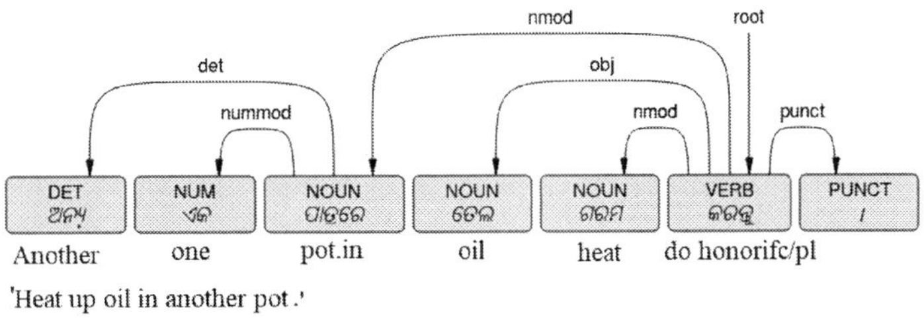

Figure 6: Finite verb with Noun modifier construction in UD Odia

5. Experiment and Results

As mentioned earlier, the Odia treebank was manually annotated using the UD annotation framework. In this, we have built Odia parser on 2026 tokens using the UDPipe open-source tool (Straka and Straková, 2017). We conducted our experiment in two parts. The first experiment was conducted on 50 sentences, while the second experiment was conducted on the rest of the dataset. We used a cross-validation 90:10 average for the data splitting where the batch size, learning rate, and dropout were 50, 0.005, and 0.10, respectively; while the other hyperparameters were randomized. The results are demonstrated in Table 4: Due to the small size of the data, the parser's accuracy is very low except on Tokenization.

6. Linguistic Analysis

We are providing few sample tree constructions along with their linguistics analysis in Figures 2 to 6

In Figure 2, *'karaajaaithilaa'* is a finite verb. So, it forms the root. The adjective *'guruttara'* modifies the noun *'abasthaare'*. The main verb has *'taanku'* as the external argument (the subject) and *'MKCG hospitalre'* as internal argument (the object) of it. It has the adverbial modifier *'prathame'*.

In Figure 3, the finite intransitive verb *'chaahinle'* 'wanted' is the root of the sentence. It takes *'shishyamaane'* 'pupils'

UD Relations	Description	Statistics
advmod	Adverbial modifier	67
advmod	Locative adverbial modifier	4
amod	Adjectival modifier of noun	109
aux	Auxiliary verb	9
case	Case marker	1
cc	Coordinating conjunction	1
ccomp	Clausal complement	2
compound	Compound	85
conj	Non-first conjunct	2
cop	Copula	1
det	Determiner	72
fixed	Non-first word of fixed expression	63
flat	non-first word of flat structure	51
goeswith	Non-first part of broken word	6
iobj	Indirect object	72
mark	Subordinating marker	52
nmod	Nominal modifier of noun	287
nsubj	Nominal subject	136
nummod	Numeric modifier	33
obj	Direct object	122
obl	Oblique nominal	1
punct	Punctuation	192
root	Root	174
xcomp	Open clausal complement	1

Table 3: UD relations used in Odia trebank

Tokenization	UPOS	XPOS	UAS	LAS
81.82%	48.25%	45.0%	36.62%	16.91%
86.6%	64.1%	63.78%	42.04%	21.34%

Table 4: Results of Odia Parser

as the subject argument. Being intransitive, it does not take any object or internal argument.

In Figure 4, *'pakaantu'* 'put' is the finite verb, which forms the root. Being an imperative sentence, the subject noun is not realized, and *'luNa o haLadi'* 'salt and turmeric' functions as the object of the sentence. *'taa pare'* 'after that' functions as the adverbial modifier. *'aabashyaka anujaayi'* 'as per the requirement' functions as a nominal modifier for *'luNa o haLadi'* 'salt and turmeric'.

In Figure 5, the main verb *'karantu'* 'do Pl/Honorific ' takes *'aapaNa'* 'you' as the subject noun and *'paaNi'* 'water' as the object. It is a negative sentence, and the negative auxiliary *'naahin'* 'be-Neg' occurs at the end of the sentence. The object *'paaNi'* 'water' is modified by the adjective *'garama'* 'hot'. *'ethipaain'* 'because of this' functions as the adverbial modifier for the sentence.

In Figure 6, *'karantu'* 'do Pl/Honorific ' which is a finite verb, forms the root of the sentence. the det *'anya'* 'another' and the numeral modifier *'eka'*'one' modify the locative modifier *'paatrare'* 'in a pot'. The nsubject *'aapaNa'* 'you Pl/Honorific ' is not realized in the sentence. The main verb *'karantu'* 'do Pl/Honorific ' takes *'tela'* 'oil' as the object and *'paatrare'* 'in a pot' as the locative modifier.

7. Conclusion and Future Work

We presented the first UD Odia treebank aimed for linguistic research and applications in NLP, primarily for POS tagging, parser, semantic analyzer, and machine translation. Also, we built a preliminary Odia parser using the UDPipe tool. The accuracy of the Odia parser is 86.6% Tokenization, 64.1% UPOS, 63.78% XPOS, 42.04% UAS and 21.34% LAS.

Future research direction includes: *i)* enrich the Odia treebank with more annotated data for training, development, and validation, *ii)* including lemma for the Odia tokens, *iii)* perform detail morphological analysis, and *iv)* experiment with neural network based models for performance evaluation.

8. Acknowledgements

Atul Kr. Ojha would like to acknowledge the EU's Horizon 2020 Research and Innovation programme through the ELEXIS project under grant agreement No. 731015.

9. References

Begum, R., Husain, S., Dhwaj, A., Sharma, D. M., Bai, L., and Sangal, R. (2008). Dependency annotation scheme for Indian languages. In *Proceedings of the Third International Joint Conference on Natural Language Processing: Volume-II*.

Bhat, R. A. (2017). *Exploiting linguistic knowledge to address representation and sparsity issues in dependency parsing of Indian languages*. Ph.D. thesis, PhD thesis, International Institute of Information Technology, India.

Buchholz, S. and Marsi, E. (2006). Conll-x shared task on multilingual dependency parsing. In *Proceedings of the tenth conference on computational natural language learning (CoNLL-X)*, pages 149–164.

Das, B. R. and Patnaik, S. (2014). A novel approach for odia part of speech tagging using artificial neural network. In *Proceedings of the International Conference on Frontiers of Intelligent Computing: Theory and Applications (FICTA) 2013*, pages 147–154. Springer.

Das, B. R., Sahoo, S., Panda, C. S., and Patnaik, S. (2015). Part of speech tagging in odia using support vector machine. *Procedia Computer Science*, 48:507–512.

de Marneffe, M.-C., Dozat, T., Silveira, N., Haverinen, K., Ginter, F., Nivre, J., and Manning, C. D. (2014). Universal Stanford dependencies: A cross-linguistic typology. In *Proceedings of the Ninth International Conference on Language Resources and Evaluation (LREC'14)*, pages 4585–4592, Reykjavik, Iceland, May. European Language Resources Association (ELRA).

Husain, S., Mannem, P., Ambati, B. R., and Gadde, P. (2010). The ICON-2010 tools contest on Indian language dependency parsing. *Proceedings of ICON-2010 Tools Contest on Indian Language Dependency Parsing, ICON*, 10:1–8.

Ojha, A. K. and Zeman, D. (2020). Universal Dependency Treebanks for Low-Resource Indian Languages: The Case of Bhojpuri. In *Proceedings of the WILDRE5– 5th Workshop on Indian Language Data: Resources and Evaluation*, pages 33–38.

Ojha, A. K., Behera, P., Singh, S., and Jha, G. N. (2015). Training & evaluation of pos taggers in indo-aryan languages: a case of hindi, odia and bhojpuri. In *the proceedings of 7th Language & Technology Conference: Human Language Technologies as a Challenge for Computer Science and Linguistics*, pages 524–529.

Parida, S., Bojar, O., and Dash, S. R. (2020a). Odiencorp: Odia–english and odia-only corpus for machine translation. In *Smart Intelligent Computing and Applications*, pages 495–504. Springer.

Parida, S., Dash, S. R., Bojar, O., Motlicek, P., Pattnaik, P., and Mallick, D. K. (2020b). OdiEnCorp 2.0: Odia-English parallel corpus for machine translation. In *Proceedings of the WILDRE5– 5th Workshop on Indian Language Data: Resources and Evaluation*, pages 14–19, Marseille, France, May. European Language Resources Association (ELRA).

Ramesh, G., Doddapaneni, S., Bheemaraj, A., Jobanputra, M., AK, R., Sharma, A., Sahoo, S., Diddee, H., Kakwani, D., Kumar, N., et al. (2021). Samanantar: The largest publicly available parallel corpora collection for 11 indic languages. *arXiv preprint arXiv:2104.05596*.

Sahoo, K. (2001). *Oriya verb morphology and complex verb constructions*. NTNU Trondheim.

Straka, M. and Straková, J. (2017). Tokenizing, POS tagging, lemmatizing and parsing UD 2.0 with UDPipe. In *Proceedings of the CoNLL 2017 Shared Task: Multilingual Parsing from Raw Text to Universal Dependencies*, pages 88–99.

Zeman, D. and et al. (2021). Universal dependencies 2.8.1. LINDAT/CLARIAH-CZ digital library at the Institute of Formal and Applied Linguistics (ÚFAL), Faculty of Mathematics and Physics, Charles University.

Proceedings of the WILDRE-6 Workshop @LREC2020, pages 90–96
Marseille, 20 June 2022

Computational Referencing System for Sanskrit Grammar

Baldev Ram Khandoliyan, Ram Kishor
SSIS, Jawaharlal Nehru University,
New Delhi
{Baldevramjnu, crks113}@gmail.com

Abstract:

The goal of this project was to reconstitute and storage the text of Aṣṭādhyāyī (AD) in a computer text system so that everyone may read it. The proposed work was to do study the structure of AD and to create a relational database system for storing and interacting with AD. The system is available online, including Devanāgari Unicode and other major Indian characters as input and output, MS SQL Server, a Relational Database Management System (RDBMS)-based system, and Java Server Pages (JSP) were used. For AD, the system works as a multi-dimensional interactive knowledge-based computer system. The approach can also be applied to all Sanskrit sūtra texts that have a similar format. Sanskrit heritage texts are projected to benefit from the system's preservation and promotion. A research is being made here for preparing an AD text as a computer aided dynamic search, learning and instruction system in the Indian context.

Keywords: Computational Linguistics, Sanskrit language, Sanskrit corpus, Sanskrit computational lexicography, Computer Text System, *Aṣṭādhyāyī,* Sanskrit grammar.

1. Introduction

Computational Linguistics (CL) does research and development to make Human Computer Intelligent Interaction (HCII) having language as the means of communication. Computational Linguists worldwide are taking great interest in Sanskrit language, texts and particularly in Sanskrit grammar. With the help of computer tasks like electronic storage, access and preservation of Sanskrit corpus, Sanskrit computational lexicography, search engines, indices and glossary etc. are going to made. A computer system for Sanskrit grammar based on the text of AD has developed to store and make accessible it in a interactive way with user friendly format. In the present time five kinds of CL research work for Sanskrit based on is in process. These are the following types:

1. analysis and description of Sanskrit structure;
2. developing learning/teaching systems within the Pāṇinian frame;
3. inferring from AD;
4. its study as a primary model of knowledge (semiotics).
5. **computerizing and storing the text;**

The last one area may be modified into the study and storing of AD as a text/as a *Śāstra*. A full access to the text will be made possible by reconstituting or organizing it into a computer text system. Computer system for AD is essential for search and e-learning/teaching of Sanskrit grammar. A tentative proposal is being made here for the reconstruction of AD text into database for a computer aided learning and instruction system in the Indian context. The reconstruction of AD into database is required for the development of the proposed system. The Reconstruction will consist, for each *sūtra*, of

(i) Analysis into *pada*
(ii) Restoring *adhikāra-anuvṛtti* elements
(iii) Identifying the *samāsa,* if required
(iv) Marking the *vibhaktis* of each *pada*
(v) Re-ordering the *pada* in Case(*Kāraka*)-orders as required-
5-7-6-1
5-7-1
6-1-7
Case 1 *Kṛtā* marks the substitute.
Case 6 *Sambandha* marks the thing that is removed due to substitution.
Case 5 *Apādāna* marks the thing that appears before the substitution.
Case 7 *Adhikaraṇa* marks the thing that appears after the substitution.[1]
(vi) Translating the *sūtras* into Hindi, English.

[1] Kapoor, Kapil, *Dimensions of Pāṇini Grammar,* p. 125

Support texts will be separately included: *Dhātu-pāṭha* (*DP*), *Gaṇapāṭha* (*GP*), *Pratyāhārasūtras* (*PS*), *Liṅgānuśāsana* (*LS*) and *Uṇādisūtras* (*US*). Also *IT-Saṁjṇā* rules and *Pāṇinīya Śikṣā* as well in original Sanskrit, with provision for recall and display along with the pertinent *sūtra*.

For reference, indices have been organized as follows[2]:

1. Alphabetical list of *sūtras*
2. Thematic grouping of *sūtras* [65 themes according to *Siddhānta Kaumudī* (*SK*)].
3. *Pratyāhāra* list and *Pratyāhāra*-generation programme
4. *IT-Saṁjās* dictionary
5. Dictionary of affixes
6. Dictionary of technical terms
7. Typical declension paradigms (83 paradigms)
8. Typical conjugation paradigms (23 paradigms)
9. Typical Examples of each of the seven kinds of *siddhi*
10. *Sandhi*-enumeration and corresponding rules
11. Concordance of *pada* in AD
12. Enumeration of representative, frequent nouns and verbs for declension and conjugation paradigms.

Further, the power of this system will increase enormously if explanatory comments in major *Ṭīkas* on different AD rules are made available as reference system for each rule that has been commented upon.

2. Structure and Organization of AD

AD has 8 chapters divided into 4 *padas*. A *sūtra* or rule is referenced as x.x.x (x *adhyāya*, x *pāda*, x *sūtra*). For example *sūtra* 1.1.1 (*vṛiddhirādaic*) is *adhyāya* one, *pāda* one and *sūtra* one.

The components of AD are as follows[3] -

1. Phonetic component
    1. Phonems (*akṣarasamāmnāya* - 14 *sūtras* called *śiva-sūtras*) (AS)
    2. *Pratāhāras* (sigla)
2. Rule base (*sūtrapāṭha* - 4000 *sūtras* - 3983 in *kāśikāvṛtti*) (SP)
    1. List
        1. Sound (*varṇa samuccaya*)
        2. Affixes – *SuP, TiṄ, Kṛt, Taddhita, Saṇ, Strī*
3. Lexicon
    1. *dhātupāṭha* (1967 verb roots - 2014 including *kaṇḍvādi* roots) (DP)
    2. *gañapāṭha* (other pertinent items like primitive nominal bases, *avyayas*) (GP)
    3. *Liṅgānuśāsana* (LS)

The AS, DP, and the GP can be called the three most basic databases of the Pāṇinian system containing duly arranged and structured data. The SP is Pāṇini's comprehensive rule base for Sanskrit.

3. The reconstruction of AD

The reconstruction of AD into database is required for the development of the proposed system. The Reconstruction will consist, for each *sūtra*, of

(vii) Analysis into *pada*
(viii) Restoring *adhikāra-anuvṛtti* elements
(ix) Identifying the *samāsa*, if required
(x) Marking the *vibhaktis* of each *pada*
(xi) Re-ordering the *pada* in
5-7-6-1
5-7-1
6-1-7
Case-orders as required.
(xii) Translating the *sūtras* into Hindi, English.

Support texts will be separately included : *Dhātu-pāṭha* (DP), *Gaṇapāṭha* (GP), *Pratyāhārasūtras* (PS), *Liṅgānuśāsana* (LS) and *Uṇādisūtras* (US). Also *IT-Saṁjṇā* rules and *Pāṇinīya Śikṣā* as well in original Sanskrit, with provision for recall and display along with the pertinent *sūtra*.

For reference, indices will be organized as follows[4]:

13. Alphabetical list of *sūtras*
14. Thematic grouping of *sūtras* [65 themes according to *Siddhānta Kaumudī* (SK)].
15. *Pratyāhāra* list and *Pratyāhāra*-generation programme

---

[2] Ibid p. 125
[3] Based on "*The system of Pāṇini*" (Language in India, volume 4:2 February 2004) at http://www.languageinindia.com/feb2004/panini.html

[4] Kapoor, Kapil, *Dimensions of Pāṇini Grammar*, p. 125

16. *IT-Saṁjās* dictionary
17. Dictionary of affixes
18. Dictionary of technical terms
19. Typical declension paradigms (83 paradigms)
20. Typical conjugation paradigms (23 paradigms)
21. Typical Examples of each of the seven kinds of *siddhi*
22. *Sandhi*-enumeration and corresponding rules
23. Concordance of *pada* in AD
24. Enumeration of representative, frequent nouns and verbs for declension and conjugation paradigms.

Further, the power of this system will increase enormously if explanatory comments in major *Ṭīkas* on different AD rules are made available as reference system for each rule that has been commented upon.

4. Research Methodology:

For the development of a computer system of AD the methodology will be used as follows:

- To study the structure of AD
- To study the structure of lexicons (DP, GP, LS)
- To study of the structure of database
- To create a database for AD system which would consist of:

(i) explicit reconstitution of the AD-*sūtra*;
(ii) *pada-artha*;
(iii) *tattvārtha* through elucidation – based on *vārttika* and *Mahābhāśya* wherever needed and available. This will be presented in two levels (a) simplified for average reader, and (b) scholarly for advanced students and scholars. Further –
(iv) *sādhāraṇa-bhāśā-ṭikā*;
(v) *uddharaṇa, pratyuddharaṇa*;
(vi) *vākya-prayoga*,
(vii) reference to further portions of texts, if necessary.

- To develop the necessary front end and search program.

The methodology of comparative study and analysis used in Sanskrit based Natural Language Processing (NLP), and techniques of software engineering will be also used for this work. The authentic edition of AD and supported texts mention above will be used.

5. Development of the *Aṣṭādhyāyī* System:

A dynamic web application cum-indexer has developed under this research. This web application is developed in the front-end of Apache Tomcat Web server using JSP and Java servlets. And its data is in Unicode data files along with RDBMS in MS SQL server. The MS-JDBC connection is used to link the front-end to the database server. The system is available online at http://sanskrit.jnu.ac.in with input and output in Devanāgarī Unicode and in other major Indian scripts. The following model describes the multi-tiered architecture of the *Aṣṭ* system is given below (Fig. 1).

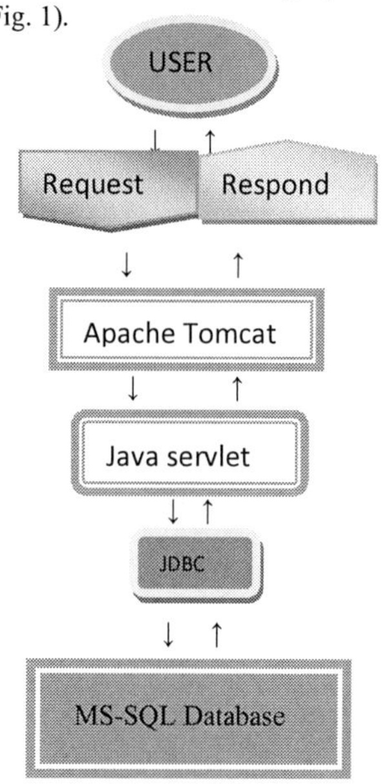

Fig. 1: Program architecture

5.1. Process flow of the system:

There are various ways to give input to the system e.g. Direct Search, Alphabet search and search by the structure of the text, tree search in Devenāgarī Unicode and major 10 Indian scripts (*Punjābī, Assamese, Beṅgālī, Oriyā, Telugu, Tamil, Kannaḍa, Malayālam, Marāṭhī, Gujarātī*).

Step I: Preprocessing.

Preprocessing a word mainly consists of transformation of a raw data required to facilitate further processing. For example – processer can remove any non Devanāgarī and other Indian scripts characters, punctuations that may have been inadvertently introduced by the user like "#" in AD.

Step II: AD Search and Database.

At this step, the system can make an indexed list of exact and partially matching words. Getting the query as an input, the system, after a light preprocessing, sends it to the database. If the word/number has its occurrence in the database, the system is giving the output.

Step III: Output level-1.

At this stage, the system is giving all the occurrences of the searched query with its numerical reference in a hyperlinked mode.

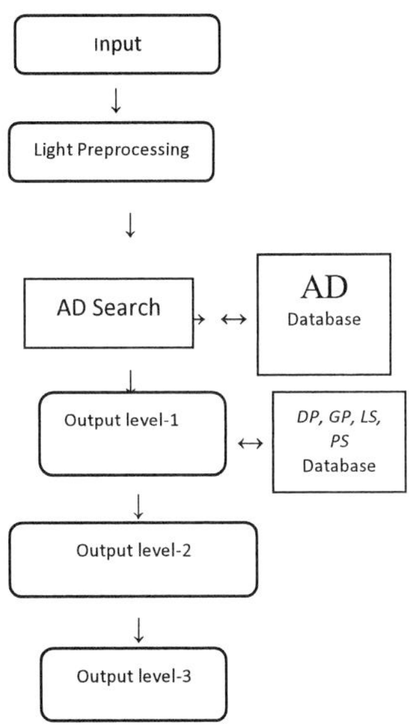

Fig.2: Process flow of the system

Step IV: Output level-2.

Clicking on hyperlinked *sūtra*/word/number, system shows its original place and its full reference in the text of AD with *sūtra viccheda* marking the *vibhaktis* of each *pada* and *adhikāra-anuvṛtti* elements of respective *sūtra*. It also asks for further information from supported texts (*DP, GP, PS, LS* and *US*) and also having link with lists of indices (like thematic grouping of *sūtras, pratyāhāra* list, *pratyāhāra*-generation programme, *IT-Saṁjās* dictionary, dictionary of affixes, dictionary of technical terms, typical declension paradigms, typical conjugation paradigms, typical examples of each of the seven kinds of *siddhi, Sandhi*-enumeration and corresponding rules, concordance of *pada* in AD, enumeration of representative, frequent nouns and verbs for declension and conjugation paradigms and supplementary texts etc.) A hyperlink also is for *IT-Saṁjṇā* rules and *Pāṇinīya Śikṣā* as well in original Sanskrit, with provision for recall and display along with the pertinent *sūtra*.

The ***Kāśikā*** is a joint work of Jayāditya and Vāmana. The ***Kāśikā*** is a running commentary on Pāṇini's *Aṣṭādhyāyī* and its merit consists in the lucid manner in which it has explained the *sūtras* of Pāṇini, clearly indicating all the *Anuvṛttis* and giving numerous illustrations for each rule. Sometimes the ***Kāśikā*** gives us information which we could not possibly have obtained from any other sources.
Hindi English translation of *sūtra* meaning The Hindi meaning of *Sūtras* is tranleted by student. The explation of *Sūtra* is given. *Sūtra Padchheda, Sūtra Vibhakti, Sūtra Sandhi, Sūtra Samasa, Anuvṛti* and *Sūtra* Sanskrit *Vṛiti* with Examples. Hindi meaning of *Sūtra* with detailed information also given. The English meaning is sudent. For Other Indian Languages translation system is used like Google translation, Bing Translation etc.

Step V: Output- final level.

Here, the system gives a list of online tools like e-learning model, TTS for reading *sūtra, vṛti* etc, and also have the facility to do morphological analysis of the query with the help of POS tagger[5] and *subanta tiṅant, sandhi, kṛdanta* analyzers[6].

5.2. Front-End of the AD System:

The front–end of the system is developed in UTF-8 enabled Java Server Pages (JSP) and HTML. The front-end of the software enables the user to interact with the computer system of AD with the help of

[5] http://sanskrit.jnu.ac.in/post/post.jsp
[6] Available at http://sanskrit.jnu.ac.in

Apache Tomcat web-server. The JSP technology helps to create web based applications combining Java code and displays the results as HTML. The web server runs the Java code and displays the results as HTML. For this system, there are two pages, one is the main search page and the other is cross-referential search/connect page which connects the searched query in different online e-learning, TTS and linguistic resources.

In the proposed program there are two layer search facility. First, the string entered in text-box will search in table1 which is available in the row of *sūtras*. These *sūtras* can be listed with Pāṇini's *sūtra* number. After clicking on desired *sūtras* at display page, then detail about that *sūtra* displays in the following form:

AD *sūtra* number and *SK sūtra* number, *sūtra* with *saṃdhi* and with *saṃdhi-viccheda*, *vṛti* with and without *saṃdhi, anuvṛta pada, anuvṛta sūtra, adhikāra sūtra* on searched *sūtra*, name of *prakaraṇa* of SK, technical term used in *sūtra* etc.

After this if user wish to know the meaning of technical term of *sūtra* or to know about *adhikāra sūtra* or detail of *anuvṛtta sūtras* than user have facility to click on desired technical term. The meaning of searched technical term displays after clicking hyperlinked term. To provide the meaning of technical term can be second level search which is from table2.

The work is connected all over world through internet after completing it so at the same time users from all over world can use the system. The program is developed on sever based for fast searching and getting the result. To damage the information of the system will not be possible as the information will be stored in database server. Here the storage and display of information is in Unicode so Font problems are resolved.

5.3. The Back-End of the System:

The back-end is built in two RDBMS tables that include co-relative data tables. Through JDBC connectivity, this Tomcat server-based programme connects to MS-SQL Server 2005 RDBMS. In the first table there is first level information with following column:

sutra_id ; sūtra_Pāṇini ; sūtra ; sūtra_kaumudi ; sūtra_type ; sūtra_sandhi ; anuvritta_pada ; anuvritta_sūtra ; sūtra_vritti ; vritti_sandhi ; vritti_tech_words ; sūtra_adhikara ; kaumudi_prakarana.

In the second table there is the explanation of technical term which displays after clicking the technical term of *sūtra*. In this table there are three columns:

tech_id ; tech_word and explaination.

6. The Snapshots of the AD Indexer

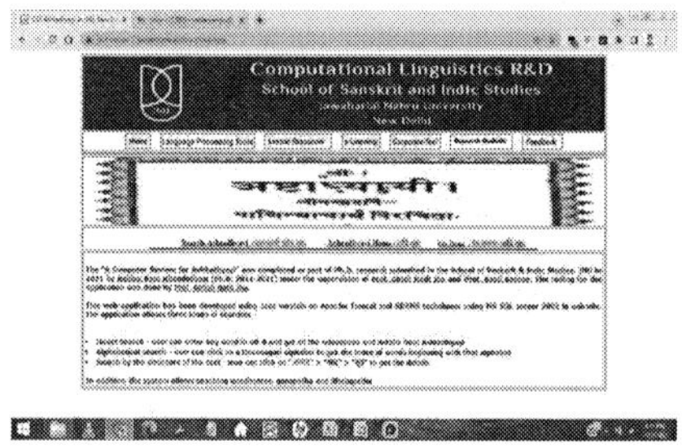

Snapshot 6.1.

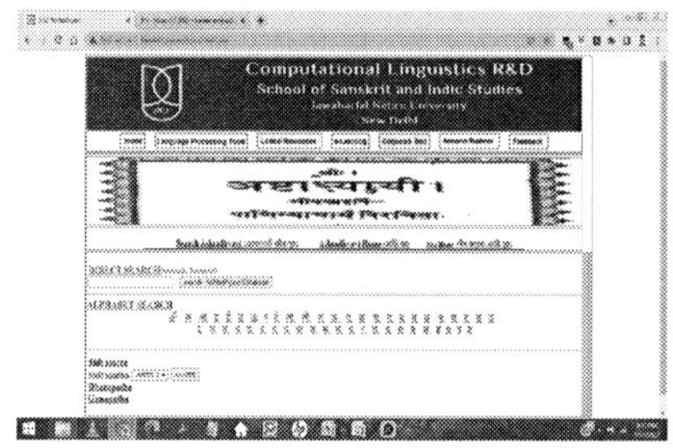

Snapshot 6.2.

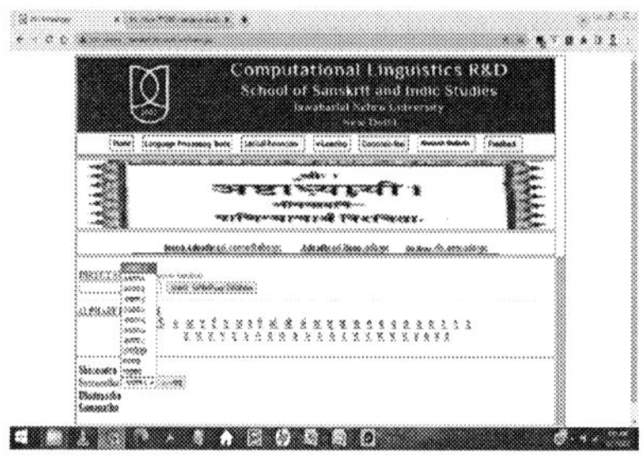

Snapshot 6.3.

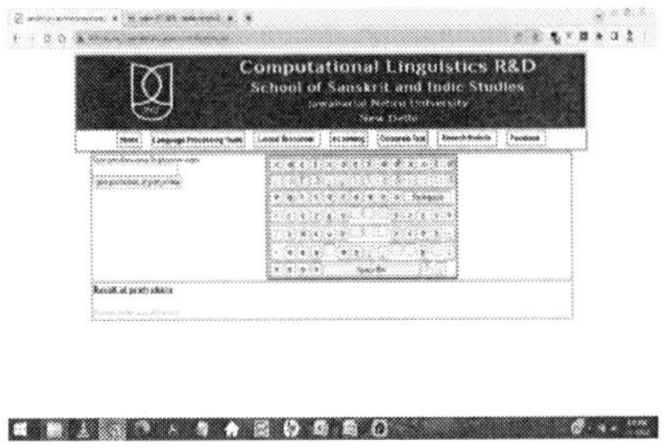

Snapshot 6.4.

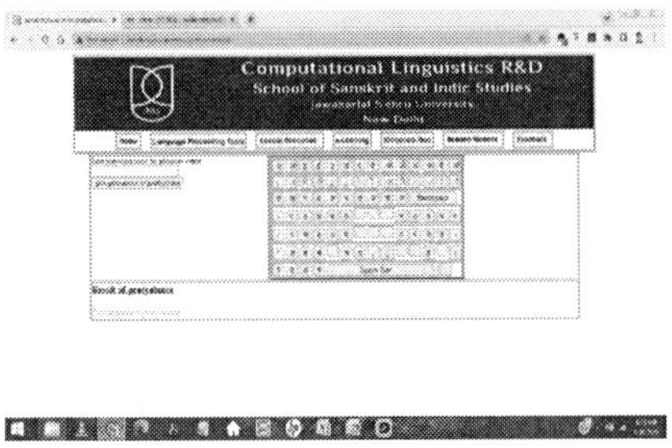

Snapshot 6.5.

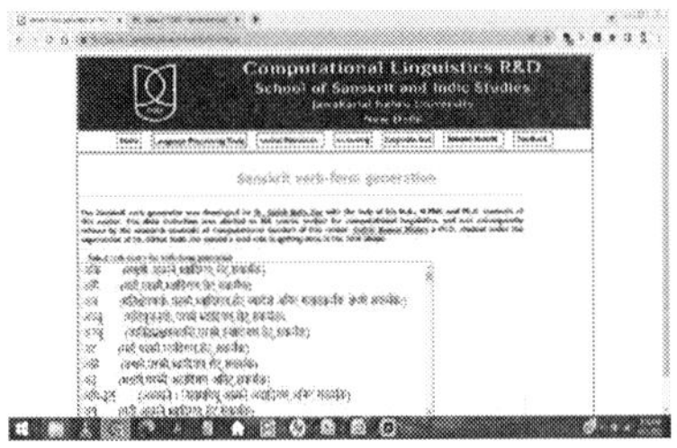

Snapshot 6.6.

7. Web Availability

Besides creating database layouts, we Also converted the data into forms that can be displayed on the web at *Sanskrit.jnu.ac.in/AD* the continuous text and *padapātha* are displayed in our general text display and additional data is displayed in the kramapatha web - based reader and index interface. The reader displays the sūtra in Devanā garī script, followed by the words with sandhi an alyzed (padapātha). Information in the comment field and several other fields from the sutra and pada files is displayed below these. Two additional rows are reserved for a presentation of a comprehend sive paraphrase of the sutra and translation, yet to be composed. Clicking a word in the padapātha displays its infectional information, stem, and lexical tag in a box beneath the word. A menu displays the possible commands, one of which allows configuring the display to suit one's preferences. Another opens a table of contents that allows one to navigate the text easily. The dynamic index to the reader allows focused access to various sorts of information. An alphabetic list of Sterns is displayed at the left. Selecting an item in the list displays the sutras in which the term occurs in the tall box in the middle sary of the stem in the box at the lower right.

References :

1. Jijnasu, Pt. Brahmadatt, (2003). Aṣṭāādhyāyi Bhāṣya Vṛtti, Ramlal Kapoor Trust, Hariyana.
2. Ketre, Sumitra M. (1989) Aṣṭāādhyāyi of Pāṇini, Motilal Banarashidas, Delhi.
3. Dīkṣita, Dr. Pushpa (2007). Aṣṭāādhyāyi Sahajabodha,vol.1-4, Pratibha Prakashan, Delhi.
4. Kumar, Prof. Avnindra (1996) Aṣṭādhyāyīpadānukramkośa, Parimal Publications, Delhi.
5. Dixit, Dr. Pushpa (2010) Aṣṭādhyāyīsūtrapāth, Samskrit Bharati, New Delhi.
6. Krishnacharya, T.R. (2005) Bṛhaddhāturūpāvaliḥ, Sri Sri Jagadguru Shankaracharya Maha Samsthanam Dakshinamnaya Sri Sharada Peetham, Sringeri.
7. Chandra Pt, Īśvara (2010) Kāśikāvṛttiḥ, Chaukhamba Sanskrit Pratishthan, Delhi.
8. Mahābhāṣyam, vol 1-7, Mimasaka, Yudhishthiro and Sudhyumanacharya, Ramlal Karpoor Trust, Bhivani, 2010
9. Jigyasu, Pt.Brahmadatta (ed.) (1998) Panini-Astadhyayi, Ramlal kapoor trust, Sonipat.
10. Vasishth, Jagdish Prasad (2013) Pāṇinīyaśīkṣā, Vandana Smriti Prakashna, Bhivani.
11. Vasudev Lakshman Shastri Panishikar (ed.) (2002) Siddhāntakaumudī, Tattvabodhinīvyākhyā, Chaukhamba Sanskrit Pratishtan, Delhi.

12. Sharma, Rama Nath (2003) The Aṣādhyāyi of Pāṇini, Munshiram Manoharlal Publishers Pvt. Ltd., Delhi.
13. Joshi, S.D. and Roodbergen J.A.F. (2007) The Aṣṭādhyāyī of Pāṇini, vol 1-12, Sahitya Akedemi.
14. Vasu Śriśā Chandra (2003). The Aṣṭādhyāyī of Pāṇini, vol. I-II, Mitilal Banarashidas, Delhi.
15. Mimasaka, Yudhishthir (2010). Uṇādi-Kośa, Ramlal Karpoor Trust, Bhivani.
16. Chaturvedi Giridharsharma (ed.) ((2004). Vaiyakarasiddhāntakaumudī with Bālamanorama and Tattvabodhini Tikā, Motilal Banarasidass, Delhi.
17. Pandey, Gopal Dutt (2007)Vaiyakarasiddhāntakaumudī with Bālamanorama Tikā, Chaukhmba Surbharati Prakashana, Varanashi.
18. Shastri, Guru Prasad (ed) (1999). Vyakaraṇa-Mahābhāṣya with Pradipoddhat Tikā, Pratibha Prakashan, Delhi.

Proceedings of the WILDRE-6 Workshop @LREC2020, pages 97–101
Marseille, 20 June 2022

L3Cube-MahaCorpus and MahaBERT: Marathi Monolingual Corpus, Marathi BERT Language Models, and Resources

Raviraj Joshi
Indian Institute of Technology Madras, Tamilnadu, India
L3Cube Pune, Maharashtra, India
ravirajoshi@gmail.com

Abstract

We present L3Cube-MahaCorpus a Marathi monolingual data set scraped from different internet sources. We expand the existing Marathi monolingual corpus with 24.8M sentences and 289M tokens. We further present, MahaBERT, MahaAlBERT, and MahaRoBerta all BERT-based masked language models, and MahaFT, the fast text word embeddings both trained on full Marathi corpus with 752M tokens. We show the effectiveness of these resources on downstream Marathi sentiment analysis, text classification, and named entity recognition (NER) tasks. We also release MahaGPT, a generative Marathi GPT model trained on Marathi corpus. Marathi is a popular language in India but still lacks these resources. This work is a step forward in building open resources for the Marathi language. The data and models are available at https://github.com/l3cube-pune/MarathiNLP.

Keywords: Marathi Monolingual Corpus, Deep Learning, Marathi NLP, Transformers, Marathi BERT, Marathi Word Embeddings, Text Classification, NER, GPT

1. Introduction

Pre-trained language models based on BERT have been widely used in NLP applications (Wolf et al., 2019; Qiu et al., 2020). These language models are fine-tuned on the target task and are reported to provide superior results. The target tasks include text classification, named entity recognition (NER), parts of speech (POS) tagging, dependency parsing, natural language inference (NLI), etc (Otter et al., 2020). The BERT-based models can be trained using un-supervised large text corpus using masked language modeling objective and next sentence prediction tasks.

The mono-lingual and multi-lingual masked language models have been very popular recently. The multilingual language models provide significant benefits for low resource languages by leveraging the learning from high resource text (Pires et al., 2019). However, models trained on a single language are shown to perform better than multi-lingual models on target tasks in corresponding language (Straka et al., 2021). Previous works have built BERT based language models in German, Vietnamese, Arabic, Dutch, French, Hindi, Bengali, etc (Scheible et al., 2020; Nguyen and Nguyen, 2020; Le et al., 2019; Delobelle et al., 2020; Abdul-Mageed et al., 2020; Jain et al., 2020). In this work, we focus on building monolingual corpus and BERT based language model in Marathi. Marathi is a low-resource Indian language and is native to the state of Maharashtra.

Marathi is the third most popular language in India after Hindi and Bengali (Kulkarni et al., 2021a; Joshi et al., 2019). It is spoken by around 83 million people in India. Despite huge representation, in terms of speaking diaspora, the language resources have not received adequate attention for the Marathi language. The language resource in the simplest form is a monolingual corpus. However, even monolingual corpus for Indian languages is mostly biased towards Hindi. This can be seen from the fact that the recently released IndicNLP data set has 62.9M Hindi sentences and only 9.9M Marathi sentences (Kakwani et al., 2020). There is a strong need to develop language resources for Marathi starting from building a monolingual corpus.

In this work, we add to the existing monolingual corpus by building L3Cube-MahaCorpus[1]. The data has been scraped from various internet sources. The corpus for Indian languages has mostly been exclusively dominated by news sources. We specifically consider this bias and also include sentences from non-news sources. L3Cube-MahaCorpus adds 24.8M sentences and 289M tokens (5.3 GB) to the existing Marathi monolingual datasets. After combining this with the existing Marathi corpus there is a total of 57.2M sentences and 752M tokens (13 GB).

We further introduce MahaBERT[2], MahaRoBERTa[3], MahaAlBERT[4 5], and MahaGPT[6] all Transformer BERT based Marathi language models trained on the full Marathi monolingual corpus. The BERT models are trained using masked language modeling objectives. These models are further evaluated on downstream tasks of text classification and named entity recognition (NER) in Marathi. We also release MahaFT, the fast text word embedding trained on the full Marathi Corpus. The dataset and resources are publicly shared to facilitate further research in Marathi NLP. The main contributions of this work are:

- We present L3Cube-MahaCorpus, a Marathi

[1] https://github.com/l3cube-pune/MarathiNLP
[2] https://huggingface.co/l3cube-pune/marathi-bert
[3] https://huggingface.co/l3cube-pune/marathi-roberta
[4] https://huggingface.co/l3cube-pune/marathi-albert
[5] https://huggingface.co/l3cube-pune/marathi-albert-v2
[6] https://huggingface.co/l3cube-pune/marathi-gpt

monolingual corpus with 24.8M sentences and 289M tokens.

- We introduce MahaBERT, MahaAlBERT, and MahaRoBERTa, the BERT variations trained on a full corpus with 752M tokens. We also release MahaGPT, a Marathi generative pre-trained transformer model trained on the full corpus.
- Finally, we release MahaFT, Marathi fast text embeddings trained on the full corpus.

2. Related Work

In this section, we review different unsupervised and supervised data sets in the Marathi language. A summary of publicly available Marathi monolingual corpus and classification data sets is provided in Kulkarni et al. (2021a). The main sources include Wikipedia text, CC-100 Dataset (Wenzek et al., 2019), OSCAR Corpus (Suárez et al., 2019), and IndicNLP Corpus (Kakwani et al., 2020). The wiki dataset consists of 85k cleaned Marathi articles. The other sources are multi-lingual datasets with Marathi as one of the languages. The CC-100 monolingual data set consists of around 50 million tokens for the Marathi language. The OSCAR corpus consists of around 82 million tokens in Marathi. The IndicNLP is perhaps the largest non-wiki source and consists of 142 million tokens.

There are limited resources for supervised tasks in Marathi. The text classification data set includes IndicNLP News Article Dataset (Kakwani et al., 2020), iNLTK Headline Dataset (Arora, 2020), L3CubeMahaSent (Kulkarni et al., 2021b). The IndicNLP News Article Dataset is a news article classification dataset in Marathi consisting of 4779 records. The iNLTK Headline Dataset categorizes news headlines and consists of 12092 records. The L3CubeMahaSent is a sentiment classification dataset in Marathi and consists of 16000 records. Another data set for Marathi NER was introduced in (Murthy et al., 2018). It consists of 5591 sentences and 3 named entities as target labels. Moreover, some hate speech detection datasets have also been released in Marathi (Gaikwad et al., 2021; Mandl et al., 2021; Pawar and Raje, 2019).

In this work, we have utilized all publicly available Marathi monolingual corpus along with the L3Cube-MahaCorpus to train the language models and word embedding. These models are evaluated on the three classification tasks and a NER task.

3. Curation of Dataset

The L3Cube-MahaCorpus is collected from news and non-news sources. The major chunk of the data is scraped from the Maharashtra Times website [7]. The non-news sources were taken from a collection website [8]. The data set was scraped using the BeautifulSoup library along with the use of Selenium for dynamic pages. The final data set was shuffled and de-duplicated. The de-duplication was also performed with the existing monolingual data set. The L3Cube-MahaCorpus adds 17.6 M sentences (212 M tokens) from the news sources and 7.2 M sentences (76.4 M tokens) from the non-news sources. These are made available separately as well. Overall it adds 24.8 M sentences and 289 M tokens. When combined with the existing monolingual dataset, we now have 57.2 M sentences and 752 M tokens in the Marathi language. These statistics are also described in Table 1.

Dataset	#tokens	#sentences
L3Cube-MahaCorpus (News)	212	17.6
L3Cube-MahaCorpus (Non-news)	76.4	7.2
L3Cube-MahaCorpus	289	24.8
Full Marathi Corpus	752	57.2

Table 1: Dataset Statistics (in millions).

4. Pre-trained Resources

The full Marathi monolingual corpus is used to train Transformer based masked language models and FastText word embeddings.

4.1. Transformer Models

The BERT represents a deep bi-directional Transformer based model trained using a large unlabelled corpus. These pre-trained models have been shown to produce state-of-the-art results on a variety of downstream tasks. There are different variations of BERT models like AlBERT and RoBERTa which are also considered in this work. From the multilingual perspective, there are three main models which can also be used with the Marathi language. These include multilingual-BERT (Devlin et al., 2019), XLM-R based on RoBERTa (Conneau et al., 2019), and IndicBERT (Kakwani et al., 2020) based on AlBERT. These three models are fine-tuned on monolingual Marathi corpus and released as a part of this work. All the models are trained for 2 epochs with standard hyper-parameters and masked language modeling objective only. The learning rate used is 2e-5 with a batch size of 64.

- mBERT[9]: It is a BERT-base vanilla model pre-trained on 104 languages using masked language modeling (MLM) and next sentence prediction (NSP) objective. The Marathi was one of the languages used in pre-training.
- XLM-RoBERTa[10]: It is a RoBERTa based model pre-trained on 100 languages using MLM objec-

[7] https://maharashtratimes.com/

[8] http://www.netshika.com/sangrah.html

[9] https://huggingface.co/bert-base-multilingual-cased

[10] https://huggingface.co/docs/transformers/model_doc/xlmroberta

Model	L3CubeMahaSent	News Articles	News Headlines	Marathi NER
mBERT	80.4	97.6	90.6	58.35
indicBERT	83.3	98.7	93.7	60.79
XLM-R	82.0	98.5	92.5	62.32
MahaBERT	82.8	98.7	94.4	62.57
MahaAlBERT	**83.7**	**99.1**	**94.7**	60.00
MahaRoBERTa	83.4	98.5	94.2	**64.34**
FB-FT + KNN	73.6	99.1	88.8	-
INLP-FT + KNN	74.9	98.9	90.7	-
MahaFT + KNN	75.1	98.9	91.2	-

Table 2: The results for different models on classification and NER tasks. The numbers for classification task L3CubeMahaSent, News Articles, and News Headlines represent the classification accuracy. The numbers for the Marathi NER task represent the macro-f1 score. The FB-FT is Marathi fast text embeddings trained on Wiki and Common Crawl Corpus released by Facebook used along with KNN(k=4). The INLP-FT represents the Marathi fast text embeddings released by IndicNLP Suite. The MahaFT are Marathi fast text embeddings released as a part of this work.

tive. The model is shown to outperform mBERT on different tasks. Even this model contains Marathi as one of the pre-training languages. The RoBERTa mainly modifies the hyper-parameters used in the original BERT and gets rid of the NSP task (Liu et al., 2019).

- IndicBERT[11]: It is a multi-lingual AlBERT model exclusively pre-trained on 12 Indian languages. The AlBERT is a lite version of the BERT model (Lan et al., 2019). It uses parameter reduction techniques like repeated layers to reduce the memory footprint. The model has been shown to work well on most of the Indic NLP tasks (Joshi et al., 2021; Kulkarni et al., 2021b; Velankar et al., 2021; Nayak and Joshi, 2021).

4.2. FastText Word Embeddings

Pre-trained word embeddings are commonly used to initialize the embedding layer of the neural networks. These distributed representations are trained on large unlabeled corpus and are useful for many downstream tasks. The FastText word embeddings are popular for morphologically rich languages (Bojanowski et al., 2017). It represents the word as a bag of character n-grams thus avoiding any out of vocabulary word. We train the FastText model on the Marathi monolingual corpus using standard hyper-parameters. A skip-gram model is trained with a window size of 5, 10 negative samples per instance, and 10 epochs.

4.3. Marathi GPT

GPT2 is a generative transformer model trained using causal language modeling (CLM) objective (Radford et al., 2019). It is also a class of self-supervised models trained to predict the next work on the unsupervised data. We train a standard GPT2 model with 12 layers and 768 internal dimension on Marathi Corpus for 5 epochs with a learning rate of 2e-5. We use a custom BPE-based tokenizer with a vocab size of 50257.

[11] https://huggingface.co/ai4bharat/indic-bert

5. Down Stream Tasks

- **IndicNLP News Article Classification**: The task consists of Marathi news articles classified as sports, entertainment, and lifestyle. There are 3823 train, 479 test, and 477 validation examples.

- **iNLTK Headline Classification**: In this classification task the Marathi news headlines are categorized as entertainment, sports, and state. The dataset consists of 9672 train, 1210 test, and 1210 validation examples.

- **L3CubeMahaSent Sentiment Analysis**: The sentiment analysis task consists of Marathi tweets categorized as positive, negative, and neutral. The dataset consists of 12114 train, 2250 test, and 1500 validation examples.

- **Marathi Named Entity Recognition**: This is a Marathi entity recognition task where each token in the sentence is categorized as Location, Person, and Organization. The dataset consists of 3588 train, 1533 test, and 470 validation examples.

5.1. Results

The L3Cube-MahaCorpus along with other publicly available Marathi corpus is used to train three variations of BERT using MLM objective. These variations are based on base-BERT, AlBERT, and RoBERTa architecture and are termed as MahaBERT, MahaAlBERT, and MahaRoBERTa respectively. The multilingual versions of these architectures mBERT, indicBERT based on AlBERT, and XLM-R based on RoBERTa are also used for baseline comparison. The

multilingual versions are fine-tuned on the Marathi corpus to get the Marathi BERT models. Similar hyperparameters are used for MLM pre-training of all these models. The results are described in Table 2. Note that the results for base models may be slightly different than ones reported in the original work as they were re-computed using a common setup and hyperparameters. These models are evaluated on three classification datasets and one named entity recognition dataset. For the classification task, the pre-trained models are further fine-tuned by the addition of a dense layer on top of [CLS] token embedding. The NER task is formulated as a token classification task and all token embeddings are passed through the dense layer for classification. Overall the monolingual versions of models perform better than the multi-lingual versions.
The fast text word embeddings trained on full Marathi corpus termed as MahaFT are evaluated on the classification datasets. In this setup, word embeddings are averaged to get the sentence representation. A KNN classifier with k=4 is used for the classification of the averaged fast text embedding. These Marathi word embeddings are compared against two other publicly available variations. The FB-FT represents Marathi fast text embeddings trained on Wiki and Common Crawl Corpus released by Facebook. The INLP-FT was released as part of IndicNLP suite. The MahaFT performs competitively with other word embeddings. Overall we show the resources released as a part of this work either perform competitively with or better than the currently available alternatives for the Marathi language.

6. Conclusion

In this paper, we have presented L3Cube-MahaCorpus, MahaBERT, and MahaFT. The MahaCorpus, is a Marathi monolingual corpus and is a significant addition to the existing monolingual corpus. The Marathi BERT is trained in three different flavors namely MahaBERT, MahaRoBERTa, and MahaAlBERT. The MahaFT is the Marathi fast text word embeddings. These resources are exclusively trained on Marathi monolingual corpus. The models are evaluated on downstream Marathi classification and NER tasks. The models are shown to work better than their multi-lingual counterparts.

Acknowledgments

Multiple L3Cube Pune, student groups have contributed to this work. We would like to thank Atharva Kulkarni, Meet Mandhane, Manali Likhitkar, and Gayatri Kshirsagar for their contribution. We also thank groups Algorithm_Unlock and Bits_To_Bytes for their support.

7. Bibliographical References

Abdul-Mageed, M., Elmadany, A., and Nagoudi, E. M. B. (2020). Arbert & marbert: deep bidirectional transformers for arabic. *arXiv preprint arXiv:2101.01785.*

Arora, G. (2020). inltk: Natural language toolkit for indic languages. *arXiv preprint arXiv:2009.12534.*

Bojanowski, P., Grave, E., Joulin, A., and Mikolov, T. (2017). Enriching word vectors with subword information. *Transactions of the Association for Computational Linguistics*, 5:135–146.

Conneau, A., Khandelwal, K., Goyal, N., Chaudhary, V., Wenzek, G., Guzmán, F., Grave, E., Ott, M., Zettlemoyer, L., and Stoyanov, V. (2019). Unsupervised cross-lingual representation learning at scale. *arXiv preprint arXiv:1911.02116.*

Delobelle, P., Winters, T., and Berendt, B. (2020). Robbert: a dutch roberta-based language model. *arXiv preprint arXiv:2001.06286.*

Devlin, J., Chang, M.-W., Lee, K., and Toutanova, K. (2019). Bert: Pre-training of deep bidirectional transformers for language understanding. In *Proceedings of the 2019 Conference of the North American Chapter of the Association for Computational Linguistics: Human Language Technologies, Volume 1 (Long and Short Papers)*, pages 4171–4186.

Gaikwad, S. S., Ranasinghe, T., Zampieri, M., and Homan, C. (2021). Cross-lingual offensive language identification for low resource languages: The case of marathi. In *Proceedings of the International Conference on Recent Advances in Natural Language Processing (RANLP 2021)*, pages 437–443.

Jain, K., Deshpande, A., Shridhar, K., Laumann, F., and Dash, A. (2020). Indic-transformers: An analysis of transformer language models for indian languages. *arXiv preprint arXiv:2011.02323.*

Joshi, R., Goel, P., and Joshi, R. (2019). Deep learning for hindi text classification: A comparison. In *International Conference on Intelligent Human Computer Interaction*, pages 94–101. Springer.

Joshi, R., Karnavat, R., Jirapure, K., and Joshi, R. (2021). Evaluation of deep learning models for hostility detection in hindi text. In *2021 6th International Conference for Convergence in Technology (I2CT)*, pages 1–5. IEEE.

Kakwani, D., Kunchukuttan, A., Golla, S., Gokul, N., Bhattacharyya, A., Khapra, M. M., and Kumar, P. (2020). inlpsuite: Monolingual corpora, evaluation benchmarks and pre-trained multilingual language models for indian languages. In *Proceedings of the 2020 Conference on Empirical Methods in Natural Language Processing: Findings*, pages 4948–4961.

Kulkarni, A., Mandhane, M., Likhitkar, M., Kshirsagar, G., Jagdale, J., and Joshi, R. (2021a). Experimental evaluation of deep learning models for marathi text classification. *arXiv preprint arXiv:2101.04899.*

Kulkarni, A., Mandhane, M., Likhitkar, M., Kshirsagar, G., and Joshi, R. (2021b). L3cubemahasent: A marathi tweet-based sentiment analysis dataset. In *Proceedings of the Eleventh Workshop on Computational Approaches to Subjectivity, Sentiment and Social Media Analysis*, pages 213–220.

Lan, Z., Chen, M., Goodman, S., Gimpel, K., Sharma, P., and Soricut, R. (2019). Albert: A lite bert for self-supervised learning of language representations. *arXiv preprint arXiv:1909.11942*.

Le, H., Vial, L., Frej, J., Segonne, V., Coavoux, M., Lecouteux, B., Allauzen, A., Crabbé, B., Besacier, L., and Schwab, D. (2019). Flaubert: Unsupervised language model pre-training for french. *arXiv preprint arXiv:1912.05372*.

Liu, Y., Ott, M., Goyal, N., Du, J., Joshi, M., Chen, D., Levy, O., Lewis, M., Zettlemoyer, L., and Stoyanov, V. (2019). Roberta: A robustly optimized bert pretraining approach. *arXiv preprint arXiv:1907.11692*.

Mandl, T., Modha, S., Shahi, G. K., Madhu, H., Satapara, S., Majumder, P., Schaefer, J., Ranasinghe, T., Zampieri, M., Nandini, D., et al. (2021). Overview of the hasoc subtrack at fire 2021: Hate speech and offensive content identification in english and indo-aryan languages. *arXiv preprint arXiv:2112.09301*.

Murthy, R., Kunchukuttan, A., and Bhattacharyya, P. (2018). Judicious selection of training data in assisting language for multilingual neural ner. In *Proceedings of the 56th Annual Meeting of the Association for Computational Linguistics (Volume 2: Short Papers)*, pages 401–406.

Nayak, R. and Joshi, R. (2021). Contextual hate speech detection in code mixed text using transformer based approaches. *arXiv preprint arXiv:2110.09338*.

Nguyen, D. Q. and Nguyen, A. T. (2020). Phobert: Pre-trained language models for vietnamese. *arXiv preprint arXiv:2003.00744*.

Otter, D. W., Medina, J. R., and Kalita, J. K. (2020). A survey of the usages of deep learning for natural language processing. *IEEE Transactions on Neural Networks and Learning Systems*, 32(2):604–624.

Pawar, R. and Raje, R. R. (2019). Multilingual cyberbullying detection system. In *2019 IEEE International Conference on Electro Information Technology (EIT)*, pages 040–044. IEEE.

Pires, T., Schlinger, E., and Garrette, D. (2019). How multilingual is multilingual bert? *arXiv preprint arXiv:1906.01502*.

Qiu, X., Sun, T., Xu, Y., Shao, Y., Dai, N., and Huang, X. (2020). Pre-trained models for natural language processing: A survey. *Science China Technological Sciences*, pages 1–26.

Radford, A., Wu, J., Child, R., Luan, D., Amodei, D., Sutskever, I., et al. (2019). Language models are unsupervised multitask learners. *OpenAI blog*, 1(8):9.

Scheible, R., Thomczyk, F., Tippmann, P., Jaravine, V., and Boeker, M. (2020). Gottbert: a pure german language model. *arXiv preprint arXiv:2012.02110*.

Straka, M., Náplava, J., Straková, J., and Samuel, D. (2021). Robeczech: Czech roberta, a monolingual contextualized language representation model. *arXiv preprint arXiv:2105.11314*.

Suárez, P. J. O., Sagot, B., and Romary, L. (2019). Asynchronous pipeline for processing huge corpora on medium to low resource infrastructures. In *7th Workshop on the Challenges in the Management of Large Corpora (CMLC-7)*. Leibniz-Institut für Deutsche Sprache.

Velankar, A., Patil, H., Gore, A., Salunke, S., and Joshi, R. (2021). Hate and offensive speech detection in hindi and marathi. *arXiv preprint arXiv:2110.12200*.

Wenzek, G., Lachaux, M.-A., Conneau, A., Chaudhary, V., Guzmán, F., Joulin, A., and Grave, E. (2019). Ccnet: Extracting high quality monolingual datasets from web crawl data. *arXiv preprint arXiv:1911.00359*.

Wolf, T., Debut, L., Sanh, V., Chaumond, J., Delangue, C., Moi, A., Cistac, P., Rault, T., Louf, R., Funtowicz, M., et al. (2019). Huggingface's transformers: State-of-the-art natural language processing. *arXiv preprint arXiv:1910.03771*.

Author Index

Association for Computational Linguistics
209 N. Eighth Street
Stroudsburg, Pennsylvania 18360

ISBN 978-1-7138-6143-0

CURRAN ASSOCIATES INC.
proceedings.com